# AFTER
# ADMISSION

# AFTER ADMISSION

## From College Access to College Success

JAMES E. ROSENBAUM, REGINA DEIL-AMEN,
AND ANN E. PERSON

RUSSELL SAGE FOUNDATION · NEW YORK

# The Russell Sage Foundation

**Library of Congress Cataloging-in-Publication Data**

Rosenbaum, James E., 1943-
  After admission : from college access to college success / James Rosenbaum, Regina Deil-Amen, and Ann Person.
      p. cm.
  Includes bibliographical references and index.
  ISBN-10: 0-87154-707-4
  ISBN-13: 978-0-87154-707-1
  1. Community colleges—United States. I. Deil-Amen, Regina. II. Person, Ann. III. Title.
  LB2328.15.U6R67 2006
  378.1'543—dc22

                    2006018384

Text design by Genna Patacsil.

RUSSELL SAGE FOUNDATION
112 East 64th Street, New York, New York 10021
10 9 8 7 6 5 4 3 2 1

# CONTENTS

# About the Authors

**James E. Rosenbaum** is professor of sociology, education, and social policy, and research fellow at the Institute for Policy Research at Northwestern University.

**Regina Deil-Amen** is assistant professor of education at the Center for the Study of Higher Education in the College of Education at the University of Arizona, Tucson.

**Ann E. Person** is a doctoral candidate in human development and social policy at Northwestern University.

# PREFACE

The conventional wisdom is that learning is one directional: students learn from teachers. The process is actually much more dynamic. This book began when a graduate student (Regina Deil-Amen) asked a professor (James Rosenbaum) for advice on her evolving study of community colleges. The professor, an expert on high schools, held the usual misconceptions that community colleges were relatively unimportant, small colleges, attended by few students. In the process of providing advice to the student, the professor learned a lot from her, and then the two devised a series of studies. Another graduate student (Ann Person) joined the project, bringing the insights of a former college administrator, and the idea for this book was generated.

The process of doing this research has taken the three authors on an exciting journey. We learned a great deal about community colleges, the ways they contributed to revolutionary changes in American society, the ways they provide new opportunities to disadvantaged groups, and the ways their traditional institutional procedures impose hidden obstacles and missed opportunities. This book attempts to share this exciting learning process with others.

We thank many colleagues who provided thoughtful suggestions along the way: Tom Bailey, Stephen Brint, Tom Cook, Stefanie DeLuca, Kevin Dougherty, Greg Duncan, Adam Gamoran, Maureen Hallinan, Mark Granovetter, Takehiko Kariya, Howard London, Mike McPherson, John Meyer, Richard Murnane, David Neumark, Gary Natriello, Gary Orfield, Aaron Pallas, Kathleen Shaw, David Stern, Art Stinchcombe, Marc Ventresca, Eric Wanner, Burton Weisbrod, Chris Winship, and James Witte.

We offer our humble appreciation to each of the colleges studied for lending us their trust and providing the access we needed to conduct our research. We also thank the many staff and students who thoughtfully and candidly answered what must have seemed like endless questions. They gave generously of their time, shared great insights, and impressed us with their dedication and commitment.

We are also indebted to Ann Pille and Linda Cheng, who helped direct the day-to-day activities required to make this study happen. We are grateful to the numerous work-study students who were tenacious enough to last through more than a few weeks of transcribing and data cleaning. We are especially indebted to Fay Cook, director of the Institute for Policy Research at Northwestern University, who provided support that greatly contributed to the project. This research also benefited from foundation support, and from the suggestions of two program officers in particular. Jesse Ausubel of the Alfred P. Sloan Foundation and Susan Dauber of the Spencer Foundation provided us with substantive comments that significantly improved the research we did. Of course, we also thank the foundations for providing the funding that was essential for this research.

Special thanks go to Norton Grubb and Julie Redline whose extensive, thoughtful comments greatly improved the entire manuscript. It is one of the great gratifications of writing to receive the kind of intellectually penetrating comments and suggestions they provided. We must take responsibility for the remaining errors, but these two are practically honorary authors because of the enormous contribution they made.

Intellectual products rarely come to fruition without personal support, and there are people in our lives who provided that for us throughout this endeavor. For this reason, Jim thanks his wife, Ginny, and daughter, Janet, and colleagues at Northwestern who discussed these ideas and provided support throughout.

Regina would like to thank her immediate family for their unquestioning acceptance and love, despite the fact that they still do not completely understand what she does and why. She also thanks her close circle of graduate school friends whose friendship extended through the years of this project and the writing of this book during her first years as an assistant professor. These women infused fun into the process, shared themselves with her, created a life-affirming space, challenged and extended her way of thinking and living, and carried her through the difficult personal times. Among these friends are Deborah Paredez, Gina Perez, Michelle Boyd, and Heather McClure.

Ann thanks her professors and colleagues in the School of Education and Social Policy at Northwestern, especially Patricia Pendry, for help thinking through both big questions and small details; and Christine Li-Grining and Jennifer Stephan for methodological support.

Throughout this research, we were continually impressed by the way progress works, particularly in the educational arena: dramatic improvements in opportunity followed by new challenges. Our goal has been to identify both. Our hope has been that in identifying these, our research can contribute to a better society for the next generation, and our book is dedicated to Janet, Soluna, and Martín, the next generation.

# CHAPTER ONE

## COMMUNITY COLLEGES: TRADITIONAL COLLEGE PROCEDURES FOR NONTRADITIONAL STUDENTS

The United States is well on its way to a previously impossible goal: universal higher education. Over 80 percent of high school graduates enter higher education in the eight years after high school (Adelman 2003, *[growth sector]* table 2.7). College enrollment has dramatically increased, and most of the gain is in a relatively new institution: community colleges.

## COMMUNITY COLLEGES TODAY: ACCESS FOR ALL

Minor institutions just a few decades ago, community colleges are now a major player in American society. A generation ago, public two-year col- *[transformation in ccs]* leges were called junior colleges, were considered unimportant, and enrolled only a small portion of college students. Now called community colleges, they have become comprehensive institutions that have greatly increased in size and importance, and serve a broad segment of the community. Where enrollment in four-year colleges has doubled since 1965, enrollment in community colleges has increased five-fold. Today, almost half of all new col- *[½]* lege students are in community colleges (NCES 2002).

Community colleges are amazing institutions designed around an idealistic goal: increasing college access. Community colleges are the primary *[clientele]* source of opportunity for ethnic minorities, immigrants, and low-income students. They offer a second chance for students who attended poor high schools, or who did poorly in high school. They also provide new benefits:

1

Besides preparing students to transfer to four-year colleges, they also offer certificates and associate's degrees in occupational fields (Brint and Karabel 1989), as well as a wide range of noncredit classes, training activities, and community services.

## BEYOND ACCESS: OLD PROBLEMS SOLVED, NEW PROBLEMS CREATED

Because of these rapid changes and new missions, community colleges are poorly understood, and policy makers struggle to figure out how to use this new institution to accomplish societal and labor market goals. College faculty and staff report vague and inconsistent descriptions of community college activities, as we shall see.

As community colleges have evolved over recent decades, old problems have been solved only to give rise to new challenges, some of which are rarely seen or understood. Despite the amazing increases in college access, most community college students do not complete degrees, and, as we detail later, many leave with no new qualifications—no degrees, and often no credits (Adelman 2003). For these students, college provides little or no labor market benefit (Marcotte et al. 2005). These colleges obviously do not work for many students. Increasing access was an important step, but it was only the first. We must now work to improve these colleges so that they can effectively educate and graduate their new students.

## UNDERSTANDING THE PROBLEMS: EXPLANATIONS AND SOLUTIONS

To solve these new problems, we must explain why they occur. This is a major undertaking. Although statistics can demonstrate the magnitude of the problems, numbers alone cannot flesh out the underlying issues. To understand such complicated and often hidden factors, one must go beyond the existing quantitative literature, which this book does, employing multiple research methods.

Throughout, we compare community colleges with private colleges that also offer accredited associate's degrees in the same occupational fields (which we call occupational colleges). Through detailed comparisons in local and national data, we discover that these two types of colleges use different procedures that handle students' problems in different ways. The community colleges we studied place responsibility on individual students, often expecting ill-prepared students to catch up on their own, and reforms focus on fixing individuals. In contrast, the occupational colleges we studied take some responsibility for student success by addressing student problems with institutional innovations rather than trying to fix the problem student by student. In other words, institutional deficiencies, rather than student deficiencies, are examined as areas for improvement.

Our research shows that students experience many problems in dealing with community college procedures; similar students respond differently to occupational colleges' different procedures—they report fewer problems at college and achieve higher degree completion rates. These findings suggest that student deficiencies are not the only cause of the problems college students face, and that programs to reduce the deficiencies of individual students may not be the most effective solution. Instead, institutional and procedural changes in community colleges may lead to greater success for their students, who are otherwise similar to their peers at occupational colleges. These comparisons bring to light the shortcomings of previous approaches and suggest some innovative alternatives.

This study has little to say about teaching and instruction (see Grubb and Associates 1999). Our focus on other aspects of the college experience helps to demonstrate one of our primary points. Colleges, and indeed all schools, are more than classrooms, and must provide more than instruction. Schools are organizations in which students have careers over several years. Aside from judging instructional quality, we should also judge schools on other criteria: students' persistence, degree completion, and employment outcomes, for example. School success in these areas may depend on whether college staff make correct assumptions about student needs and capacities and devise appropriate organizational procedures.

This chapter first examines three revolutionary changes in American society which have transformed community colleges and have given them a central role in society. We discuss the innovative ways that community colleges have dramatically improved college access for new groups of students. Yet, despite this remarkable success, students with degree aspirations have dismal rates of degree completion at community colleges. We consider two explanations. The first comes from a youth development or individual approach, which blames students' deficiencies for their failure at college and proposes to increase college completion rates by improving individuals' capabilities. These strategies, however, are difficult to fit into students' already overburdened lives, and it is questionable whether this approach seriously considers the adult responsibilities that many students must manage while in college.

The second explanation comes from an institutional approach, which examines how colleges' organizational procedures may not match the needs of the new students in these colleges. Consistent with this, we demonstrate how occupational colleges, which are similar to community colleges in the students they serve and the occupational programs they offer, have much better degree completion rates and different organizational procedures. As we will show, many problems that are blamed on student deficiencies are less likely to arise in occupational colleges. These problems also seem to be reduced by certain organizational procedures, which could be adapted for use in community colleges.

## THE RISE OF COMMUNITY COLLEGES: AN UNFINISHED REVOLUTION

American society is now in the midst of major transformations. In one generation, American society has been radically transformed by three revolutions, each related to community colleges.

1.  The labor market has increasingly demanded college degrees.
2.  Community colleges have emerged as a major societal institution.
3.  Community colleges have adopted a revolutionary policy of open admissions.

First, the labor market has dramatically changed. Just forty years ago, most jobs required little education. For example, high school dropouts with poor academic skills could get high-paid jobs in factories. This is no longer true. Most of those manufacturing jobs are gone, and the remaining ones require academic, problem-solving, technical, and social skills. These new basic skills include academic skills at only the tenth grade level, but the majority of high school graduates lack such competencies (Murnane and Levy 1996). Although students formerly acquired these skills in high school, many no longer do, and employers increasingly seek out college graduates. Today, the fastest growing jobs are those that require at least some postsecondary education (Barton 2005; Carnevale 2001), and the demand and wage premium for college degrees is growing (Grubb 1996).

Second, community colleges have emerged as a major societal institution. Since 1965, while enrollments at four-year colleges doubled, community college enrollments increased five-fold (NCES 2002, table 173). Although community colleges began as a small part of higher education, today almost half of new college students attend community colleges (NCES 2002, table

190). The proportion is higher for nontraditional students (economically disadvantaged, ethnic minorities, immigrants, older individuals), who are the fastest-growing segment of students in higher education. Providing access into higher education for over five million students every year, community colleges have become a central component of American society.

Third, whereas four-year colleges increased opportunity by tinkering with admissions criteria, community colleges adopted a revolutionary policy of open admissions, admitting all interested applicants regardless of academic achievement. This is the most amazing change, removing virtually all obstacles to college. For the 86 percent of young adults with a high school diploma or GED (NCES 2002, table 8), college access has almost become an entitlement. High school was the highest level of education that most Americans attended in 1965, but today most young people attend college. The first half of the twentieth century led to universal access to secondary education; in the second half, the United States is approaching an age of nearly universal college attendance.

## Innovations of College Access

Community colleges have transformed higher education. Community colleges offer many new options, including one-year certificates and two-year associate's degrees, in addition to preparation for transfer to four-year colleges. With their low cost and convenient locations, they have reduced financial and spatial barriers, allowing students to attend college while living at home and continuing their family or work duties, with no additional housing costs or job-related sacrifices. With open admissions, community colleges remove academic barriers and offer second chances for college to students who did poorly in high school.

Community colleges have shifted traditional notions about college in both space and time. Initially each state had only a few public colleges, but today every state has numerous community colleges, many with multiple campuses. More than 1,100 public two-year colleges are located in cities and towns across the nation, and many have satellite locations (NCES 2002, table 246). Instead of offering courses only on a college campus, community colleges are also located in storefronts or office buildings convenient to homes or workplaces. Such satellite locations allow students to fit college into their daily lives with less commuting and fewer sacrifices. The emergence and expansion of online options has extended this access into students' homes.

Besides spatial convenience, community colleges have also shifted time schedules. They offer classes before 9 a.m. and after 5 p.m. on weekdays,

Saturdays, and even Sundays. Some campuses offer Internet classes, lessons, and help sessions that are available around the clock. College has shifted from a nine to five schedule to 24/7.

Community colleges have also transformed high schools. "College for all" has become the guiding principle in high schools, and guidance counselors have changed their advice. Whereas old studies found that guidance counselors acted as gatekeepers to keep students out of college (Cicourel and Kitsuse 1963), by the 1990s some guidance counselors were, one study found, urging most students to attend (Rosenbaum 2001). Obviously such expansion means more students enter college. It also means new kinds of students. This diversity has further increased with the changing ethnic composition of the United States.

In studying community colleges, we were impressed with the ambitious idealistic goals of these institutions, the extensive breadth of program offerings, the extraordinary dedication and efforts of some faculty and administrators to extend themselves well beyond formal job duties to support students in college and into careers. We were impressed by the sense of mission that many faculty and administrators demonstrated. Some devoted sixty hours a week to making sure that they reached students and helped them succeed. The deeper we delved, the more impressed we were with the heroic efforts of community college faculty, staff, and administrators. A simple focus on average statistics misses the important and inspiring achievements we describe later in this volume.

*a way out of poverty*

We also marvel at their impressive successes. As we interviewed students, we were repeatedly impressed by the dramatic changes in opportunities offered to students who came from very disadvantaged backgrounds. If it were not for these institutions, many of these disadvantaged students would have no chance to escape poverty.

*high college-going rates*

College attendance is now possible for most high school graduates. Indeed, recent analyses indicate that over 80 percent of high school graduates attend college, and most surprisingly, the racial gap in college attendance has largely disappeared. Eighty-three and a half percent of whites attend college in the eight years after high school, and the numbers are only 3 percent lower for blacks and Hispanics (80.2 percent and 80.6 percent; Adelman 2003, table 2.7). Although blacks and Hispanics face greater barriers in graduating from high school, high school graduates find that the major barriers to entering college have fallen, and college attendance is universally high across most ethnic groups. Because of community colleges, the major barriers to entering college have fallen.

## Access, but Poor Completion

Despite these achievements, degree completion is disappointing in community colleges. A national survey found that, of students who began in public two-year colleges, only 26 percent completed any degree five years after entrance (NCES 2002). Moreover, there are serious racial gaps. Whereas 28 percent of whites complete degrees, only 11 percent of blacks and 21 percent of Hispanics do so (NCES 2002; see also Bailey et al. 2003; Dougherty 1994; Dowd 2003; Grubb 1996). Following students over a longer period increases degree completion, but the results are still poor, and sometimes dismal. Analyzing high school graduates who had degree plans and entered public two-year colleges immediately after graduation, one study finds that only 40.8 percent of students complete any degree over the next eight years (Rosenbaum and Stephan 2005). Moreover, the racial gap is huge: 45.2 percent of whites complete degrees, but only 32.6 percent of Hispanics and 18.7 percent of blacks do so (2005).

Indeed, many students barely enter college. Defining incidental students as those with ten or fewer credits eight years after graduating high school, Clifford Adelman (2003, table 3.1) finds that about 20 percent of African American and Latino college students are incidental students, but fewer than 10 percent of whites are. Moreover, 75 percent of incidental students attend community colleges (Adelman 2003, table 3.2). Community colleges provide access to higher education for many new groups of students, but it is not clear whether these students are actually in college, and whether they accumulate enough credits to improve their job opportunities (compare Marcotte et al. 2005).

These statistics indicate an amazing success and a startling failure. Community colleges have dramatically lowered barriers to college access. They serve nontraditional students, who are often the first generation in their families to attend college (Dougherty 1994). They also serve nontraditional purposes, offering occupational programs that respond to labor market needs (Bailey, Badway, and Gumport 2002; Brint and Karabel 1989; Grubb 1996; Jacobs and Winslow 2003; Shaw and Rab 2003; Wilms 1974). However, degree completion is shockingly low for whites, and abysmal for blacks and Hispanics.

## BLAMING STUDENT DEFICIENCIES: THE INDIVIDUAL APPROACH

To understand such problems, one approach is to study individuals, explaining outcomes with multivariate analyses of student attributes (disadvantaged backgrounds, poor achievement, and the like). This approach assumes that students have deficiencies that must be repaired. However, this implicit blame of students does not inform colleges and policy makers what actions can remedy the problems because the deficiencies arise before students enter college and may not be easily redressed. This individual model has serious limitations, which suggest the need for other, more structural, approaches.

Psychologists have focused on identifying the problems that minority and disadvantaged students face. Their studies have led to a wide variety of ambitious youth-development programs that target risk factors and seek to build youths' capacity to surmount educational obstacles. For example, a National Research Council report enumerates a long list of goals for improving the lives of young people. It includes twenty-eight attributes in four broad categories: physical health, intellectual development, psychological and emotional development, and social development—to be targeted for improvement (Eccles and Appleton Gootman 2002).

In an ideal world, these approaches are obviously desirable; it is always valuable to improve individuals' capabilities. However, in the real world that disadvantaged students inhabit, this approach is often unworkable. It demands precious time and money from low-income youths for whom resources are already scarce, and may make further demands on the support from significant others. The additional demands of youth development programs may impose new costs and fail to improve students' success.

An illustrative example comes from our interview with Sheila, a student who faces difficulties similar to many others we interviewed (all respondent names in this book are pseudonyms). Sheila was a twenty-two-year-old African American from a low-income background. She did poorly in high school, has never married, and had two babies before she was twenty. Although she received only occasional childcare help, she managed to attend college full-time, work forty hours a week, run a household, prepare meals, and read to her two preschool children. Sheila struggled with her college coursework, and managed a B average. She blamed herself for not working harder in college, but could not start her schoolwork until the children went to bed, and blamed herself for sometimes falling asleep over homework. Her two-year degree would take at least four years to complete, if she could persevere that long. She did not realize that many of the courses she had to take for the academic associate's degree did not confer college credits, nor did she know that the college offered an applied associate's degree that did not require some of these remedial courses, yet would confer virtually the same, if not better, benefits in the labor market. If she had known, she might have chosen the latter and completed the degree by the time of our interview. Meanwhile, her mother was helping with child care, but, as Sheila began her fourth year in college, her mother repeatedly asked how much longer the "two-year degree" would take.

The typical youth development approach would provide Sheila with better academic skills for getting through college and better life skills for managing the many competing demands on her time. These would be useful, but it is hard to imagine where she would fit this program into her already busy schedule, and whether she (or her mother) would be patient about extending her college career with another noncredit delay. This approach would provide Sheila with a great deal of information about college procedures, much of which would be of little use later in life.

Moreover, this individualistic approach has some limitations that are often ignored. First, despite claims about focusing on the positive, many youth development programs pose a daunting array of ambitious goals that might be overwhelming and discouraging to practitioners and students, particularly students who have failed in the past. Second, though this approach intends to operate in all domains, the emphasis has been on providing small, add-on social services programs (during or after school), rather than on fundamental redesign of major societal institutions such as schools. As such, there is a risk that it will not reach all students in the way that institutional changes do.

## BEYOND INDIVIDUAL BLAME: AN INSTITUTIONAL APPROACH

Instead of focusing only on improving individuals, the problem may reside in the person-environment fit. Describing research on the motivational effects of small schools, teacher efficacy, and junior high school structures, one review concludes that many of the typical problems faced by young people are not developmental, but rather, the result of a poor match between young people's needs and institutional structures (Eccles et al. 1993).

Rather than analyzing individual traits, this book takes a different approach, examining different institutions and how they may contribute to college failures for disadvantaged students. Instead of seeing students' actions as related solely to internal motivation, individuals also respond to external incentives. A sociological analysis can uncover the ways that different organizations provide students with opportunities and incentives, yet also pose obstacles, including some that may be unnecessary and unintended. As we illustrate, organizations may contribute to students' successes and failures, and studies of their alternative procedures can suggest practical steps that schools can take to improve student outcomes.

For Sheila, and for many students like her, a structural approach of studying and remedying college organizational procedures has obvious attraction. Instead of adding a new program to provide Sheila with the many skills and extensive information she would need to cope with community college, colleges may be redesigned so they demand less prerequisite information, make it difficult to make mistakes, and reduce the impact of mistakes. This study will enable colleges to identify institutional barriers and make organizational changes to help students who lack the time or resources to attend additional intervention programs.

## INSTITUTIONAL DIFFERENCES: PROCEDURES AND OUTCOMES

We seek to understand the ways that institutions contribute to students' outcomes by comparing two types of institutions: public community colleges and private occupational colleges. Although the public and private two-year colleges we studied offer accredited programs in the same occupational fields and enroll similar students (as we show later), they handle the same issues in different ways. We examine the ways that each type of college tries to engage students who had previous difficulties in school, to respond to students' difficulties, to bolster students' confidence in college payoffs, and to teach them social and cultural skills required in school and in the college labor market. We examine how these colleges provide institutional contacts with employers, and we compare how they operate across different occupations and in different college structures. This comparison lets us see the ways similar students respond to very different organizational procedures. Instead of blaming students for their outcomes, private occupational colleges address problematic outcomes by using procedures distinctly different from those used in public two-year colleges. These procedures seem to lead similar students to fewer problems and greater progress.

### Community Colleges

Community colleges are accredited, public, two-year colleges that began as feeder schools (junior colleges) into traditional four-year colleges and have evolved to offer extensive occupational programs (Brint and Karabel 1989). They frequently have been the focus of research (Dougherty 1994; Grubb 1996). Our sample of community colleges covers a large metropolitan area and is racially and socioeconomically highly diverse.

## Occupational Colleges

Occupational colleges are also accredited two-year colleges that offer occupational programs, but are private rather than public. Many began as traditional business or technical schools, but unlike most schools of this sort, these colleges are now accredited to offer associate's degrees by national associations, similar to the regional groups that accredit most community colleges. They have a long history of providing postsecondary education in occupational fields to students who generally come from less advantaged backgrounds.

Readers may think of these colleges as trade schools, vocational colleges, business colleges, technical schools, or health services schools; however, there is an important difference. Although they began as business and technical schools, they have changed over the past fifteen years. Now these and many like them have upgraded their programs to offer accredited associate's degrees. Accreditation is important, because it sets these occupational colleges apart from over 90 percent of private postsecondary institutions, which offer no degree above a certificate (Apling 1993). Beyond accreditation, occupational colleges are also similar to community colleges in that they increasingly offer transfer opportunities for four-year degrees (mostly in applied occupational fields), and prepare students for the same jobs, in the same local labor market, for the same high-demand skilled occupations (for example, health services, technicians, computer information systems, administrative, paralegal). However, these occupational colleges do not offer the other programs offered by community colleges (for example, liberal arts, remedial, GED, adult education, hobbies, self improvement, second language programs). Most interestingly for this inquiry, these private colleges design their programs and services differently (as we will discuss later), which may account for their better degree completion rates.

Although in earlier decades some private schools offered poor training (or even fraudulent practices), federal regulations in the early 1990s radically altered these institutions, forcing 1,300 out of business and imposing performance criteria that improved the others (Kelly 2001). The institutions in our sample have a history of serving low-income and minority students, and have successfully met these performance requirements.

Our study has nothing to say about private colleges generally; we are studying some of the best ones—an ideal type. This point must be emphasized. Although our community colleges may be typical, our private colleges are not a representative sample of such institutions. Rather, we focus on a small, handpicked group of private colleges. These colleges are not a random sample and do not represent private for-profit or nonprofit colleges nationwide. We chose colleges offering some of the best programs in occupational fields, and those most comparable to community colleges.

The ideal type provided by the private colleges in our study presents a different perspective on how two-year colleges can operate, which we contrast with our community colleges. Our aim is not to compare average private and public colleges, nor to discount the other extensive educational functions community colleges provide that occupational colleges do not. Our aim is instead to compare private and public colleges that are highly similar in terms of the accredited occupational programs they offer, the students they enroll, and the geographic region and labor market they serve. At the same time, we seek to contrast how these colleges use different procedures, to understand how these procedures operate, how students respond to them, and how students' experiences and outcomes differ in comparable colleges using different procedures.

*Goal:*
*SRQ*

## Comparing Degree Completion Rates

Private two-year, degree-granting colleges (for-profit and nonprofit) have higher graduation rates, and possibly smaller racial gaps, than community colleges. Analyzing high school graduates with degree plans who entered two-year, degree-granting colleges right after graduation, James Rosenbaum and Jennifer Stephan (2005) find that only 40.8 percent of community-college students complete degrees (associate's or above), but 58.0 percent of private-college students do so in the eight years after high school. The racial gap also may be smaller, although small numbers make this inference less certain (table 1.1).

Other research suggests similar conclusions. Using National Education Longitudinal Study (NELS) data, Stephan and Rosenbaum (2006) found that students attending public and private two-year colleges are highly comparable. After creating a multivariate logistic model of students' propensity to attend community colleges (versus private two-year colleges), the study found many students in each college type at every propensity level, and the two groups of students were not significantly different on any of the extensive array of pre-existing attributes tested. Moreover, after matching groups of students who were highly comparable in propensity and balanced on forty-five relevant attributes, the study found that degree completion was significantly higher in private than in public two-year colleges in every comparison (Stephan and Rosenbaum 2006).

In our local sample, only one occupational college provided degree completion data. That college shows dramatically higher six-year completion

TABLE 1.1    Degree Completion Rates

|  | Whites | Hispanics | African Americans |
|---|---|---|---|
| Public colleges | 46.7% | 32.5% | 18.9% |
|  | (1207) | (270) | (110) |
| Private colleges | 58.7% | 25.0% | 64.3% |
|  | (81) | (13) | (12) |

*Source:* Rosenbaum and Stephan (2005).
*Note:* Numbers taken eight years after college entry. Number of cases unweighted.

rates than the above community college rates, especially among minority students (65.1 percent for all students, 57.0 percent for blacks, 77.9 percent Hispanics).

The Illinois Board of Higher Education collects systematic data that permits computing graduation-enrollment ratios for all colleges in the state (2002). While these ratios are not the same as degree completion rates for a cohort, they are a rough approximation. Analyzing all colleges in Illinois, Davis Jenkins (2002) finds that private two-year colleges have much higher graduates–enrollment ratios than community colleges, especially for African American and Hispanic students.

All these analyses lead to the same conclusions. First, private colleges *conclusions* have higher completion rates than public colleges. Second, the racial gap in degree completion may be smaller in private colleges than in public ones. Each of these analyses has potential sources of error. Yet it is noteworthy that the same conclusions are suggested in analyses with different sources of error—small numbers of minorities in the national data, only one college in our data, and uncertainties about graduates-enrollment ratios.

## Explaining Completion Rate Differences

Some critics argue that these degree completion rates ignore students who seek only certificates. Yet the evidence indicates that certificates have less certain labor-market value than most associate's degrees (Marcotte et al. 2005, table 3). Moreover, students rarely aspire to certificates alone (Grubb 1996; Rosenbaum and Stephan 2005; Tuma 1993), and they do not often complete them (Grubb 1996). Other critics contend that students do not get degrees because they chose to use college to explore their interests, prior to or instead of pursuing a particular degree (Adelman 2003). However, some results seem hard to explain as informed choices. For instance, among high school graduates in the class of 1992 who entered postsecondary education, though only 8 percent had completed associate's degrees by the year 2000, another 10 percent had enough credits (sixty or more), but no degree (Adelman 2003, 34). Although they may have chosen to accumulate unrelated credits, one must wonder whether students would have chosen different courses if they realized that, more than eight years after high school, they still would not have the labor market payoffs that one gets only from a full degree.

In sum, earning the degree is important. Moreover, the evidence strongly indicates that completion rates are higher and the race gap may be smaller in private colleges than in their public counterparts. This volume seeks to explain these institutional differences.

## UNDERSTANDING INSTITUTIONAL DIFFERENCES

Previous researchers have identified three different institutional explanations for community college difficulties. Steven Brint and Jerome Karabel (1989) trace the history of community colleges from their origins as transfer institutions for providing access to four-year colleges to a new emphasis on occupational goals. Analyzing historical materials and interviews with top administrators, they show that the new occupational mission has emerged victorious, supplanting the prior transfer mission. They titled their book *The Diverted Dream* and conclude that the original dream of transfer to bachelor's programs was diverted to vocational purposes.

Unlike Brint and Karabel, Kevin Dougherty (1994) contends that the occupational mission did not replace the transfer mission; both missions occur simultaneously, forcing the institution to embody many contradictions. Dougherty maintains that the conflicting goals of community colleges interfere with their success by overextending their resources. Indeed, community colleges seem to be the repository for many new goals continuously added to the college mission. Dougherty suggests that these new programs raise questions about priorities and coordination. Like Brint and Karabel, Dougherty not only suggests that the transfer mission should be primary, but also shows that students encounter many institutional barriers to transferring credits for particular courses, to obtaining financial aid, and even to getting dormitory rooms when they enter four-year colleges.

Unlike either Brint and Karabel or Dougherty, Norton Grubb (1996) sees community colleges' occupational mission as valuable: it is a way to provide significant opportunities to disadvantaged students. He demonstrates that the sector of skilled jobs requiring some college is growing, that there are clear economic payoffs to the associate's degree in certain fields (business, health, and some technical fields), and that many students have entered community colleges with the goal of gaining preparation for good jobs. Interviewing faculty and staff, he shows that community colleges try to provide occupational training that meets the needs of the labor market, but that their efforts are repeatedly hampered by inadequate resources. Moreover, community colleges sometimes take on new missions without the resources to fund new programs or to integrate them with the existing institution.

[handwritten margin note: *resource constraints*]

## JUGGLING MULTIPLE MISSIONS

As these models indicate, community colleges have responded to the influx of nontraditional students by adding new programs and missions that sometimes conflict with traditional programs and missions. However, as the following chapters will show, although we find some support for the three diagnoses (diverted goal, contradictory goals, and scarce resources), our analyses suggest that none completely explains students' difficulties in making good use of community colleges. True, as Brint and Karabel note, community colleges have devised new occupational goals, which are departures from traditional transfer goals, but this transformation is far from complete—it neither precludes transfer nor does it provide unambiguous support for occupational goals.

[handwritten margin note: *fuzzy focus*]

[handwritten margin note: *2 competing objectives*]

Indeed, both missions coexist in our community colleges, which are similar to many others statewide and nationwide: 50 percent of our community college students are enrolled in transfer programs, and the average for the entire state is also 50 percent (IBHE 2002, table VI-2). Nationally, the transfer emphasis is even stronger: 71 percent of community college students expect to earn a bachelor's degree or higher (NCES 2002, 27). Our findings are compatible with national studies. A study of administrators in eighteen community colleges across the United States (Cross and Fideler 1989) and a national sample of 1,725 faculty in ninety-two community colleges (Brewer 1999) both report that administrators and faculty are nearly evenly split in their ranking of transfer and workplace preparation as the top institutional priorities. Contrary to the reports of Brint and Karabel's presidents, transfer and occupational programs are evenly balanced.

These findings support Dougherty and Grubb, who both note that community colleges have taken on contradictory missions, which create administrative difficulties in coordinating offerings and allocating resources. However, our study questions whether these contradictions necessarily pose problems for students.

## FITTING NONTRADITIONAL PEGS IN TRADITIONAL HOLES

The key issue is how colleges integrate their contradictions for students and whether they implement procedures to make each component operate effectively. Despite nontraditional students and nontraditional goals, community colleges have preserved many aspects of the traditional four-year college model—similar variety of courses, ways of choosing classes, registration and guidance procedures, academic emphasis, and career counseling. Their students, however, may have different backgrounds, needs, and goals than traditional college students, and this model may not work for many of them.

As we shall show, the integration of students, goals, and organization is incomplete at community colleges, and may be why so few students complete degrees. The contradictions of community colleges not only strain resources, as Grubb notes. They also confuse and distract students, obscure goals and pathways to goals, and prevent colleges from focusing on improving clarity and benefits. The unresolved contradictions, unfocused programs, and poor labor market linkages may leave students with serious shortages of information about the marketplace. Such contradictions could confuse any student, but are especially confusing for nontraditional students who often cannot rely on parents as a resource for college information and plans.

## INTEGRATED MISSIONS AND NONTRADITIONAL PROCEDURES

Private two-year colleges, on the other hand, offer a variety of occupational programs and even four-year degrees without posing time conflicts, confusing choices, or ambiguity about payoffs for students. Institutions can offer multiple missions without harming students. If a college offers a clear way for students to choose among the college's missions, and an effective pathway to each program's goal (four-year college or occupation), students can navigate effectively through college. Although the range of programs is narrower than at community colleges, these colleges demonstrate that multiple missions do not necessarily mean that the contradiction is imposed on students, confusing them and impeding their progress.

Whereas community colleges provide traditional college procedures to nontraditional students, the occupational colleges in this study have adopted a nontraditional approach to integrate new students and goals into their institution, and to shift some responsibility away from students. These colleges have devised ways to reduce the need for information and to streamline the gathering of information so that nontraditional students are not hurt by their lack of "college knowledge." Where Dougherty analyzes students' difficulties in completing degrees and transferring to four-year colleges, and Grubb analyzes students' difficulties getting preparation and entering the labor market, we examine ways these outcomes may be affected by different organizational procedures.

We find that colleges' organizational procedures may have an important impact on students. All organizations have procedures that provide certain kinds of assistance to clients and make regular demands on them. Colleges' organizational procedures include rules, ways of handling various tasks (for example, course and program choices), resources for assisting these tasks (staff and their duties), and the like. This volume identifies alternative procedures in different colleges and examines the implications for informing students' plans and choices, bolstering motivation with clear incentives, teaching requisite social skills, and facilitating job placement.

The procedures we observe in community colleges and occupational colleges seem to arise from the organizational history and culture of these types of colleges. These procedures include a wide variety of details—curricula, prerequisites, program selection, course sequences, information collection and dissemination, and job duties of various staff. Although these procedures are often dismissed as details that are taken for granted and assumed to be unavoidable and unimportant in understanding student success, we find that both assumptions are wrong. We find that alternatives are possible: these colleges use different organizational procedures to help the same kind of students handle the same organizational problems. We also find that these procedures are important: alternative procedures make different demands on students, lead to different perceived incentives, and students report responding differently to them and having different consequences.

## LEARNING FROM INNOVATION

As advocates often claim, private schools have the freedom to innovate. However, innovation can be positive or negative—indeed, it is often both. Innovation refers to departures from tradition, and though some traditions stifle responsiveness, others preserve deeply held values. Unfortunately, the for-profit sector of postsecondary education, especially at the subbaccalaureate level, has sometimes devised innovative fraudulent practices—for example, deceptive claims, poor employment rates, low standards, and the saddling of students with large debts. While free markets or government regulation may drive fraudulent colleges out of business, these corrections take time during which many students can suffer. As noted, federal regulations in the early 1990s curtailed fraudulent practices, forced 1,300 schools out of business, and encouraged those that remained to engage in practices to improve graduation and employment rates. Today, the incidence of fraud is likely to be much less, but examples are still reported with some frequency, and the full extent of fraud is unknown. Many public concerns are still raised about some for-profit college practices regarding overly aggressive recruiting and misleading promises.

However, innovation can also be highly beneficial and regulatory procedures may stifle it. A community college instructor told us of his efforts to launch a new occupational program. After enormous efforts over many months, dealing with five levels of bureaucracy, the program was finally blocked at the sixth. He vowed never to innovate again because of how thankless and futile the effort had been for him. Those six levels of bureaucracy, meant to prevent wasteful and redundant programs and to ensure program quality, unintentionally stifle progress and improvements. By contrast, in occupational colleges, innovation is simple. Someone proposes an idea to the college president, who makes a decision, perhaps after consulting a few people, and the change is made.

Sometimes it is hard to tell if innovation is positive or negative. Private two-year colleges are criticized for lowering academic standards. In some cases, however, lower academic demands may be appropriate, for example, if jobs do not require high academic skills. If a business program required calculus merely because it is a traditional college requirement, but few business jobs need calculus, calculus would be an unnecessary barrier preventing access for otherwise qualified students. Unlike trade schools, these occupational colleges require some general education courses in English, humanities, social science, and math—accreditation demands it. We did not study academic standards and cannot say if occupational colleges have lower academic standards than community colleges, but the strong responsiveness of occupational colleges to employers' demands makes them unlikely to reduce standards to levels that would disappoint employers. We would be surprised if graduates of occupational colleges lacked the basic skills in reading, writing, and math employers require. This is a complex issue, requiring detailed information on job demands. It is beyond the scope of our study (compare Maxwell 2006).

## COMPARING INSTITUTIONAL ASSUMPTIONS: INDIVIDUAL CHOICE VERSUS PACKAGE DEALS

Some community colleges have tried one or two of the procedures we find in occupational colleges (Palmer 1990; Roueche and Baker 1987), but have not implemented them as a complete package. Indeed, a combination of many procedures (for example, curriculum structure, information systems, mandatory advising, peer cohorts, and job placement) may have more than an additive effect: there may be a package effect. Even if students face strong pressures from work or family, they may find it difficult to walk away from an occupational college where many procedures operate: where they meet regularly with an advisor and a peer cohort, where their progress is closely monitored, where required courses are always offered at predictable times, where milestones come quickly, where most students complete degrees, where the college offers extensive job placement assistance and promises [and delivers] 95 percent job placement. Meanwhile, it may be easier to walk away from a community college that only provides two reforms (for example, an advisory meeting and a tracking system).

Just as a travel agent can eliminate headaches and crises associated with traveling by arranging a package deal for vacationers, occupational colleges provide complete packages in which many details are arranged and guaranteed, reducing the burden of collecting information and the risk of mistakes for students. The traveler and the student both have confidence that they will be taken care of and that little can go wrong. If a traveler were to have only flight arrangements, he would still be responsible for arranging the rest of the journey and thus open to making mistakes that could put the vacation in jeopardy. Similarly, the student who only has one or two aspects of the college process guaranteed may run into problems with other aspects, and, just as important, may lose confidence in the entire college experience.

Indeed, the comparison of the traditional practices of community colleges and the nontraditional innovations of occupational colleges suggests two different models with different assumptions. Community colleges use procedures that seem to be based on the assumption that students already have certain attributes—plans, motivations, information, social skills, and job search skills. Students who do not have them have difficulties in community colleges. Even current reforms continue to assume that students come to college fully prepared. In contrast, occupational colleges do not assume that students have these attributes initially but ensure that they develop them.

Although the community college approach lends itself to blaming student failures on their deficiencies, these occupational colleges devise organizational procedures to help students succeed in each of these realms, regardless of personal background or preparation.

We discover that private colleges handle these issues differently, using procedures that make having prior knowledge and skills less necessary.

1. While community colleges assume that students can make effective plans on their own, occupational colleges give students a package deal plan for attaining an explicit educational and career goal in a clear time frame.

2. While community colleges assume that students are motivated, occupational colleges foster motivation by bolstering incentives and students' confidence that they can earn their degree.

3. While community colleges assume that students have enough information to make choices on their own, occupational colleges devise extensive procedures to inform students, guide their choices, and prevent mistakes.

4. While community colleges assume that students have professional social skills, occupational colleges teach these skills.

5. While community colleges assume that graduates have job-search skills and can get jobs on their own, occupational colleges actively help graduates get jobs related to their studies.

Despite the inevitable uncertainties in inferring causality, these findings identify entirely new college organizational procedures that may have a large impact on students. These procedures are strikingly different from the traditional approaches of community colleges, and our findings suggest that new types of students have fewer difficulties with occupational college procedures. This volume examines each of the assumptions discussed and their corresponding procedures.

## BEYOND EXPLORATION AND CHOICE

Occupational colleges pose serious challenges to our ideas about what college is and how college can assist students. We often assume that college entails choice, and choice is desirable. However, in looking at students' experiences, we find that students report many difficulties when confronted with choices that occupational colleges address in novel and effective ways.

In *The Paradox of Choice*, Barry Schwartz (2004) notes that when people are offered many options, they sometimes want an option that spares them from the burden of so many choices. Although community colleges offer many choices, we find that they rarely offer one: highly structured programs that curtail choice but promise timely graduation and an appropriate job.

To many readers, the students we interviewed may seem narrowly focused on pragmatic and vocational goals. As R. D. Cox (2004) has shown, community college students want occupational training, not exploration. This should not be surprising. Vocationalism has become an overwhelming part of education in the United States, in two-year and four-year colleges (Grubb and Lazerson 2004). Hearing that the labor market punishes individuals who do not attend college, many students enter college who might not have done so otherwise. Over 70 percent of students in our sample said that they entered college to get a good job. It is not surprising that they did not want to explore academic options. Such students have every reason to be pragmatic, given that financial circumstances may demand that they proceed quickly into a career, and any delay poses the constant threat of crises, interruptions, and dropping out. Regardless of whether we like vocationalism, we must recognize that students shoulder serious constraints on their time, resources, and social support.

Sometimes our ideals, no matter how good they may seem, do not apply to other people's life circumstances and should not be imposed on them. Phrases like Dewey's—"What the best and wisest parent wants for his own child, that must the community want for all of its children"— expresses an appealing ideal, but ignores the reality of social context. Yes, we should all want the possibility of limitless opportunity for all of our citizens, but at whose expense? Does our idealism sometimes blind us to the reality that those most in need and most likely to fail in their attempt at a college education are, in some sense, victims of that idealism? When so many leave college without attaining their goals, is the possibility of opportunity enough, or should we consider ways to offer more effective, albeit possibly less idealistic, pathways to success? Studying students' experiences in community colleges leads us to ask new questions. Should colleges offer open-ended exploration without time limits to students whose life circumstances impose time limits? For nontraditional students who need many remedial courses, and face acute pressures to complete degrees on a short timetable, does the rhetoric of exploration offer false promises? Does the same kind of education have the same value and payoff for all?

## LARGER IMPLICATIONS

These findings have general implications for our understanding of how to apply sociological insights. For social scientists, private colleges' procedures are especially interesting because they seem to reflect sociological insights. These colleges respond to important factors that are often the focus of sociological analyses, such as organizational requirements, students' social worlds, and information processes. The private colleges in our sample seem to respond to implicit organizational requirements for the information and social skills that students need to graduate. The colleges also seem to respond to students' social worlds, recognizing how school success depends on the student's ability to balance home, work, commuting, and peer influences. The occupational colleges respond to information processes, devising effective social mechanisms to provide information. Their procedures pay explicit attention to the kinds of information students need, the kinds of mistakes students make, and the kinds of concerns students have.

If the successes of occupational colleges are due to specific organizational procedures, community colleges may also be able use them to provide similar benefits for their students. In other words, the shortcomings of community colleges may not be inevitable. These findings suggest policy alternatives that are not usually considered.

Although we are only studying two-year colleges, our findings may have implications for other institutions. Many four-year colleges strive to assist disadvantaged students, who experience similar problems to those we see in two-year colleges, perhaps for similar organizational reasons. Many high schools are concerned about students' poor choices and guidance counselors' difficulties in assisting student progress, which resemble some of the problems we observe. Even job training programs offer either skill training or employer contacts, but rarely connect the two. Our studies offer new ideas about how organizational procedures can address these difficulties.

Community colleges, four-year colleges, high schools, and job training programs can use these findings to transform good intentions into sound understandings, and disorganization into effective procedures. These various institutions have well-meaning goals, but their traditional procedures create difficulties for students, which they do not always see. That is the great advantage of this research. Our studies permit us to examine multiple levels of influence: organizational policies and procedures, faculty and staff actions, and student perceptions and behaviors. In some cases, faculty and staff are aware of students' difficulties, but do not know how to respond, do not see alternative procedures, or assume another office is handling the

problem when in fact no one is. Solutions can come from institutional procedures rather than from painstaking efforts to fix each individual student.
Many of our results suggest some potential remedies that would not be
difficult to try in these organizations.

## BOOK OUTLINE

As institutions develop, the problems they confront unfold in a dynamic
sequence, which the following chapters show and discuss. The problems used
to be what Burton Clark (1960) called cooling out student plans and stigmatizing students with remedial needs. Community colleges have found ways
to avoid them (see chapters 3 and 4). New problems arise from the new procedures, however. We find that avoiding cooled plans and stigma may sometimes prevent students from having realistic expectations and timetables.

Another former problem, limited college access, has been dramatically
lessened. The problem in its place is completing college. The assumptions
that emerged from nineteenth-century elite colleges are not particularly
appropriate for community colleges whose nontraditional students and
occupational programs call for nontraditional procedures. Chapters 5
through 10 indicate that community colleges make many mistaken assumptions about student information, college information procedures, college-
to-career procedures, and student social skills. These assumptions lead to
serious problems for nontraditional students in community colleges, though
private occupational colleges avoid the assumptions and the corresponding
problems for similar students. Analyzing private occupational colleges, we
discover new institutional procedures that community colleges could use to
reduce student problems. This dynamic sequence is unavoidable—clearly,
it is impossible to talk about completion when no one yet has access. We
believe, however, that the time has come to stop fighting old battles and turn
to the new challenges that confront us.

Some of these new procedures will make readers cringe and wonder, "Is
this really college?" Yet that discomfort may be necessary. If colleges are
going to include new groups of students, we may have to question some of
the traditional practices that we have assumed are a necessary part of college.

Because society's shift to college-for-all policies is rarely stated explicitly,
no one has considered whether it creates difficult contradictions. All students
are admitted to college, but remedial programs are the only accommodation
for the new students. Obviously, this is not working. Students mistakenly
expect to get a degree, when in fact, large portions fail every year, blame
themselves, and do not realize these failures were easily predictable. Only
41 percent of students entering community colleges manage to complete

any degree in eight years (and only 19 percent of African Americans do so), yet the labor market payoffs are primarily to those who get degrees. Clearly, we need to think about other procedures to improve completion rates.

Colleges need to examine which procedures are essential to higher education and which are not, and which new procedures would better accommodate the needs of these new students so that college can offer them meaningful opportunities rather than empty promises. In comparing these two types of college, we find that we are comparing two models of schooling: individual and institutional. The first assumes that individual students determine their own outcomes; the second shifts some responsibility to the institution, on the assumption that institutional arrangements can affect students' outcomes. This volume examines various issues about which these models conflict: plans, motivation, information, social skills, and finding jobs.

Chapter 2 describes our research methods. By gathering data from different actors in fourteen colleges, we are able to discover aspects of these institutions that are not generally seen by any single group of individuals (for example, students, teachers, or administrators alone). By comparing alternative types of colleges, using both qualitative and quantitative data, we are able to examine alternative procedures that are not usually considered. We also use a national longitudinal survey to examine generalizability and longer-term outcomes.

Chapters 3 and 4 focus on community colleges and describe the ways they handle students' plans and motivation. Community colleges are often criticized for cooling out students' plans. Chapter 3 finds that warming up is actually more common, and faculty engage in extensive efforts to elevate students' plans. Chapter 4 then describes some dilemmas that emerge from warming up and sustaining students' high hopes as faculty and staff seek to protect remedial students with procedures that do not stigmatize. These procedures solve some problems but provide new ones, preventing students from getting information and anticipating the implications of their placements. Surprisingly, we find that cooling out has some benefits for degree completion, and nonstigmatizing procedures have some costs. However, solving students' problems by changing their aspirations is not enough to result in increased graduation rates. The remaining chapters examine whether another kind of college with different procedures can reduce students' problems and improve their outcomes.

Chapter 5 considers the problem of informed choice and suggests that students' selection into the different college types entails a certain degree of randomness. Although they were criticized for blocking students' choices in the past (Pincus 1980; Brint and Karabel 1989), we find that community col-

leges now provide ample choices, but that students lack the information they need to make the choices that best suit their needs. Overall, students report that serious information problems and community college procedures are sometimes responsible, but those in occupational colleges report fewer information problems and planning difficulties, even net of student attributes.

Chapter 6 examines difficulties that arise from community college procedures as they relate to students' college knowledge after enrollment. We find that community college procedures implicitly require students to have various kinds of social know-how, but that occupational colleges use different procedures that reduce information gaps and the risk of mistakes in student choices.

The next four chapters describe how the organizational procedures address the transition from school to employment. Chapter 7 contrasts the emphasis of community colleges on career counseling with the highly developed job placement procedures of occupational colleges. Chapter 8 describes the informal faculty activities to improve job outcomes in both types of institution. Chapter 9 examines how these job placement activities might affect students while they are still in college, possibly improving motivation and confidence (in our local sample) and degree completion (in national data).

Chapter 10 examines organizational procedures for ensuring that students meet the soft skills requirements of the labor market. Where community colleges assume that students have professionally relevant social skills, occupational colleges train such skills with mandatory procedures.

Chapter 11 pulls our findings together and considers implications for policy and future research. We find that many of the complaints against community colleges are misdirected. Rather than being concerned about excessive cooling out, stigmatizing, structuring, and socialization, the occupational college model suggests that disadvantaged students need information, supportive structures, social skills, and dependable job placement to succeed in earning college degrees and getting relevant jobs. Although community colleges should not totally emulate occupational colleges, we suggest ways that community colleges might help some students by creating programs that use the findings of this research.

Given the dismal completion rates at community colleges, it is important for research to examine how college procedures may be contributing to these outcomes. Our results are not definitive, but they do at least provide new ideas and evidence about what is happening. Rather than being the last word, these findings are closer to the first word on a number of topics that merit careful study.

# CHAPTER TWO

## RESEARCH METHODS

Most research on subbaccalaureate education focuses on community colleges. This approach is appropriate, considering that community colleges enroll about half of all college students, as well as about 95 percent of all two-year college students. There is certainly great variation in the ways that community colleges can and do operate, and much could be learned from comparative analysis of different community colleges. On the other hand, community colleges contrast sharply with their private counterparts—accredited, degree-granting occupational colleges. Both community and occupational colleges serve a relatively disadvantaged and nontraditional student population, and both seek to educate these students for skilled jobs in local labor markets. Yet, compared to community colleges, occupational colleges on average graduate far greater proportions of their students, especially the new disadvantaged and nontraditional students who have only recently gained access to postsecondary education (Bailey, Badway, and Gumport 2002; The Futures Project 2000; Stephan and Rosenbaum 2006; Tinto 1993). Unfortunately, such private two-year colleges have rarely been studied. By comparing the way a select group of these colleges approach a similar goal for similar students, we hope to discover some of the practices that support two-year college student success more generally.

Although we draw from national data and earlier ethnographic data, the majority of our findings come from qualitative and survey research conducted at fourteen two-year colleges in a major Illinois city and its sur-

TABLE 2.1    Detail of Institutional Sample

|  | Community Colleges | Occupational Colleges |
| --- | --- | --- |
| Number of colleges studied | 7 | 7 |
| Mean number of full-time students | 3409 | 1495 |
| Median number of faculty | 331 | 54 |
| Average tuition[a] | $3,571 | $25,601 |

*Source:* Authors' compilations.
[a]Does not include financial aid

rounding suburbs over the three years from 2000 to 2002. In selecting these colleges, we sought variety in terms of college location and type, but also wanted a group small enough that we could visit the schools repeatedly and get to know them well. In the end, we selected a group of seven public community colleges and seven private occupational colleges (see table 2.1). Of the second group, four are for-profit institutions and three are nonprofit. Four were founded in Illinois and have historically served the local labor market by focusing on business and secretarial training, but more recently they have branched out into other occupational fields, like health, electronics, and computer technology. The other three are members of for-profit corporations with campuses across the United States. Although they all grant primarily associate degrees, four of the seven occupational colleges have begun to offer applied bachelor's degrees in a limited number of the same fields as their associate's degrees; the other three have developed articulation agreements with some local four-year colleges that allow students to transfer to bachelor's programs without repeating coursework. Although smaller in scale and more recently developed, these agreements are similar to those of all seven of the public community colleges in our study.

Although the community colleges in our sample are, on average, much larger than the occupational colleges, the difference is less stark for full-time students: the community colleges average about 3,409, and the private about 1,495 (compare Illinois Board of Higher Education 2002, table 2.1). We certainly recognize the potentially important influence of college size for the analyses discussed in this text. Still, we feel that our qualitative focus may actually shed light on which aspects of size are important with respect to questions about linking between colleges and labor markets.

Aside from their geographic proximity and articulation with four-year schools, these fourteen colleges are also similar in offering accredited associate's degrees in similar occupational fields. These include business, accounting, computer information systems, computer-aided drafting, court reporting and paralegal, office technology, electronics, engineering, and a variety of health programs (see table 2.2). Because they offer similar associate's level programs in the same geographical area, these colleges are also comparable in serving the same or very similar labor markets.

Because occupational programs are important in their own right, and are comparable in the two types of colleges, they are the focus of this study. Whereas occupational colleges only offer programs in occupational fields, community colleges also offer other kinds of programs—liberal arts, adult education, GED programs, English as a second language, and the like— that are not studied here.

## Organizational Analysis: Multiple Levels, Multiple Views

Organizations encompass a wide range of people, perceptions, and behaviors, and organizational analyses must take this into account. Studies of organizations must consider that perceptions and behaviors vary at different levels. If one studies only a single level, important parts of the story at other levels will be overlooked. All of the colleges in this study are complex hierarchies, and we suspect that personnel at different levels in the college have different perceptions as well.

One way to study colleges is to look at the goals posed by organizational leaders. Steven Brint and Jerome Karabel (1989) focused on college presidents, administrators, and other leaders, who described the goals and policies at their colleges. Brint and Karabel did not, however, study the extent to which these goals and policies were accepted or implemented at lower levels. Even if college presidents set a clear occupational mission for their institutions, the operation of the college also depends upon the actions of lower administrators, program heads, faculty, and staff. Moreover, all of these actors may also be affected by public officials, as well as by their various constituencies (Dougherty 1994).

Indeed, there are indications that the emphasis of college presidents on occupational programs and their de-emphasis of academic transfer programs do not reflect a similar consensus at lower levels in community colleges, as Brint (2003) has noted. Two national surveys found that lower administrators and faculty were highly divided on their college's mission (Cross and Fideler 1989; Brewer 1999). Given such inconsistencies, we hoped to gain a variety of perspectives as we examined our fourteen colleges.

TABLE 2.2    Detail of Majors and Programs in Study

|  | Community Colleges | Occupational Colleges |
|---|---|---|
| Business–secretarial | Business, accounting, management and marketing, administrative–executive assisting, office technology | Business administration, accounting, management, administrative assisting, office technology, paralegal–legal office assisting, court reporting |
| Health | Medical assisting, health information technology, occupational–physical therapy assisting, cardiac technology, radiography | Medical assisting, health information technology |
| Computer–electronics | Computer-aided drafting, architectural drafting, electronics–computer technology, mechanical engineering technology, computer information systems | Computer-aided drafting and design, electronics, computer and electronics engineering technology, computer information systems, information technology, business computer programming, computer networking |

*Source:* Authors' compilations.

## College Personnel Perspectives

To more completely understand college organization, we interviewed three kinds of college staff in each type of college: administrators, advisory staff, and program chairs (who are also faculty; see table 2.3). We follow the lead of past research in talking with high-level administrators—presidents, deans, and so on—at each institution to gauge institutional missions and priorities as they are officially articulated. Research has also examined community college faculty (for example, Brewer and Gray 1999), and we do as well, but we focus on faculty who are also program chairs to get a better sense of the development of occupational programs in the two college types. Because our ultimate interest is in how these colleges operate at the ground level to influence their students' experiences and outcomes, we include the college staff who interact most with students to provide key assistance—for example, admissions counselors, academic advisors, career services staff, and so on. These are the individuals who implement student services procedures in each college, and their activities have strong poten-

TABLE 2.3    Detail of Interview Sample

|  | Community Colleges | Occupational Colleges |
|---|---|---|
| Students | 85 | 40 |
| Advisors–career services[a] | 14 | 21 |
| Administrators[b] | 16 | 16 |
| Program chairs: |  |  |
| Business–secretarial | 12 | 6 |
| Computer–electronics | 10 | 10 |
| Health | 6 | 2 |
| Total | 28 | 18 |

*Source:* Authors' compilations.
[a]Academic and career advisors and counselors, job placement or career services staff, faculty or deans–directors
[b]Any other administrators or administrative faculty

tial to influence students. In addition to gauging how college procedures are articulated and implemented at different organizational levels, multiple vantage points also allow reports to be cross validated. Individuals' reports may be distorted, whether to make the person look good or because the individual has limited experience, but we are able to examine whether these reports are corroborated by others, including students.

College personnel interviews were semistructured and open-ended, allowing us to probe a variety of issues in depth. The interviews were typically one to two hours long, tape-recorded, and transcribed verbatim. We coded interview data both deductively and inductively, first examining responses to specific questions of interest that were put to all respondents, then coding for related themes that emerged across cases.

## Student Perspectives

In addition to examining college organization through the eyes of various personnel, it is important to understand how college procedures affect students. Toward that end, we interviewed a large and diverse group of students from a wide variety of programs at the two college types, surveying more than 4,000 students at the fourteen colleges.

We interviewed a saturation sample of 125 students. Some were initially selected as part of Deil-Amen's earlier dissertation study, but eighty-six were selected based on criteria to ensure variability in race, socioeconomic status, gender, age, and major across institution types (that is, private and public colleges). Again, interviews were about an hour long, were taped and transcribed verbatim, and then coded deductively and inductively.

The interview sample may not be representative of students in these colleges, but nonetheless provides rich data, which we seek to triangulate with other interviews as well as the student survey. Findings from the student interviews are most often used in interpreting the results of survey analyses, or in understanding how students perceive and respond to particular institutional procedures. (Later, in chapters 3 and 4, we include the additional student interviews from a partial subsample of the community colleges to probe specific issues. These were conducted from 1999 to 2000 as part of a dissertation that essentially served as a pilot study and formed the basis for the broader research project that is the source of all other data described here.)

Our survey sample included 4,365 students from comparable occupational classes at the fourteen institutions. The surveys asked about students' goals, background, attitudes, experiences, course-taking patterns, and perceptions of college and the labor market. The surveys were conducted during class sessions. We surveyed students in both basic and advanced courses, most of which were core requirements for the selected occupational programs and would enroll mostly occupational students. Classes were selected to target a cross-section of credit-level students in comparable occupational programs across both types of colleges. We obtained responses from nearly all students attending class, and 96 percent of surveys provided usable information on most items. We believe this sample is representative of the particular occupational programs studied in these particular colleges, at least for students who attend classes, though we have not attempted to test this. Faculty reported that attendance was high in the classes studied (over 85 percent), but we were not given class lists for comparison. Of course, our sample does not represent students who have dropped out and underrepresents those with poor attendance records.

## Archival Materials and Field Observations

We also conducted an extensive review of college materials (including, for example, program guides, course schedules, Internet sites, and the like), and we made repeated observations of campus activities, taking detailed field notes. This permitted another validity check on respondents' reports, which sometimes produced new findings about discrepancies.

## National Longitudinal Data

Finally, three chapters in this book (3, 4, and 9) use data from the National Center for Education Statistics (NCES) to compare the findings from our local cross-sectional data to a nationally representative longitudinal sample. The data used are drawn from the Beginning Postsecondary Students Longitudinal Study 1996–2001 (BPS) (NCES 1996a), as well as the Integrated Postsecondary Data System (IPEDS), also for 1996 (NCES 1996b).

The BPS data include a sample of first-time beginners in postsecondary education who enrolled during the 1995–1996 school year. Unlike the national longitudinal studies of high school graduates that follow a single age cohort, the BPS sample analyzes all students entering college at a single time, thus reflects more accurately the true population of community college students, including older students. IPEDS includes institution-level data from all postsecondary institutions nationwide. Chapters 3 and 4 rely only on the BPS data for national analyses, and—in line with the chapters' themes—the sample is limited to community college students. Chapter 9 integrates the BPS and IPEDS data using institutional identifiers included in both datasets, and the analyses include degree-seeking students enrolled in both public and private two-year colleges. The complex sampling strategy of the BPS—with different probabilities of selection at both the institutional and individual levels (NCES 2002)—prompts certain methodological considerations. To support projection of findings from the sample to the broader student population, BPS analytic weights are applied and adjustments are made for the primary sampling unit and sampling strata, as well as the subpopulation in question (using Stata 9.0 survey commands).

## UNDERSTANDING FINDINGS AND IMPLICATIONS

Before interpreting the research findings and policy implications presented in this book, it is important to note the advantages and disadvantages of this type of research. Although this study is not experimental, analyses of student traits and comparisons to findings in national data allow some inferences to be made about the causality and generalizability of our findings. Moreover, this study does offer some notable advantages that would not be possible with different research designs.

### Inferring Causality

Besides describing empirical relationships, we sometimes wish to make inferences about causal relationships. To infer causality, we must have reason to believe that the outcomes observed are caused by the colleges, not due to the pre-entry attributes of the students in these two types of colleges. One way of doing this is with multivariate analyses that statistically control for student attributes. We use this approach throughout. However, such statistical procedures cannot account for the possible influence of unmeasured attributes on which students may systematically differ.

The best way of inferring causality is random assignment. If individuals are randomly assigned into two conditions, we can assume the two groups are comparable, and any observed outcome differences can be attributed to the different conditions. Although we cannot randomly assign students to public and private colleges, there are reasons to believe that the students are similar. As we shall show, analyses suggest that these two sets of colleges offer similar occupational programs, that students enter these colleges for similar reasons, and that the students who do enter are highly similar to each other. Students attended some of the same high schools and seek to enter the same local labor market and many of the same jobs.

One might worry that private colleges would enroll higher income students because of their higher tuition. Private two-year colleges are more expensive, with net tuition (that is, published tuition minus financial aid) exceeding that at public two-year colleges by more than $4,000 in the 1995–1996 academic year in national comparisons (Bailey, Badway, and Gumport 2002).

Surprisingly, private colleges do not draw students from more advantaged backgrounds. In part, this is because they aggressively use state and federal funding for students. Like community colleges, private colleges' existence depends very much on public funds. Indeed, analyses of state (Jenkins 2002) and national data (Bailey, Badway, and Gumport 2002) show that for-profit degree-granting institutions enroll somewhat higher proportions of low-income and minority college students than their public counterparts. Analyses of national data (NELS) find that public and private two-year colleges enroll students who are not significantly different in test scores, grades, SES background, and a wide range of other attributes (Stephan and Rosenbaum 2006).

In our local sample, we also find that these private colleges actually enroll the same or higher proportions of disadvantaged groups as community colleges do. In our survey of nearly 4,400 students, compared with community college students, occupational college students are slightly more likely to be disadvantaged on a number of dimensions. Specifically, they are more likely to have low high school grades (27 percent versus 25 percent), to be nonwhite (69 percent versus 52 percent), to have parents with

TABLE 2.4    Detail of Student Survey Sample

|  | Community Colleges | Occupational Colleges |
|---|---|---|
| Male | 45% | 46% |
| Racial-ethnic minority | 52% | 69% |
| High school grades C- or below | 25% | 27% |
| Parent education high school or less | 48% | 57% |
| Parent income $30K per year or less | 40% | 44% |
| Mean age | 25 | 24 |
| N | 1,562 | 2,803 |

*Source:* Authors' compilations.

incomes under $30,000 a year (44 percent versus 40 percent), and to have parents with high school education or less (57 percent versus 48 percent); see table 2.4. Moreover, we could not even find much difference in the top or bottom range of the grade distributions. The general conclusion is that students in both types of college are from similarly low socioeconomic backgrounds and have similarly low high school achievement. However, to the extent that the small differences are important, they would suggest that students at private occupational colleges are somewhat more disadvantaged, and any apparent positive effects we find in favor of occupational colleges may be underestimates. In addition, students at the two college types have similar goals. Occupational college students were only slightly more likely than their community college counterparts to report they were in college "to get a better job" (80 percent versus 70 percent).

Although students are not randomly assigned to the two types of colleges, the process students describe for selecting colleges appears random (see chapter 5). Unlike the deliberate way some middle-class students select four-year colleges, with students and their parents gathering large amounts of information about multiple options, many of these two-year college students reported that they only considered one college, and the decision was made quickly, often without consulting parents or anyone else, and without gathering much information. Moreover, students learn about these colleges through quasi-random processes, such as an advertisement on the radio or television, a mass-mailing, or word from a relative, friend, or acquaintance.

Obviously, none of these mechanisms is perfectly random—there may be some hidden systematic biases in who listens to the radio, receives mass mailings, or has acquaintances attending a certain college. However, we find that if such biases exist, they do not result in large differences in student attributes in the two types of colleges. Of course, very few studies can randomly assign individuals to conditions; it is neither feasible nor ethical. Like such research, we cannot definitively reject the possibility of un-measured differences between students.

However, the larger question is whether one believes that the substantial differences in outcomes we observe can be explained by whatever subtle systematic differences may underlie our analyses. Although that possibility cannot be excluded, we have difficulty imagining what unmeasured attributes could explain these large and varied outcome differences, and have even greater difficulty dismissing the influence of the dramatic observed differences in institutional procedures between the two types of colleges. Readers must of course draw their own inferences on these points.

Another way of making causal inferences is through propensity score analysis. This method can both assess whether students are comparable in the two types of colleges and compare outcomes among similar students at different college types. As noted in chapter 1, a carefully controlled analysis using propensity score methods finds that among comparable students with equal propensity to attend community colleges, degree completion rates are significantly and substantially higher in private than in public two-year colleges (Stephan and Rosenbaum 2006).

There is a fourth basis for inferring causality: a detailed understanding of forces. We find that certain organizational procedures sometimes make causal inference plausible, and even hard to avoid. For instance, when we see students expressing more confidence about the job payoffs of their colleges' employer contacts (see chapter 9), and private colleges that make substantial investments in staff whose major duty is job placement (see chapters 7 and 8), we find it difficult to avoid inferring that job placement staff have a causal influence on students' confidence about the job payoffs of their colleges' contacts. Again, readers can draw their own conclusions.

In summary, these analyses indicate high comparability of students in the two types of college and support causal inferences about the effect of institutional differences. These findings are supported by a large body of qualitative evidence, presented primarily in chapter 5 of this volume, which describes how students enrolling in both public and private colleges often select their college, their major, and their career field based on very little information and with a very minimal degree of forethought. In this sense, chapter 5 suggests that for many students entering two-year colleges, their selection of one college over another does indeed include a certain degree of randomness. Other chapters use qualitative and quantitative analyses to describe both the complex interactions that occur between college students and personnel, and the procedures that might explain the pathways by which such similar students arrive at very different outcomes in the two types of college.

## Inferring Generalizability

Besides offering empirical observations, we sometimes wish to make inferences that such findings generalize beyond the particular cases we are studying. To infer generalizability, we must have reason to believe that these particular community colleges are typical of most, or at least a large segment of such institutions.

As noted in chapter 1, our private colleges are not typical. Some are part of national chains, and these corporations insist on conformity to the corporate model on all campuses. However, generalizability to the entire private sector is not our goal. Rather, we study private colleges accredited by associations similar to those accrediting community colleges. This makes these private occupational colleges comparable to our community colleges, but atypical when compared to other private two-year colleges.

As noted, we believe our community colleges may be typical—a point for which we have some evidence, but no proof. There are several reasons to support such an inference. First, this book repeatedly draws on findings from other studies to show similarities and differences to our observations. Second, we note the heterogeneity of the community colleges in our sample, which captures some of the variation noted by other researchers. Third, as noted, we also use national surveys to analyze some of the issues raised in our study and to examine whether our findings might generalize (see chapters 3, 4, and 9).

However, our method of drawing our sample of local community colleges does not necessarily support the generalizability of the study. We selected these colleges to reflect diverse types, but limited our sample to a single geographical region. Although this has the great advantage of allowing easy access for gathering multiple kinds of information over time (cross-checking new information as we learn it), it hurts our ability to infer generalizability. To the extent that community colleges and occupational colleges may differ in other regions of the country, the generalizability of our findings will be limited. It is our hope that future research will address this issue on a wider scale.

Although it is always hard to tell if case studies are typical, the value of case studies does not necessarily depend upon typicality. Community colleges do not have to be typical if our goal is to discover possible mechanisms that may explain well-known problems, or to discover that our implicit assumptions are sometimes seriously mistaken.

Similarly, occupational colleges do not have to be typical to identify alternative procedures that force us to question traditional procedures and allow us to discover new variations, why they exist, how they operate, how they influence students, and their apparent outcomes. Rather than ask about generalizability, such variations reveal a number of available alternatives that might not otherwise be seen, and indicate how they operate, and the trade-offs involved with each. As community colleges struggle with mixed success to use traditional college procedures to help nontraditional students obtain nontraditional goals, these alternatives, their operation, and the related trade-offs should be considered and examined. Ultimately, awareness of them must come before attempts to implement similar procedures in the public sector can occur.

Additionally, many of our local findings indicate processes and outcomes that can be further studied in national data sets. For example, chapter 4 finds that many students in a few colleges do not understand the implications of their remedial placements, a finding that led us to test the actual impact of multiple remedial coursework in national survey data. The findings also suggest the need to include measures of students' perceptions of their remedial placements to better learn how such awareness may or may not affect eventual degree attainment.

One could imagine other designs for such a study. However, our goal is to learn about alternative organizational procedures and how they affect similar students seeking similar goals. We use these private colleges to demonstrate alternatives that the local community colleges might implement to prepare students for entry into the same local labor market.

## Limitations

This study is not a general assessment of these two types of colleges and does not address many of their features. First, as noted, we are not describing average private colleges but are instead studying some of the best private occupational colleges most comparable to community colleges.

Second, we are not studying financial costs and benefits. This is more difficult than it seems. Our calculations suggest that private colleges pay two to three times more per student for instruction (FTE data not available), but this is misleading. One must be cautious in examining public and private two-year college expenditures because so many public college students are part-time, in remedial or other noncredit classes, or in humanities classes, all of which reduce instructional costs per student. Still, ratios within college types are interesting. In our colleges, the ratio of expenses for student services to student instruction is roughly equal to 1.0 in private colleges, but only .20 in public colleges, suggesting that private colleges invest five times more in support services proportionately. If support services improve timely degree completion, as our findings will suggest, and if degree completion improves students' earnings (Grubb 1996; Marcotte et al. 2005), then these investments may be cost effective. One study indicated that the high tuitions of private colleges are cost effective because they reduce the time it takes to get degrees, but this is an old study (Wilms 1974). We haven't seen a more recent cost-benefit analysis, and have not done one.

Third, we are not studying long-term outcomes. Some occupational colleges have begun to offer applied bachelor's degrees, and some have articulation agreements with four-year colleges to recognize their graduates' credits. We don't study whether transfers occur. We also do not study labor market outcomes. Our interviews with a few employers suggest that some employers do not make distinctions between the degrees at the two types of colleges, but we lack strong evidence on this.

Fourth, we are not studying the wide variety of programs offered at community colleges, including GED, ESL, short-term certificate, and transfer programs. This study focuses on occupational programs conferring accredited associate's degrees. Nationally, 61 percent of community college students are in occupational programs (Grubb and Lazerson 2004, 89), and most associate degrees are in occupational fields (NCES 2002, table 251). In this sense, we are studying the largest segment of the community college student population, but it is only one of many segments. Still, the portion of students we have studied is large and important, and we believe our findings may help to improve their chances for success at college.

## Advantages

Despite its limitations, our study overcomes many shortcomings of earlier research. National survey data mostly rely on student reports, so can rarely detect student misperceptions, and obtain little or no information about institutions or institutional processes. Virtually none of the national surveys—National Longitudinal Survey of Youth (NLSY), Beginning Postsecondary Students (BPS), or National Education Longitudinal Study (NELS)—contain data about whether students get jobs through school-employer contacts, for example. In prior work, we analyzed one survey that does have such an indicator (HSB, compare Rosenbaum 2001), but it indicates only high school contacts, not college contacts, and says nothing about the kind of contact or how it operates. Many surveys have indicators of student plans, but these are usually derived from multiple-choice response sets, with no indication of students' understanding or commitment to the response they checked. Our findings provide evidence that student plans are often vague, unrealistic, or misinformed, and they are often contradicted by procedures in their colleges. These problems cannot be detected in most national surveys.

Moreover, by detailed analyses of organizations, we discover the organizational processes that shape individuals' behaviors. Regardless of whether students in public and private two-year colleges differ in subtle and unmeasured ways, the differences of organizational procedures in the two types of college are not subtle and impose strong unavoidable impacts. Occupational colleges use powerful procedures that radically alter student experiences: unambiguous course requirements each term and unavoidable procedures that quickly redirect students if they are not on track to make regular progress. These procedures prevent mistakes, quickly remedy problems, and virtually ensure dependable progress toward degree goals. After seeing these procedures in occupational colleges and contrasting them with the lack of comparable procedures in community colleges for ensuring timely progress, causal inference is hard to avoid.

As we have indicated, we are able to get beyond the limitations of any single method by using a combination. We can use various methods in conjunction to get a better overall understanding of our research questions. By studying multiple vantage points, we can gain a better sense of how procedures are developed and implemented at various levels of the college organization. In comparing these multiple data sources, we are able to verify our information and can also diagnose some of the problems and misconceptions that would go undetected by other approaches.

# CHAPTER THREE

## "WARMING UP" THE ASPIRATIONS OF COMMUNITY COLLEGE STUDENTS

We begin the discussion of the individual versus institutional model by exploring the role that community colleges can play in shifting individual students' goals and aspirations. In exploring this process, we reveal how community colleges act to positively encourage and perhaps change students, but also suggest that such informal strategies do not necessarily translate directly into students' eventual goal attainment. Later in this volume, we suggest the various ways in which more formal and systematic institutional procedures might have an influence on students' success above and beyond the encouragement of aspirations.

Research on community colleges has historically focused a critical eye on these schools, regarding them as second-tier institutions that distract students from higher attainment, dampen and discourage student ambitions, and prevent disadvantaged individuals from gaining upward mobility (Karabel 1972). Most of the literature on community colleges has focused on the schools' function of discouraging and limiting students.

Central to this perspective is what is known as the cooling out function, introduced in Burton Clark's institutional case study of San Jose Junior College, *The Open Door College* (1960). The process of cooling out junior college students' ambitions occurs during counseling, testing, assigning students to remedial classes, and other policies that convince underprepared students who aspire to bachelor's degrees to relinquish their initial goals and pursue alternatives, that is, a lower degree program or departure from college without graduating.

Clark's seminal book set the stage for future educational research on community colleges, inspiring quantitative and qualitative research on the cooling out function. His discoveries motivated many quantitative researchers to examine the long-term educational attainments of community college entrants. Several analyses of national and institutional data have inferred a cooling-out process from findings that students who enter community college are less likely to complete a bachelor's degree than those who begin at a four-year institution. These quantitative, and several qualitative, studies, dominate the research literature on community colleges.

However, the primary empirical evidence that Clark provides to demonstrate the cooling-out process is the language of the counseling manual in the one junior college he studied. This evidence is not only institution-specific, but also dated, and lacks description of how these policies play out in interactions between administrators and counselors and between counselors and students. Subsequent research about community colleges has tended to assume the existence and nature of cooling out.

Cooling out may exist, and it may be widespread. In fact, one study did directly examine the lowering of students' aspirations and found that community college beginners with bachelor's degree plans are significantly more likely to lower their plans compared to similar students who begin at four-year institutions (Pascarella et al. 1998). However the details of the processes by which students' aspirations are lowered have not been a focus of the literature, particularly in recent years. It is unfortunate that the "vast majority of research on community college effects on students has tended to treat community colleges as a homogeneous set of institutions that are most effectively grouped together in between-sector comparisons with 4-year colleges and universities" (Pascarella, Wolniak, and Pierson 2003).

Little research has examined the process within community colleges or the extent to which cooling out occurs. This is particularly relevant in a community college context in which many occupational programs offer transfer to four-year degrees. In fact, high growth programs such as business, health, and computer technology offer effective pathways to transfer that did not exist at the time of Clark's study.

Here we reconsider some of the original assumptions about cooling out, and also reveal a previously unexplored process—warming up. Warming up is the raising of students' initial aspirations after they enroll in a college. We analyze a different type of national data, look for multiple directions of aspiration changes, and study administrator reports, official college documents, student reported aspirations, and faculty, counselor, and student reports of their actions, interactions, intentions, experiences, and perceptions. In doing so, we demonstrate that community colleges may not be cooling out aspirations as much as previously assumed, and in fact may be warming them up just as frequently. However, as Barbara Schneider and David Stevenson (1999) note, the problem is not simply getting students to be ambitious, because they are already ambitious. The question is how schools and colleges direct students onto pathways toward realistic goals.

## PRIOR RESEARCH: THE ORIGINS AND CRITIQUES OF COOLING OUT

Previous research has defined cooling out as a process of lowering student aspirations. Clark relates the process specifically to dissuading students from maintaining unrealistically high expectations of transferring and earning bachelor's degrees (1960). Colleges accomplish this with a combination of pre-entrance testing, counseling, orientation classes, notices of unsatisfactory work, further counseling referrals, and probation. These steps serve to convince those students who aspire to transfer to four-year colleges to "accept their limitations and strive for success in other worthwhile objectives that are within their grasp" (1973, 367).

Quantitative findings have shown that beginning at a community college, rather than a four-year college or university, reduces the probability that an individual will actually earn a bachelor's degree. These researchers suggest that community colleges passively discourage student success by setting institutional roadblocks in the way of those with bachelor's degree aspirations (Alba and Lavin 1981; Anderson 1984, 1981; Astin 1977, 1972; Crook and Lavin 1989; Dougherty 1994, 1992; Karabel 1972; Monk-Turner 1983; Nunley and Breneman 1988; Richardson, Fisk, and Okum 1983; Velez 1985).

Brint and Karabel (1989) and Dougherty (1994) build on Clark's original theme by detailing the ways in which promoting and expanding vocational or occupational programs dampens the transfer function of community colleges and fosters an environment that distracts students from baccalaureate transfer options. These authors generate their frameworks from their own qualitative, historical case study research, but also rely on quantitative studies to document their claims about the impact of community colleges on students.

Beyond identifying and defining the process, the existing literature criticizes the intentions and implications of it. Cooling out has primarily been attacked for discouraging capable students and setting low standards. Clark (1960) writes that this latent function acts as a screening device for four-year colleges and universities, enabling the entire system of higher education to be both ostensibly democratic and effectively selective. Karabel (1977) argues that cooling out reinforces stratification, guiding students—primarily those of working-class or lower middle-class origins—into lower status tracks. Karabel is most critical of the role that cooling out plays in actively pressuring students to sort themselves out of the competition for transfer based on their substandard performance. If students do not seek out guidance, "the counselor with the authority of the disciplinary apparatus behind him, requests to see the student . . . [informing him that he] . . . had his chance [and he did not] . . . measure up."

> Community colleges . . . developed cooling out as a means not only of allocating people to slots in the occupational structure, but also of legitimating the process [and causing] people to blame themselves rather than the system for their "failure." (1977, 240)

By convincing students that lower track vocational courses are their best alternatives, cooling out gets students to accept the college's assessment as serving their own self-interest (Erickson 1973).

In addition, Dougherty (1994) highlights the prevalence of community college faculty's low expectations of students and the negative impact this has on student performance. Dougherty's analysis draws on the research of Howard London (1978) and Lois Weis (1985), which suggests that community college teachers respond to students' low skill levels by concentrating on a few promising students, and largely giving up on the rest.

> The sad irony is that these low expectations feed a self-fulfilling prophecy. In a process well described by labeling theorists within the sociology of education, . . . low expectations tend to lead teachers to withdraw attention and praise from poorer students, which in turn reinforces the very poverty of the student performance that is being decried. (Dougherty 1994, 90–91)

## A RESPONSE TO COOLING OUT: NEW PERSPECTIVES

Despite this vast body of research on cooling out, shortcomings in the existing literature remain. First, most studies fail to ask students about their goals, assuming that students who are either enrolled in an academic (rather than occupational) program or who have completed twelve credit hours have plans to transfer and eventually earn a bachelor's degree. This assumption is problematic. Simply because students begin college in an academic program or complete one semester's worth of credits, they did not necessarily intend to pursue a bachelor's degree initially, or even at all. As noted, one study actually measures changes in students' degree plans and suggests that cooling out does occur, but only 119 two-year college students were included in the final sample (Pascarella et al. 1998). Second, quantitative research has neglected the possibility that some students may actually change their aspirations in the opposite direction, warming up, and the relative extent of cooling out versus warming up has not been studied. Third, Clark's account gives a great deal of influence to guidance counselors, without considering other actors. As Norton Grubb notes, many students do not "make much use of counselors. . . . Counseling resources in many community colleges are sparse. It seems absurd to place the burden for cooling out on counselors; they simply do not have power or influence enough to accomplish all that they have been blamed for" (1996, 66).

Here we address these problems. Using NCES's Beginning Postsecondary Student (BPS) survey (1996a), a national sample of beginning community college students, we are able to revise previous assumptions about cooling out by taking students' stated degree goals into account rather than assuming that all students have bachelor's degree goals. Using BPS, we also address changes in aspirations that occur in both directions, examining the extent to which warming up happens relative to cooling out.

We find that warming indeed happens in community colleges, and build on this finding with qualitative research to understand the processes involved in this change in student aspirations. Existing literature does not address these processes, nor does it examine a key component in student information and plans: college faculty. Some previous researchers have focused on the role of state officials and community college administrators to influence institutional priorities and resources (Dougherty 1994; Brint and Karabel 1989, 1991; Labaree 1990), and others on the influence of student cultures in discouraging BA aspirations (London 1978; Weis 1985). Meanwhile, little is known about the process by which college faculty members influence student aspirations. Using qualitative data from fieldwork at three community colleges, we describe warming patterns and processes, as well as faculty behaviors that have not previously been noted.

Although changes of aspirations certainly occur, we find that they do not always happen in the ways that previous researchers have suggested, and they do not necessarily have the disastrous consequences implied in previous literature. The key issue is whether students complete degrees, and we explore the ways cooling out and warming up are related to subsequent degree completion.

## DATA AND METHODS

Here we use data from BPS, a nationally representative longitudinal sample of more than 7,200 college students. BPS offers a more accurate view of community college students than other national data sets because it surveys beginning college students (rather than a high school cohort), so it includes older students.

We also use qualitative research from fieldwork conducted at three community colleges over a three-year period. These three colleges were part of the research for Regina Deil-Amen's dissertation (2002). Two of these colleges were included in the larger sample of seven community colleges described in chapter 2.

All three colleges are urban community colleges although they vary in ethnic composition. The composition of college credit students at Northwest are 47 percent white, 9 percent black, 30 percent Hispanic, and 12 percent Asian, and 43 percent of these students reported incomes below $15,000. At Central, the composition was 24 percent white, 46 percent black, 15 percent Hispanic, and 11 percent Asian, and about half report annual incomes of less than $12,000 and only 18 percent report incomes over $30,000. The third college, Southside, is located in a high poverty neighborhood and enrolls students who are 97 percent black (Office of Planning and Research 1997).

Two kinds of warming up can occur. The first involves encouraging high school students who are not college-bound to attend college. This has been studied in earlier research (Rosenbaum 2001), and our research design does not address it. The second involves warming up in colleges, and that is our focus. Similarly, cooling out can take two forms. The first is guiding students from four-year degree goals to two-year degree goals, and that is our focus. An alternative version, guiding them from academic or transfer programs to occupational or applied programs in community colleges is not studied here, due to its complexity and ambiguity. Increasing numbers of occupational programs are transferable—business, information technology, and health, for example—and do not necessarily involve compromises in students' aspirations. Indeed, we found many students who enrolled in occupational programs after earning bachelors' degrees in academic fields that didn't lead to jobs. Instead, we focus on changes in students' goals from bachelor's degrees to associate's degrees or lower goals.

## Cooling Out Versus Warming Up: Examining National Data

The BPS data indicate that, though cooling out still exists, many community college beginners experience warming up. Selecting only students who began in a community college, their initial degree goals are compared with those after five years. Students initially aiming for an associate's degree who after five years had either a bachelor's degree or a goal of earning one were considered warm-ups. Those initially aiming for a bachelor's degree who ended up with an associate's degree or lesser goal were considered cool-outs.

In this national sample of community college beginners, some cooling out exists—21.6 percent of students with an initial bachelor's degree goal had achieved or were pursuing a lower degree goal. However, almost as much warming up occurred: the percentage of students initially seeking an associate's degree who were warmed up to a bachelor's degree or bachelor's degree goal within the same five-year period was, at 18.4 percent, only slightly lower percent (see table 3.1).

Furthermore, warm-ups (from associate's and certificate goals) make up a higher percentage of all community college beginners (10.5 percent) than cool-outs (from bachelor's goals—5.0 percent; see table 3.2). Approximately twice the percentage of students who begin in community colleges are warmed up than cooled out. Overall, warming up is more frequent than cooling out. It is evident from table 3.3 that most students who did not drop out experienced no goal change. However, among those who did change goals, warming up (16.7 percent) is slightly more prevalent than cooling out (13.1 percent).

## Cooling Out, Warming Up and Dropping Out

Previous research has criticized cooling out in part because it was believed that it promoted dropping out. We find the opposite. As indicated in table 3.4, cooling plans actually reduces dropout for associate's degree planners and has no statistically significant effect on those planning bachelor's degrees.[1] As one might expect, table 3.5 reveals that warming up reduces dropout for those students who begin college with no degree goal, no certificate goals, or no associate's degree goals. Of course, we cannot be certain that students who haven't dropped out will complete a degree.[2]

Indeed, table 3.4 indicates that failure to cool one's plans may itself lead to dropping out. We saw this in interviews. For instance, we interviewed some students whose academic skills were enough to meet the associate's degree

TABLE 3.1    Students' Goal or Degree Status

| | | Degree Goals and Status Five Years Later | | | | |
|---|---|---|---|---|---|---|
| Beginning Goal | Dropped Out | Certificate Goal or Certificate | AA Goal or AA Degree | BA Goal (or More) or BA Degree (or More) | Total Percentage | n |
| No degree goal | 60.4 | 13.3 | 16.2 | 10.1 | 100.0 | 487 |
| Certificate goal | 57.5 | 30.9 | 9.8 | 1.7 | 100.0 | 346 |
| Associate's goal | 42.5 | 10.1 | 29.0 | 18.4 | 100.0 | 1555 |
| Bachelor's goal or more | 37.3 | 6.8 | 14.8 | 41.1 | 100.0 | 716 |

*Source:* Beginning Postsecondary Survey (BPS); Author's compilations.

TABLE 3.2    Students' Warm-Up and Cool-Out Status as a Percentage of All Cases

| | | Degree Goals and Status Five Years Later | | | |
|---|---|---|---|---|---|
| Beginning Goal | Dropped Out | Certificate Goal or Certificate | AA Goal or AA Degree | BA Goal (or More) or BA Degree (or More) | Total Percentage |
| No degree goal | 9.5 | 2.1 | 2.5 | 1.6 | 15.7 |
| Certificate goal | 6.4 | 3.4 | 1.1 | .2 | 11.1 |
| Associate's goal | 21.3 | 5.1 | 14.5 | 9.2 | 50.1 |
| Bachelor's goal or more | 8.6 | 1.6 | 3.4 | 9.5 | 23.1 |

*Source:* BPS; Author's compilations.

TABLE 3.3    Dropouts, Cool-Outs, and Warm-Ups as a Percentage of All Cases

| | No Goal Change | Cool-Outs | Warm-Ups |
|---|---|---|---|
| Dropouts | 40.7% | | |
| Nondropouts | 29.5% | | |
| Less than associate aspirants | | | 6.9% |
| Associate aspirants | | 6.7% | 9.8% |
| Bachelor aspirants | | 6.4% | |
| Total | 70.2% | 13.1% | 16.7% |

*Source:* BPS; Author's compilations.

TABLE 3.4     Mean Dropout by Degree Goal
and Cool-Out Status

|  | Mean Dropout |
| --- | --- |
| No degree goal | .58 |
| Certificate goal | .34 |
| Associate's goal | |
|     Not cooled out | .34 |
|     Cooled out | .25 |
| Bachelor's or more goal | |
|     Not cooled out | .33 |
|     Cooled out | .39 |

*Source:* BPS; Author's compilations.

TABLE 3.5     Mean Dropout by Degree Goal
and Warm-Up Status

|  | Mean Dropout |
| --- | --- |
| No degree goal | |
|     Not warmed up | .90 |
|     Warmed up | .25 |
| Certificate goal | |
|     Not warmed up | .35 |
|     Warmed up | .30 |
| Associate's goal | |
|     Not warmed up | .41 |
|     Warmed up | .06 |
| Bachelor's or more goal | .34 |

*Source:* BPS; Author's compilations.

requirements, but not bachelor's degree requirements (at least not without extensive remedial coursework over one to two additional years). If they didn't cool their aspirations, they would either find themselves in difficult courses for which they were poorly prepared, or else in remedial courses that would add several noncredit years to their degree timetable (see chapter 4).

These findings indicate that the forty-year focus on cooling out in community colleges has neglected several key points. First, cooling out may not be as negative a function as assumed. It is in fact associated with decreased dropout rates, and may even be necessary for some students for whom poor information has led them down paths for which they are not prepared. Furthermore, the narrow focus on cooling out over the past forty years has blinded researchers from identifying the opposite function, which community colleges also perform—warming up. We begin to fill this major gap by detailing the warming-up process observed at three local community colleges. These findings highlight the central role of faculty in students' accounts of their warming-up experience and in observations of daily life within the colleges.

## INVESTIGATING THE PROCESS OF WARMING UP

Social scientists have ignored warming up. Two kinds of warming up have occurred. First, increased college plans among high school students: by the 1990s, 95 percent of high school seniors planned to attend college, even if they don't know what college will require and how long it will take (Rosenbaum 2001). This pre-college warming up creates problems for colleges, and may increase the need for cooling out, but this is not our focus here. Second, warming up occurs in college, and we may wonder why social scientists have focused on cooling out in community colleges but ignored warming up. Clark's pioneering case study and other institutional research has relied primarily on administrator reports and college documents (1960, 1973; Karabel 1972). Obviously, these are old findings, and community colleges have changed. Although they have increased emphasis on occupational programs (Brint and Karabel 1989), occupational education has also changed. In recent years, 85 percent of enrollments are in occupational fields where academic work is necessary and where there are four-year programs (Grubb 1996). Occupational programs are no longer terminal— transfer rates from some occupational areas are higher than from academic subjects (Grubb 1991; 1996, 65).

Research has also tended to ignore not only faculty resistance to administrators' preferences, but also the importance of that antagonism for influencing the culture and priorities of particular community colleges. Furthermore, Clark's case study of a single college leaves open the possibility that in other community college settings, counselors may approach students in distinctly different ways than those he found. In fact, just as some high school counselors have abandoned gatekeeping to prevent college access (Rosenbaum 2001, chapter 4), college counselors may have abandoned cooling out and changed the ways they encourage or discourage student aspirations.

Here we focus on faculty's role in shaping students' experience with a consideration of counselor's role as well. Two of the colleges studied have preserved very strong transfer missions, and the qualitative data include numerous examples of students whose aspirations had increased as a result of their enrollment. In the third college, the occupational function is a higher priority. However, warming up is also evident at this college, though less frequently than at the other two.

Coincidentally, these findings are relevant to one of the major studies of community colleges, because the district studied here was also studied by Dougherty (1994). However, where Dougherty did not focus on faculty and counselors' reported actions, this study does. This study also shows other aspects not considered in his work.

## BEYOND THE DIVERTED DREAM

In *The Diverted Dream*, Brint and Karabel (1989) describe how community college administrators and the American Association of Community Colleges (AACC) aligned with the interests of state universities and government officials to support an emphasis on learning a vocation in community colleges—transforming them away from their original transfer-focused junior college mission and toward more terminal occupational programs. Dougherty (1994) built on this framework by noting the relative autonomy of state and federal officials to influence the direction of community college growth and expansion. These authors relate the growth of occupational programs to the neglect of the community college's liberal arts curriculum and transfer function. Dougherty, for example, summarizing previous studies, boldly asserts that

> most community colleges provide little encouragement to their baccalaureate aspirants. Baccalaureate aspirants entering the community college fail to have their transfer hopes strongly bolstered and in fact are pulled in the opposite direction by the community college's strong promotion of vocational education. (1994, 94)

These authors have been central to our understanding of these institutions. On the other hand, Brint and Karabel note that both faculty and students resisted the push toward terminal programs:

> The faculty were, at the beginning, predominantly oriented to the liberal arts and were, accordingly, more often aligned with student opposition to vocationalization than with administrative enthusiasm for it. (1991, 350)

Despite a few provocative statements like this, the authors fail to examine diversity among administrators and faculty, or conflicts between them. In particular, they fail to suggest variability within the monolithic image of community colleges as cooling out and vocationalized institutions.

In contrast, two major surveys find considerable diversity in attitudes. A study of administrators in eighteen community colleges nationally (Cross and Fideler 1989) and a national sample of 1,725 faculty in ninety-two community colleges (Brewer and Gray 1999) reported that administrators and faculty are nearly evenly split in their ranking of transfer (general education) and workplace preparation as the top institutional priorities. These findings indicate that the vocationalizing of community colleges is far from complete.

Although states vary in their focus on transfer and occupational goals, and the state we studied may be more transfer-oriented than some, the faculty support for transfer is consistent with the national findings. Despite the public statements of top administrators in favor of a vocational mission, community college faculty and lower administrators often do not all concur. We find, in fact, that counselor and faculty behaviors toward students actually encourage a warming up of students' aspirations that has not been noted.

## SORTING AND SOCIALIZING

Having established that warming up is more common than cooling out in a nationally representative sample, we now look at how warming up is experienced and how it is encouraged. We study these issues in a sample of three colleges (a subset of our full sample), which vary in their transfer emphasis and the transfer intentions of the student body. While at Northwest, 48 percent of students intend to transfer, 30 percent of Central's students intend to transfer, and at Southside, only 24 percent of students intend to transfer. These differences are likely to result from two processes—sorting and socializing.

Although these community colleges were all within the same metropolitan area, they differed along several dimensions, including student demographics, the neighborhoods served, the proportion of occupational versus traditional academic transfer enrollments, and the emphasis on transfer as the college's top priority. Due to these differences, each campus is likely to attract students and faculty with different characteristics and generally predisposed to the mission of the particular campus. Furthermore, colleges with weak reputations and those in neighborhoods with higher poverty rates are more likely to attract students with less academic preparation and the type of negative experiences that incline them to seek one- and two-year degrees rather than transfer. Such circumstances illustrate the impact of sorting on educational outcomes, a self-selection process. Because this research design did not allow us to examine sorting effects, we can only acknowledge that it probably occurs.

Educational institutions can also have a socializing impact. Here we focus on this process and explore how colleges influence students and their aspirations and plans.

## STUDENT PERSPECTIVES ON WARMING UP: QUALITATIVE FINDINGS

We now focus on the twenty-two students who experienced warming-up, that is, who, having begun their postsecondary education without a bachelor's degree in mind, later established earning one as their goal. Of the 132 students interviewed, twenty-two had experienced warming up. That this 17 percent of the total sample is not far from the 18.4 percent in the nationally representative sample is not necessarily meaningful because the local sample was not randomly selected. Although we cannot assume that our findings for this 17 percent are representative, the detailed description gives insight into the process of warming up.

The purpose of this discussion is not to make causal inferences, but rather to describe a process—the warming-up process. The rich knowledge acquired about each institutional setting and students' detailed accounts repeatedly point to the faculty's role in the process—a finding that persists across all three colleges, despite the variations in college composition, structure, and culture.

We saw three key aspects of the process: students initially had little confidence that they could succeed in college, college faculty provided a support and improved their confidence, and college faculty actively encouraged students to pursue the bachelor's degree. These occurred at all three colleges.[3] We also found that counselor advice was consistent with faculty encouragement of bachelor's degree aspirations, and that counselors rarely tried to actively redirect students toward lower, or more short-term degree goals. However, counselors played a decisively smaller role than faculty because their interactions with students were less extensive.

### 1. No Initial Confidence that They Belong in College, a Weak Commitment to College

Many of the students who experienced warming up initially suffered from a weak commitment to their academic pursuits. They doubted whether they belonged in college and whether they could succeed in this context, and their doubts were sometimes reinforced by their strong ties to home and work.

Many performed poorly in high school and were seeking a second chance in college. Some, like Jamal, invested little effort in high school: "I didn't do hardly nothing, until my final year [in high school], and that's when I realized I really wasn't learning much" (Central College).

Others, like Natasha, couldn't pinpoint exactly why they did poorly in high school, but said that their low grades diminished their confidence:

> I did horrible in high school. I just lost my confidence. I think that's what it was when I dropped out of high school—I lost my confidence completely. All I was getting was Fs, and on my papers Ds and Cs, and wondering why. . . . I thought I was going to do the same thing in here, but I didn't. (Central College)

These students initially felt uncomfortable in college. They entered community college timidly testing their potential and fearing failure, like Ivan, a student at Southside who explained it this way: "Well, I started off by just taking one class, it was a continuing ed. class, and I didn't know if I had what it took to go to college."

It is precisely because community colleges provide access for non-traditional students that they attract students with histories of poor academic achievement, students who lack confidence that they belong in college. Community colleges' low tuition and convenient locations allow students to test whether they can handle college (Manski 1989), risking little money, while continuing their jobs.

However, many of these students are also facing financial obligations that traditional college students are not. For instance, Natasha was an unmarried mother with a toddler, living in public housing. Marta was divorced with one young daughter and one teenager. Jamal was paying the entire costs of tuition and rent with a full-time job.

The proximity of community colleges also tends to attract students who cannot cut ties to community, family, or work. The option of spending four consecutive years living away from home on a far-away campus, largely separated from home and family, is a situation that many students are not ready for, emotionally, socially, or financially. Community colleges allow students to pursue postsecondary education yet retain ties to work and family. For example, Marta's responsibilities as a mother, her financial status, and her need to continue working obviously limited her college possibilities, and her doubts about her ability to succeed also kept her from fully committing to college. Bridgette, a student at Northwest, says, "I was not ready to lose my friends. . . . It really wasn't just leaving my friends, it was just that I did not feel personally ready to leave to go away. The other reason was really financial." Another Northwest student, Beatriz, indicated some of the more pressing constraints under which young students attend college, particularly those whose families do not support their aspirations:

> Since I come from a Mexican family of eight, it was almost impossible to think of finishing high school, much less to enter college! In my house, school was not really emphasized. Work, on the other hand, was all my parents talked about. . . . I knew my parents would not be able to help me financially, so I decided to find a cheaper school I could afford on my own. Fortunately, a friend told me . . . that Northwest had a lot of programs that would help me decide on my career and also the low tuition I had to pay to enter. . . . Staying in college was not an easy task either. Many times my father would yell at me telling me I was just wasting my time and money and I was gonna go nowhere. . . . [He] wanted me to quit school to get a job to help him at home. No matter what happened, I had no intention of ever quitting school. Even though I got a full time job I continue to go to school part time.

As researchers have noted, many students report continuing pressure interfering with their college efforts (Brint and Karabel 1989, 180; London 1978; Neumann and Riesman 1980, 58; Weis 1985). Marta, a Puerto Rican woman, was a high school dropout with little family support for academic goals. She grew up in a broken and verbally and sexually abusive home with a mother who provided no support for college-related goals. Before attending college, Marta had already struggled through a strained relationship with her family, dropping out of high school and marrying at the age of seventeen, the birth of her two children, a divorce, unemployment, and desires to commit suicide. Her ex-husband, the father of her children, like her mother, did not support her ideas about college. "He was always saying I was going to quit school, like my mom. . . . My mom discouraged education. It was kind of like, 'find a husband,' that type of thing." Marta showed up at Central with a crippled self-esteem and a lack of a support network to affirm her efforts.

Marta got her GED just before enrolling at Central, and her high scores earned her a tuition scholarship that she has retained each semester by maintaining at least a B average. She felt that her ability to do well when she first started in college was the fuel that kept her motivated to pursue her goals:

> Like one week before I walked into the school I was thinking of killing myself. So, yes, it just totally changed it and I'm so glad because I can't even believe that I thought that back then, that I even had that desire. Now I'm completely turned around and I'm not stopping. . . . The grades helped me. The first grades I got, they were A's. It was the one thing in my life I could control, that I could change. I didn't even have a job when I first came here. Oh my God, if I did nothing else right, I was doing this right. So that's what kept me going.

Community college literally saved Marta's life. In the debate about whether education affects life chances, her story, as an example, clearly documents an extreme form of impact. Moreover, since she entered community college, Marta has also encouraged one of her sisters also to enroll.

For these students, a bachelor's degree often seems implausible given their doubts about whether they even belong in college. Their confidence and commitment to their educational pursuits is tenuous, and is challenged both by their previous academic experiences and by significant others.

## 2. College Faculty Provided Support to Improve Student Confidence

Before students can warm up their aspirations, they must acquire confidence that they belong in college. Over 70 percent (sixteen of twenty-two) reported that community college faculty were critical in helping them become confident.

How can students with such poor academic records and experiences acquire confidence that they belong in college? Faculty help students acquire confidence by explaining to students that their poor performance is due to poor high schools. Faculty were acutely aware of students' backgrounds and the difficulties they present. A math professor at Northwest talked about how students who perform poorly often come from "weak educational backgrounds."

> [The students] were not raised in either a cultural atmosphere conducive to education, or the school was overcrowded, or there were too many kids in the classroom. They were improperly developed. We meet those needs here too. I have taken students from 098 [remedial math]

all the way through differential equations. This can be done, but it requires historically redoing a lot of things.

Rather than criticizing students for low achievement and the negative pressures in their outside environments, faculty accepted these factors and incorporated these realities into their teaching strategies. Faculty reported that it is their job to help the student overcome such disadvantages. Students must be given the time, attention, and assistance they need to succeed. Faculty were committed to this idea and saw it as one of the main functions of a community college.

Counselors tended to espouse a similar philosophy, usually dealing with difficult-to-convey messages about students' remedial placements to soften the blow to their confidence by focusing blame on the high school and emphasizing future success. A good example of this approach is clear in one counselor's response about whether a student's placement test scores influenced her encouraging or discouraging the student's degree goals during an advising session. The counselor explained how she didn't want students to get discouraged just because the remedial classes they need to take might delay the degree needed to accomplish their career goals:

> No, I don't discourage them, I try to make them understand, "You just came in here with some things that you didn't take care of when you were in high school. So we gotta make sure you have them. Otherwise, I'm just setting you up for failure, and that's something I don't want to do. So we have to make sure your reading and your writing are strong so when you go into those classes, you can be successful." . . . So placement tests dictate our academic advising, but it shouldn't dictate career advising, at least not from our philosophical point of view.

This consistency between faculty and counselor's messages seemed to reinforce the idea that maintaining students' confidence and heightening students' awareness was, in fact, the aim of the college staff.

Indeed, many students attributed their increased confidence to faculty members who gave them the extra support they needed. They noted various aspects of faculty efforts, sometimes noting that such efforts aren't necessarily available to four-year college students. Structurally, the small class sizes at community colleges permitted instructors to give students more attention. In addition, the students reported that faculty extended themselves in four ways: care, patience, personal attention, and structuring.

*Teacher Caring*   Many students mentioned that teachers extended themselves in ways that indicated they cared about students' succeeding in community college. Bridgett said, "All the teachers are helpful and seem like they really care if you pass or fail." Echoing similar sentiments, Gail said this about her remedial English class at Northwest:

> It helped a lot. The teacher was very enthusiastic. In high school, the reason I had trouble was because my high school teachers, they didn't really show how they were proud of you or whatever, but this teacher, like every little effort you made he was just like "Wow, I'm so proud of you" . . . and that just really helps to know that the teacher *cares*.

Brook, another Northwest student, conveys her positive opinions:

> From my experience . . . if you are struggling, they will help you. One of my biology teachers is willing to meet before class, after class, or when you are available to meet. He will help you to understand it by going over it again and again until you understand.

*Teachers' Patience*   Teachers were also willing to give students individual attention during class time and even adjust their teaching pace to students' needs. Elisa, a Central student who had been in a remedial math class, remembered:

> [Math] 110 was great because of [math teacher]. . . . He just helped us. Like he was there until we got it. If we had any questions he wouldn't move on. He'd be like, over and over he would tell us until we finally got it. That's what I liked about him. He cared if we knew it or not.

Dwight, a nursing student at Southside, shared similar remarks:

> I thought the classes were difficult at first, you know, just coming back to classes. Like I said, the instructors and staff, they were helpful. As a matter of fact, Dr. Parris, who was my biology 111 instructor—and consider that about 95 of the people failed his first test. And he felt bad about it. He went back over this material all over again slowly, and he was helpful. Put it like that, he was just real helpful. He was patient, very patient.

*Personal Attention*   Many students noted how important it was for them to feel that they were not considered "just a number" and that personal interaction with their teachers was important in addressing personal difficulties. Personal attention also encouraged students to continue despite struggles. Monica, now an honor student, fondly remembered the support she received during her first year at Northwest:

> Even though I did do bad in a lot of their classes in the first semester, ... [teachers] could tell I was trying. ... I know a lot of the teachers here, they actually *do* care. ... That's the advantage of [Northwest] The classes are small. You get to be more personal with the teacher. The teacher gets to know you, name basis. ... They're very very supportive.

Several students had transferred from four-year universities to community colleges, and particularly emphasized the smaller classes in community college and the personal attention they received from faculty. Dawn, who transferred to a local university after attending Northwest, recalled:

> For the most part I just felt like at the community college, they cared about you more than they do at the university. You know they took a little bit more time in talking to you. ... At the university they barely even know who you are. It's so big, the classes and stuff. It was a little bit more homey, you know?

Tyrone, who voluntarily went from a local state university to Northwest, said:

> What influenced me to come to [Northwest] is last semester I was attending [local university]. It was big and hard. I felt that the teachers weren't giving me enough attention. I guess the fact that it was so big, you didn't have time to talk to the professor, and when you did it was so crowded around him. Then I decided to come to [Northwest]. I felt that I could get more attention from my teachers because the classes were smaller. ... I like it. ... I think I'll stay here to get all my basic courses that I need and then I might decide to go back and attend [local university].

Robin, a student in her third semester, shared similar remarks:

> I think [Central] has some of the best teachers. They come from the best schools. People say "community college" and they think it's like

second class. I think it's better than some places. Like [local state university], where my sister went to school in a lecture hall with 500 students. I don't want that. It wouldn't be my type. I need that interaction. Maybe I'm spoiled, but I need a lot of interaction from my teacher. I want to know that the guy that's teaching me is the guy I'm going to ask questions to, that they're going to be there when I need them. That's the beauty of Central, the teachers here are great.

*Additional Structure and Mentor Relationships*    Students reported a number of ways that faculty structure their courses and the activities surrounding the courses. Dan suggested that his instructors were able to subtly tailor the educational process to his needs without compromising academic standards. He emphasized that community college is a happy medium between high school and university expectations. The standards at community college, he says, are "not just a continuation of high school." Unlike universities, students are given some autonomy, but not too much.

> When I was at [local university] it was like, well here's the syllabus and here's the book. If you don't want to come to class at all it's up to you. If you don't want to do anything, don't do it at all. . . . At the end you had to write a paper. Well you could not go to class during the whole thing and at the end just turn in a paper as long as you've read the material. You could read it all in the last week or the first week. . . . [Here at community college,] there's still some sort of structure because there's definite assignments and a little more pacing. . . . It's not one big project at the end . . . I think it helps me a lot more.

Some faculty initiate additional activities to develop personal relationships with students. Marta reported that her English professor's role as advisor to the student group she joined gave her the opportunity to talk with him frequently. Although he was close to retiring, he continued to forge relationships with his students:

> Sometimes in the morning we'd be there by ourselves and he'd read poetry. He knows I love reading. . . . he actually asks my opinion of certain stories and poems. . . . He's like that with everybody. He takes them in. He gives you that unconditional love, and for me that's really important because I didn't have it. It's like the way I try to be with my children. You can mess up, and he'll be there if you do. He's not going to shun you or make you feel bad about it or lecture or anything like that.

So when you have that, you do strive to do better, way better than you even thought possible. I really mean it when I say I didn't even know I had so many opinions. Now I'm constantly, "No, I used to do it this way" or "Yes, I agree." I never did that before. Not like that.

Marta's relationship with a faculty member and her involvement in a student club gave her a sense of affirmation, which was helpful in counteracting both her lack of academic self-confidence and the damage done by her family's failure to support her intellectual pursuits. This extracurricular activity provided a new social group with which to identify, one closely connected with their faculty advisor:

Then when I joined the club, it was like finding family in the school. You get that close knit group. It does a lot for your self-esteem. It really does. . . . I can't say enough about [the club]. . . . The friends I've met there and the professor I'll know for the rest of my life. It's important. Sometimes I need advice from him, even on a personal level, and he's there. . . . I come from a family of eight and I'm not close at all [to them]. . . . So it's important that I have some kind of a family, wherever I go, that I develop a sense of some kind of foundation. And I got it here, thank God.

Many other students reported having had similar feelings—of belonging to a safe and effective support network that helped them develop confidence to pursue higher educational goals. However, the stability, activeness, and strength of student groups depended heavily on the involvement of faculty. Groups without ongoing and dedicated faculty leadership were more vulnerable to dissolution and stagnation. A stable pool of full-time faculty make a critical contribution to the quality of the student community on campus and to the opportunities for social and intellectual exchanges and relationships between faculty and students.

Like Marta, other students at the other colleges spoke of the essential role that such relationships played in their ability to negotiate their college pursuits. Loretta, a student at Southside, explained the pivotal role of her informal mentor relationship:

This instructor was a role model for me . . . and so he has been my mentor for the two and a half years that I'm here. . . . He's given me a lot of encouragement . . . you know, when I really felt I couldn't go on, when I felt that it wasn't any use, or that I was having difficulty in a class or whatever, I could always talk to him. If my home life was too hectic or my schedule was too chaotic, I always found a listening ear and some support and some suggestions. I would say that he also is a friend, not only an instructor.

At Southside, John called the chair of his department his guardian angel:

No matter how hard she was working, . . . [she had] the passion to help you get to where you needed to be, because she saw the talent. Like, [she'd say] "We're going to sit down and talk about every problem that you have, what you need to do, where you're going when you get out of this college, and what can I do to help you?" . . . [She'd say] "I'm your friend. You need somebody to cry, you need somebody to talk, this is the person." And you can see the passion because every person she meets, it's, "Hey, how are you, what's your name?" That's what I really respect, and that's something that I look for. The passion to help, the passion to serve us well. . . . Not just there collecting a check.

John reported that other faculty also "pushed" him to pursue his degree goals and "guided" him "through the school."

Teachers at all three community colleges gave students opportunities to receive help in improving their academic performance and in incorporating school into their already demanding lives. Faculty reported a commitment to working with students who needed additional help, and emphasized their availability to students, both on an academic and a personal level. They provided additional tutoring and remedial classes without stigma, and they initiated mentor relationships with students to alleviate their fears and let students know that they care about them and are personally invested in their success. Faculty were aware of the challenges students face, and their personal support enhanced students' confidence in their potential and reinforced their commitment to their goals, despite competing demands on students' time and emotional resources.

### 3. Faculty Actively Encouraged Students to Pursue Transfer

As they became more confident that they belonged in college, their plans warmed up. Many students reported that community college faculty were critical in helping them raise their aspirations, define success as earning a bachelor's degree, and pursue that goal. Students reported that faculty repeatedly took extensive efforts to encourage students to pursue four-year degrees.

In observing classroom interactions, we often saw faculty make statements that conveyed an assumption that most, if not all, the students in their classes intended to transfer. For example, despite the fact that college algebra fulfills the degree requirements for a host of different degrees, including applied degrees not designed for transfer, a professor at Central who taught this course said, "If you're in this class, I assume you want to try to transfer these credits to another college." In one freshman-level English course, a professor told students, "I'm sure more than 80 percent of you share a common goal—to transfer to a four-year college. You are going to help each other get there by working in groups." Even if students did not intend to transfer, faculty made it clear that they should. Students talked about how, in classes, faculty pushed students to transfer rather than terminate their education after two years. One student at Southside reported that his biology teacher, "was always telling everyone in his class to further their education after they leave [Southside]. Don't just let it stop there."

In contrast to earlier accounts that assumed that vocational course faculty do not encourage transfer (Dougherty 1994), the pattern of encouragement toward transfer witnessed among the liberal arts transfer faculty could also be seen among faculty who taught more occupationally focused classes required in programs designed to lead to terminal degrees.

At Southside, for example, John reported that faculty encouraged him to pursue a bachelor's degree even though he was already enrolled in a terminal applied science degree program. Tina, while earning a two-year degree in secretarial science and a certificate in child development at Southside, was encouraged by a professor who taught in the secretarial program to stay in college beyond the two-year level: "Any questions and everything I need to ask, I went straight to her, you know, about my credits, and everything." Apparently, this faculty member, and others like her, consistently encouraged the secretarial students to go beyond the associate's degree. Tina decided to pursue a bachelor's degree at the local state university campus.

Charles, another Southside student, described how his social service professor inspired him to pursue higher educational goals:

> My ideal was to come here, to get my GED, and get a two-year liberal arts degree and go on to social work . . . to become a social service aide. And then, as I got into the program, I just got inspired more and more, and realized that really what I wanted to do . . . would take more than just an AA. And my mentor, he was very good at that, at saying, "Well,

you can't stop until you get a master's." . . . And just by staying here
and being involved in the program . . . I've upgraded my dream.

Surprisingly, faculty subvert the ostensible occupational mission of their
programs by encouraging students to pursue bachelor's degrees. These findings were true even for Southside, which emphasized occupational programs.
Previous literature assumes that the transfer function has been diminished,
based on community college presidents' accounts and on the shifting enrollments toward occupational programs. However, these data suggest that
from the actions of faculty a "hidden curriculum" of transfer emerges.

Furthermore, encouragement for warming up extends beyond the classroom. In interactions with counselors, students encountered a bias toward
transfer so strong that one counselor metaphorically joked about it being
akin to a religion. She described this common scenario involving students
who come in with two-year degree intentions whom she encourages toward
the idea of transfer:

It's interesting, in the beginning, they may come in thinking terminal,
meaning associates of applied science. After we talk somewhat about
pros and cons, short medium long term, they end up converting to
Christianity. I'm kidding about that but . . .

Outside of the classroom, full-time faculty with strong transfer orien-
tations are also active as advisors in student government, clubs, and other
activities. This allows for extensive social interaction between students
and faculty, who serve as intellectual role models. Under these conditions,
the academic integration and social integration processes that Vincent
Tinto (1993) highlights as so important, become intertwined and mutu-
ally reinforcing.

To summarize, it is important not to underestimate the day-to-day
influence of faculty as they interact and communicate with students, and
this research suggests that the warming-up process is inextricable from
the faculty's mission to make students feel they belong in college. Overall, the encouragement of transfer aspirations pervaded faculty interactions with students, whether one on one, in connection with club activities,
or in a classroom setting, faculty sent clear messages to students that
transferring to a four-year college epitomized success. Maintaining a core
of full-time transfer-oriented faculty, and providing additional opportunities for those faculty to develop relationships with students—small class

sizes and involvement in student activities, for example—appear to support the warming-up process.

## Implications of Warming Up

National survey data suggest that warming may occur more than cooling out in today's community colleges. If cooling out has declined, that should be no mystery. No one likes to give bad news, and cooling out has gotten a bad reputation. However, these results (and those in the next chapter) suggest that avoiding giving realistic information about outcomes may also be harmful. Such findings challenge the usual one-sided portrayal of community colleges in existing research as institutions that promote a cooling-out function. They also indicate that cooling out does not necessarily increase dropping out, and in some cases may reduce it.

Having found that warming up is relatively common in community colleges, we have tried to understand how and why it happens. Here we must rely on qualitative research, because no national study has examined factors encouraging warming up.

These findings add to the literature by addressing the important role of faculty and, to a lesser extent, counselors, in shaping institutional priorities as they're realized in the day-to-day life of the college, particularly in interactions with students. At all three campuses, despite variations in geographic location, student demographics, institutional history, and the power of administrators to advocate for an occupational curriculum, full-time faculty and counselors encouraged these students to pursue bachelor's degrees, even for those in applied occupational programs. Although warming up occurred less frequently at the campus dominated by applied programs, even there, faculty encouraged students to transfer. We have emphasized student interviews, but faculty interviews and field observations also indicate faculty's commitment to encouraging warming up.

The institutions' formal policies and job descriptions did not anticipate such behavior, and perhaps administrators were not even aware that it was happening. Yet the faculty report engaging in many activities to support warming up, and, most important, students report that these faculty actions were critical in their own decisions to stay in college and to raise their aspirations. The findings of this research are a testament to the power that faculty, particularly full-time faculty, can and do exert on students' plans and trajectories in two-year colleges.

These findings indicate that the long-held assumption of cooling out and the belief in its influence on degree completion must evolve alongside the changing institutions to which they apply. Cooling out may not lead to dropping out, and sometimes may even be necessary to avoid failure. Furthermore, cooling out does not tell the whole story: warming up also happens. The key issue is whether students complete degrees, and we find that cooling does not guarantee dropout and warming does not preclude it. In light of these findings, research needs to shift its focus to the broader issue of how to help students create clear plans, strive for realistic targets, and follow through on their goals. Beyond measuring changes of aspirations in one direction or another, researchers and policymakers must instead focus on informing and guiding students, and, as we shall see in the chapters that follow, this may involve devising procedures that can provide more clarity about choices and outcomes.

# CHAPTER FOUR

## THE UNINTENDED CONSEQUENCES
## OF STIGMA-FREE REMEDIATION

As Norton Grubb (1996) notes, the concept of cooling out student ambitions was generated from a study of a single junior college in the 1950s, and emphasizes the central role of counselors in this process. Since that time, little research has examined either the internal practices of faculty and counselors or the perceptions of students with regard to this issue. In the study that did attempt such an examination, the author concluded that counselors may not play a central role because students' interactions with them are limited: "They simply do not have power or influence enough to accomplish all that they have been blamed for" (Grubb 1996, 66). Suggesting that "the mechanisms of cooling-out are probably more complex than those suggested by many critics," Grubb (1996, 66) encourages researchers to explore factors other than lowered aspirations that may contribute to the low completion rates in community colleges.

Clark's 1960 study stressed, in addition to counselor impact, that the assignment of students to remedial classes was an important step in the cooling-out process. Research, however, has not examined this connection. Here we seek to fill this gap. Drawing from our interviews with administrators, faculty, and counselors, we consider the organizational context and cultural norms through which community colleges provide remedial education, interview students to explore the ways students perceive this process, and use multiple sources of data in examining the potential impact of these dynamics on students' prospects for degree completion.

As part of their effort to provide access to new groups of students, community colleges have developed remedial programs. Remediation is a key step toward the goal of opening access; it permits students who would be otherwise held back by specific academic deficiencies to enter colleges. However, remediation creates a dilemma. It is both necessary and stratifying, and the effects of these conflicting influences partly depend upon the ways remediation is implemented and presented to students. As noted earlier, community colleges have long been criticized for cooling out, and we commend them for their efforts to push an opposite agenda of warming up. Here, however, we illuminate some of the unintended negative consequences of these and related efforts as they pertain to remedial programs. We show that efforts to reduce the outward stigmas attached to remedial placement sometimes hide the students' degree completion timetables, and can lead to unanticipated delays and costs, and ultimately, to dropping out. Although this approach may appear more benign than cooling out, it may be detrimental to students who often do not receive college information from family members or peers, and for whom making mistakes can be extremely costly. Nonstigmatized approaches associated with both warming up and benignly sustaining students' high hopes may be no less harmful than the historically criticized cooling out processes.

## Uninformed Students

Although the literature on cooling out that we reviewed in chapter 3 focuses on activities during college, the reasons for changes in students' aspirations in fact begin much earlier. In the age of college for all, overburdened high school counselors often do not offer realistic advice to students about college preparation, demands, or plans. Unlike some middle-class students at four-year universities, many community college students do not receive information about college from family members or peers. Many students therefore arrive at community colleges with unrealistic goals based on too little accurate information, a topic we address in detail in chapter 5. Their uninformed ideas are particularly susceptible to influence by college staff, who can either inflate or deflate the students' aspirations.

Two institutional aspects of high schools contribute to the low levels of information and the shifted burden of cooling out onto colleges. First, various studies have noted the extremely low ratio of high school counselors to students (McDonough 1997), which reduces student-counselor discussion of college planning. Second, guidance counselor practices favor an approach that does not interfere with students' ambitions to attend college. Although several decades ago, high school counselors acted as gatekeepers (Cicourel and Kitsuse 1963; Rosenbaum 1976), recent research indicates that high school counselors often avoid giving unpleasant news, and advise nearly all students to try out college, even if they expect students to fail (Rosenbaum, Miller, and Krei 1996). In various ways, counselors deny the responsibility for advising students to consider modifying their plans, though some confide that they have misgivings about not warning students they doubt have any chance of succeeding.

## Uninformed Choices

As a result of these high school practices, many students decide to pursue college degrees, and many are doing so despite low high school achievement. The proportion of students planning to get college degrees has dramatically increased over the past two decades (NCES 2002). By 1992, 84 percent of high school seniors in the NELS sample planned to get a college degree and 68 percent expected a bachelor's degree (Schneider and Stevenson 1999). Part of the reason for these high expectations is that students think their low high school achievement won't hurt their educational attainment (Rosenbaum 1998; Steinberg 1996). Students know that open admissions will allow them access to college, and they report that they can wait to exert effort until they get to college (Steinberg 1996). However, recent research reveals that high school grades strongly affect college degree completion. In the High School & Beyond (HSB) ten-year follow-up, seniors with poor grades (Cs or lower) who plan college degrees have only a 14 percent chance of achieving these plans even ten years after high school (Rosenbaum 2001). Indeed, about 31 percent of these students get zero college credits (Rosenbaum 2001). This reality is not communicated to students in high school, and the result is that many students attend college without the tools to succeed or any awareness of the risk of not succeeding.

The lack of counseling in high school has created problems at the college level. Many unprepared students who enroll in college do not enter college-credit classes but instead are placed in noncredit remedial courses. In fact, over 60 percent of community college students have taken at least one remedial course (U.S. Department of Education 1998). Indeed, remedial placements are increasing: between 1990 and 1995, more than half of community colleges reported that remedial enrollments had increased, and only 5 percent reported that they had decreased (NCES 1996a, 11, table 4). The growth of remedial programs in community colleges has created new challenges for colleges and students; colleges now strive to avoid attaching stigma to remedial classes, and students struggle to understand their remedial status and what this means for their degree progress.

Students' lack of awareness about remedial placements and degree progress is evident in national data. Although students in remedial classes seem on one level to be college students, given that they are enrolled in a college, they are in fact taking high school (remedial) courses and earning no college credit for them. Many of these students, particularly those enrolled in multiple remedial courses, have degree plans and timetables that are inconsistent with their remedial class enrollments. Indeed, students who take remedial courses in several fields are unlikely to complete their stated degree, or indeed any college degree. This set of conditions—low levels of information and unrealistic plans—provides community colleges with an opportunity to manage information and affect students' perceptions of their situation. Community colleges are in the position to inform those students whose high expectations are not in line with their circumstances.

## THE ROLE OF COLLEGES IN INFORMING STUDENTS

This study suggests that policy makers and practitioners may not be doing enough to inform students and help them to develop realistic college plans. Students are not getting college information at home or in high school; community college is the last place for them to receive it and to establish achievable goals. As we will show, however, college staff members are failing to inform students of the implications of their remedial placements, obscuring or concealing the fact that they are in remedial courses and that they are not earning college credit and thus not progressing toward a college degree as quickly as they assume. When college staff members do discuss long-term plans with students, they may focus too narrowly on preserving students' original degree plans and fail to warn them about the realistic implications of their poor academic preparation.

This process of obscuring information and preserving students' naïve plans may be a way to avoid the stigma associated with remedial placements, and may indeed boost student confidence. The effort appears well intentioned, and may well be a reaction to the long criticized cooling out process (that is, the forced recognition of academic shortcomings and poor outcomes). The pendulum seems to have swung toward the other extreme, and students now may be shielded too much from their academic potentials and propensities to succeed. As we shall see, the result is that remedial students are free of stigma, but also deprived of essential information.

Actions that preserve high expectations may avoid discouraging students, but in the process may harm students by delaying their recognition. Such delays can not only lead to unanticipated costs but also prevent students from choosing an alternative degree and career goal that might better match the timetable students, their families, and others expect. The delayed recognition reinforces students' focus on impossible plans and unlikely goals and precludes constructive responses.

Here we explore the unintended consequences associated with the good intention of maintaining students' high aspirations. Although it is difficult to strike the right balance between informing and discouraging students, what we suggest here is that the solution may be more nuanced than simply warming up all students.

## DATA AND METHODS

Data were collected from multiple sources in two of the three community colleges described in chapter 3. We analyzed college catalogs and class schedules at these two colleges, here called Northwest and Central, to examine how these documents create ambiguities about remedial courses that allow students to retain their plans despite their low likelihood of attainment. We also use interviews with more than 130 students and fifty-four faculty and staff, observation in classrooms, informal conversations with and observations of students, faculty and staff, focus groups with students, attendance at meetings and school events, and surveys of students in these two colleges. The surveys included questions about students' goals, attitudes, experiences, and course-taking patterns and their remedial status. Additional primary research regarding the district's funding system and the organizational structure of higher education further reveal facts about the institutions that serve to support such an approach.

This chapter, unlike those that follow, focuses only on two of our fourteen colleges because of the need for a fine-grained analysis of the remedial course structure. Indeed, the difficulty of understanding this course structure is an important finding.

## THE CONTEXT OF SUSTAINING HIGH HOPES

Although we cannot say whether Northwest and Central represent the community college sector as a whole, these colleges do give us a better understanding of the structural and cultural conditions that encourage the unintended consequences we describe. Ironically, these colleges' emphasis on the transfer mission fosters high expectations but also fuels an approach with some risks.

## Institutional Support for High Expectations

The strong transfer emphasis orients the faculty at these colleges toward the task of preparing students to meet the standards and requirements of the senior colleges to which they intend to transfer. Such an orientation is reflected in the rigid and highly complex hierarchy of course levels intended to move remedial students into the college level courses accepted for transfer credit by senior institutions. In our interviews, virtually all faculty highly approve of this system, which prevents "watering down" of what these faculty value: the idea that their institution continues to provide its students with college education, not a less-than-college education. The following quotations exemplify this attitude:

> We spend a lot of time talking about how you keep standards up because the last thing this population needs is further fraud perpetrated upon them where they've been told "O.K. you've passed" when in fact they haven't mastered what they're going to need to survive out there. And pretty soon someone's gonna throw them out there and they're gonna sink. And I won't be part of that fraud and I don't think many of my colleagues will. (department chair)
>
> I think almost everybody sees that there is a commitment and dedication to the same type of ideals of helping the students and holding certain standards so that the students are not just passed along. I know in English we talk about it all the time. We do the student no favor to pass them along to the next level when they're not really prepared for it. So there's a lot of that making sure the student is academically prepared for the next level even here at the college so that they will then be successful. Because you sort of program them for failure if you're going to let them go on and they don't have the skills necessary. (English professor)

In short, faculty and counselors view their mission as helping remedial students slowly but surely achieve their educational goals by guiding them through a series of short-term improvements. Judging, evaluating, or altering students' long-term aspirations is not part of how they define their role, especially if students hope to transfer. Counselors and faculty at these community colleges feel that they should not underestimate students' potential to achieve their college degree goals despite a history of poor academic performance. As one department chair noted when asked whether he makes judgments about students who might not complete their degree, "Some people are late bloomers. Some people just take a long time to click and get into it. . . . So I don't make those kind of determinations." A counselor at Northwest articulated a similar philosophy:

> You could easily misjudge or judge too fast an academic history by the fact that they didn't do too well the first couple of times. You'd be surprised. I try to stay away from that. Students can blow you away, and then you fall into the trap of making judgment calls and decisions that are not in your judgment call to begin with—to tell a student whether or not they can become a doctor simply because they had a bad semester. . . . Although there is the time that you gotta be real with them and tell them, get real. . . . I hate those times, that's when I hate my profession. But other than that, you know, some people have bad semesters, but then they come around and do a 4.0 and do so well. . . . It doesn't happen all the time but it happens.

No one wants to be the bearer of bad news. Many counselors and faculty we interviewed tend to avoid such unpleasant actions, expressing optimistic hopes that students will eventually improve their performance.

## The Nonstigmatizing Approach in Community Colleges

Traditionally, colleges were candid about remedial courses, which communicated clear stigma. This is still true at many four-year colleges. Some students at the two community colleges in our sample first attended four-year colleges, where they reported that they had negative experiences regarding their low performance on placement tests. They were made to feel bad about themselves because they were in remedial classes. Steve, for example, recalled his experience with a remedial English instructor at a four-year college who would discourage him by words and attitude:

> I took the placement test and they placed me in her class and she felt that . . . she had the right to say things, to say that we were below all the other students in [the college] because we were placed in her class. I felt that wasn't a good positive thing to say about students that come to your class. You've got to teach them or help them go to the next class.

Steve dropped out of that college after one semester. His experience was stressful and he did not find the college's atmosphere supportive.

In contrast, these community colleges de-emphasize failure and emphasize students' need to improve their existing skills. Their practices remove the stigma and negative labels of these courses, and may have resulted from faculty's reluctance to cool out students' ambitions and their desire to encourage transfer. In our interviews with community college staff, we were surprised to discover that community colleges have developed innovative ways to avoid conveying stigma.

The community colleges studied offer a large number of remedial classes, which do not count as credit toward a degree or transfer. However, a student's own remedial placement and the status of remedial classes within the larger structure of the college are not always clearly stated. The term *remedial* is rarely used in conversations between staff and students, and does not appear in catalogs, course descriptions, and class schedules. Instead, the word *developmental* is sometimes used as a euphemism, removing the customary stigma and perhaps avoiding the cooling down of aspirations.

This approach seems desirable. It is a form of information management that downplays the negative and highlights the positive aspects of students' placement. It avoids the tendency to blame students for their deficiencies. Realizing that students' skill deficiencies may be due to life circumstances or low high school standards, college staff encourage students to try to achieve more in college than they have in the past. The term *developmental* is used to imply some temporary stage from which individuals will emerge with assistance. It seems to reflect several underlying beliefs.

First, faculty and counselors always try to communicate their high expectations of students in order to combat their students' tendency to lack academic self-confidence. An English professor at Northwest explained the logic:

> As your student population becomes less elite, you can't assume a common background . . . and you have so-so students who are not completely confident of themselves as students then you're going to have to support them. . . . We assume we're not getting all the A students [and we're getting students] who aren't confident and you have to kind of keep them afloat, particularly when it gets to be hard.

Second, most faculty and counselors truly believe that remedial placement is preferable to placing students in classes for which they are underprepared and in which they are likely to get frustrated and give up. Attempts to improve remedial English classes tend to focus on moving students steadily through a sequence of remedial courses, giving them the opportunity to develop their skills and transition into college-level English. The faculty member in charge of remedial English at Central described the logic:

> We feel that they get much more out of their experience because it's so connected with what they did the prior semester. . . . What I'm hoping is that we'll . . . work on our curriculum, so that it goes all the way . . . up to 102 with the same basic aims, the same basic abilities that are being developed at higher and higher levels as the student goes through the curriculum.

A counselor at Northwest commented on the importance of not moving students too quickly into college-level courses that might be too difficult for them to handle:

> There are a number of factors why students drop out. There's the frustration level. They just give up and walk away. . . . If students are given the kind of course work or the opportunities to improve certain skills that they are lacking, then we have a better chance.

Faculty, who view the testing and placement system as legitimate and in the student's own best interest, try to inform students of their remedial placement gently by presenting it as a positive and necessary step in fulfilling their ultimate goals. A faculty member who teaches remedial English talked about the way she tries to communicate her program during registration: "We try to build in that it's a positive experience."

Apparently the efforts of faculty and counselors work as intended: students don't feel stigmatized or demoralized on learning of their remedial placement. In interviews, students explained their remedial placement by repeating the positive language they heard from college staff. Steve, for example, later enrolled at Central College, where he felt he was treated much more positively when his remedial placement, based on his placement test results, was explained to him:

> They told me I would need help in English classes—not saying that I wasn't capable of doing the work, but . . . I would need that help first before I could just jump into something like [English 101].

As is true for many students, Steve's encounter was with an English department faculty member who taught developmental (remedial) classes and who was in charge of registering students into the developmental courses. Due to the small numbers of counselors at each college, much of the advice during registration came from faculty given the temporary task of getting students registered during this busy time, when counselors could not possibly serve all students. Given the limited number of counselors, community college's stratifying practices must inevitably extend well beyond the counselor-student interaction that Clark's study highlighted. However, in the present study, although these stratifying encounters had similar outcomes, the message conveyed was not one of realistic caution and redirection, but rather one of universal optimistic encouragement. Regardless of which actors (faculty, counselors, or other staff) served as the source of the message, we found that the message was consistently positive and tended to downplay the student's academic deficiencies. Many other students, such as Tomisha, voiced similar explanations:

> When I came back up here to pick up my test scores, they told me that my test scores were pretty high, but I didn't test in the high end, which is [English] 101 [the lowest college-credit English course].

Latoya said much the same:

> Ms. Bartlett discussed my scores [on the placement test]. She said they weren't weak, but they weren't at the strongest point.

Community colleges convey a stigma-free message: college can be a second chance to improve minor weaknesses and enhance one's skills.

This stigma-free technique seems to be an appropriate strategy, given the lack of confidence and fragile academic egos that many students have when they walk through the community college's open door. For instance, when Enrique first started, he was concerned because he had been out of school for so long. He actually expected that he would do so poorly that he would get Ds and then have to take his classes over again. However, after getting his placement test scores, he was reassured by his instructor's comments about how he was only one level below regular English, saying, "I guess I'm not that bad." Because of his positive experience with his current English class, he felt more confident. "I feel more tenacious. . . . I'm trying to find a word for it. I don't feel that I don't belong here. I feel like this is what I want to do and I'm going to do it. I'm looking forward to succeeding." Traci contrasted her experience at Central Community College with her GED:

> I hated it [the GED program]. It was like being inside a little jail or something. Even the teachers treated you like you were a nobody because you didn't finish school. . . . They thought everybody was all ignorant and everything. Even when I tried to show them that I'm not that ignorant person, they still treated me like I was nothing and I didn't like that.

She felt that she was treated differently at Central College from the start. Other students who didn't do very well on the placement exam, like Sylvester, agreed:

> When I got here it was like the staff was more helpful. . . . It was no problem going through what I had to go through to start. So the staff was very welcoming, . . . hope you stay here and good luck, etc.

The softer approach has clear advantages over one that discourages students by labeling them as deficient, disregards their ability to improve, and reinforces their own doubts about their potential. The nonstigmatizing approach is likely to improve morale and the institutional culture as well. Students feel good about themselves and their goals rather than focusing on their limitations. Similarly, faculty and staff do not have to be the bearers of bad news regarding students' weak prospects for success but instead are satisfied with their ability to keep students' expectations high rather than tracking them toward lower goals. It may also interrupt the negative cycle of low expectations exacerbating students' poor academic performance and failure, which researchers have described (Dougherty 1994; London 1978; Weis 1985). Counselors, advisors, and instructors at Central and Northwest Colleges have clearly taken steps to communicate high expectations and minimize negative labeling.

These new stigma-free approaches solve some of the previous problems associated with community colleges, but in interviewing students we discovered a serious disadvantage to this approach. Many students did not understand certain implications of their remedial courses. Avoiding language that might have negative connotations can prevent students' from understanding their status in college and thus hinder them in making successful plans.

## Analysis of College Catalogs: All Credits Are Not Created Equal

This softer approach is built into the very structure of course offerings and the labels attached to them. The college catalog and course schedule guide students' decisions and strategies, but Central's and Northwest's catalogs and course schedules are unclear and potentially misleading about which courses count and for what purposes. As one might assume, remedial classes fall at the bottom of a hierarchical system of course offerings. Furthermore, remedial instruction itself is arranged hierarchically, and students are allocated a place within this hierarchy through their performance on a placement test.

The hierarchy, however, is hard to recognize, and students often fail to recognize their position within this system. The system itself is not clearly defined. After extensive effort to analyze the course offerings and to interview staff about the meaning of certain terms and descriptions, we discerned the main elements of the course hierarchy. For simplicity, we have grouped the community colleges' course offerings into four general categories: pre-credit remedial, college remedial, ambiguous college credit, and definite college credit. We can describe these categories succinctly, but the distinctions are not readily apparent to students. Ambiguity is a major attribute of some of these categories.

At the lowest end, there is no ambiguity. Pre-credit remedial courses are tuition-free and are housed in a separate noncredit division of the college. The pre-credit classes do not count for credit nor do they count toward any degree or certificate. Students who score below a tenth-grade threshold on the reading, writing, or math placement test are placed in a pre-credit curriculum at either the eighth- or ninth-grade level. According to Northwest's assistant to the dean of instruction, such scores are "below the required level for college level." The catalog states that pre-credit students must pass a progress test to advance to the college's collegiate programs or credit division. The pre-credit classes are not ambiguous.

On the other hand, at the next two levels, the distinction between remedial and nonremedial classes becomes much more blurred. At the second level, college remedial classes, though offered with credit classes and labeled similarly to them, offer credits that do not count toward degree or transfer. Students who score above tenth-grade level on the placement test, but below a college skill threshold, are placed in courses that are labeled *college credit*, yet do not count toward any degree or transfer requirements. These classes appear in the class schedule along with all other college credit classes, with no indication that they differ in any way from other classes (except that lower level classes serve as prerequisites for higher level classes). The terms *remedial* and *noncredit* never appear. Indeed, on the contrary, next to each course name, in parentheses is a notation—3 cr hrs; 4 cr hrs; or 6 cr hrs—which seems to imply credit, even for courses that do not offer college credit toward a degree. These classes count for credit hours just like the rest, yet cannot be used as credit toward a degree or transfer. They are labeled as credit so that the institution can get state funding and the students can get financial aid.

Consequently, students cannot distinguish between remedial and non-remedial classes. For example, Raymond did not know how some remedial courses differ from other courses in terms of credit. During registration, when he found that a course he needed was closed, he chose to sign up for a reading class instead, not realizing that it was remedial and he would be paying for a course that would not count for degree or transfer credit:

> I wanted a math class, but they said the math classes were too full. . . .
> I didn't really need the reading though because they said I scored high
> and I didn't need the reading. I just took it anyway because they didn't
> have math. So I took it.

Included in this "credit, but not really credit" college remedial category are Reading 099, 125, 126. and English 098, 100, which actually account for about 60 percent of all English sections offered at Central College. In math, these courses include Math 100 and 110.

Third, the ambiguous college credit classes count as credit toward some degrees and majors, but not others, and may or may not count for transfer for some programs of study and for some four-year colleges. Math 112, for instance, counts as credit only toward the associate's in general studies (AGS), but not toward an associate's of applied sciences (AAS), associate's of arts (AA), or associate's of sciences (AS). Including Math 112, these remedial and ambiguous classes make up 55 percent of all mathematics sections at Central.

Fourth, definite college credit courses count for both degree credit and transfer. Confusion is less likely to occur for classes at this level.

A perceptive observer looking over the course numbers might infer that numbers below 100 were below college level, and the others were not. This is a reasonable inference, but it is wrong. Indeed, numbers vary among departments, so Math 112 is the first college-level course, yet Reading 126 is not college level. To further complicate matters, math courses below Math 204 do not count toward an AS degree, but Math 118, 125 and 135 do count toward an AA degree.

Actually, if students were to ask college staff about credit, they would have to be pretty sophisticated to get adequate information. They must ask if the course gives credit for a particular certificate or program, and which degree. In addition, just because a particular class counts as credit toward a degree does not necessarily guarantee that it will be transferable to a four-year college or university. The transferability of particular courses varies by each four-year college and each program type. At the time of the study, neither community college indicated in their catalog course descriptions which courses were transferable. Furthermore, the course descriptions do not specify whether a course is remedial or whether it does or does not count as credit toward any degree.

Such ambiguity encourages students to enroll in courses without clearly informing them whether they will receive real credits, and whether these credits will count toward their goals. In community colleges, the reason for this action may be to save face or simple oversight, but it is likely to mislead students into believing that they will get more for their course efforts (and tuition) than they ultimately receive.

## Unintended Consequences

This nonstigmatizing approach has further unintended consequences. The lack of clarity leaves students with ambiguous ideas about their status. Remedial students enrolled at these colleges may benefit from this approach, and certainly feel better about themselves and their potential. Many students are confused, however, and lack the structured guidance they need to make timely and informed decisions about their path through college.

Although the ambiguity we have noted in the catalogs and in students' perceptions could be overcome by effective guidance, these colleges do not offer what is needed to help students navigate the organizational structure and procedures. College staff usually assume that students will take it upon themselves to discover the degree, certification, and transfer requirements for their program of interest. Many students eventually do, but many wait too long, wasting time and money in the process. This problem is especially acute among students in remedial classes, the second category. In our interviews, faculty and staff report a hesitancy to highlight the negative implications of remedial courses, including the lack of real degree or transfer credits earned in such courses. They fear that such an approach will unduly discourage students.

However, students experience some difficulties from this delayed information. Ivette, in her second full-time semester and aiming for an AA degree, responded to the question about how long she thought it would take to complete her degree: "I still haven't seen what credits I need for the classes." Darius was also starting his second semester and, though he had definite plans to transfer to a specific university, had not found out anything about the requirements for transfer. He thought that he would transfer to a four-year college with junior status the following year. Unfortunately, he was not aware that after his full year of full-time coursework—which he thought had given him twenty-four credits—he actually only accumulated nine that were transferable. Five of his eight classes were either remedial or too low to count toward transfer.

Students often go for several months, a full semester, or even a full year without knowing that their remedial courses are not counting toward a degree or their transfer goals. Donald, a former remedial student, was in his fourth semester at Northwest and had not yet talked to a counselor to find out which classes would be accepted at the university to which he wanted to transfer. Students with very low achievement in English or math might need to take three terms of remedial courses before being able to earn college credits, but few of these students recognized this delayed timetable. Several students who were enrolled in a special program that combined several different classes along with remedial English and reading complained that they were not informed about the credit status of their classes:

> John: We had five classes. For each class we're supposed to get three credit hours. We came up with just four credit hours [instead of the fifteen he was expecting].
>
> Vanessa: We didn't even know that they were college prep classes.
>
> John: We didn't know. Like, they told us that we were in [this program]. They didn't explain exactly like, "You're going to take this, but you're not going to be credited for this." So like at the end when [the counselor said we] . . . only get four [credits], everybody is like, "Wait. [We weren't aware of this.]"

Marta related a similar experience of not finding this information out until after she enrolled in English 101:

> When I first came here, I was so happy to be in college. . . . Now I know I really wasn't [in college]. It kind of disappointed me to know that those classes, I'm not going to get no credit for. But, although they

helped me, it would help me a lot if I could get credit for them too. So I know I'm in college now. I didn't know [I wasn't in college] then.

Some of this confusion stems from the diffuse, unorganized way that students tend to get information about what courses to take and how best to go about their plans. First, students tend not to read the catalog very carefully, if at all. When they do, they are often immediately confused and frustrated. This is not surprising. As researchers, we had to conduct actual content analysis of the catalog and course schedule to understand the implications of the course credit numbering system and its relationship to remedial status and various degree requirements.

Second, visits with counselors are voluntary and limited. Students' limited use of the counselors is built into the structure of the colleges. Both Central and Northwest each have eight counselors for more than 7,000 students in a given semester (Office of Planning and Research 1997)—that is, one counselor for 875 students. This ratio obviously limits the amount of counseling that students can get from counselors. As one counselor at Central explained,

> Unlike high school, students will come to us voluntarily. We don't have a command performance. Obviously we couldn't have with just eight of us for over 6,000 students [*sic*, actually over 7,000]. So students do come to us when there's a problem, either personal, academic, or vocational.

Although counselors are officially the main staff responsible for providing information, in practice they are not. During registration, full-time faculty, counselors, and administrators sit at the registration tables to help students select courses. This is often a chaotic period, and the particular staff person who advises a student is somewhat arbitrarily assigned. That is, the available information and advice depends on a random process, with many faculty knowing very little about remedial courses and their implications. In addition, students who get their advice before the registration period get more advice, in bits and pieces, from faculty members with incomplete knowledge of remedial courses. Furthermore, like Ivette and Darius, many students choose not to visit counselors until they are well on their way toward their degree or toward transfer.

Third, even among students who are clear about their program and degree requirements early on, confusion and frustration sometimes arise

from their lack of familiarity with the college environment. This is com-
pounded by the vague language faculty use during registration to avoid
the stigma of remedial placement. Annette, for instance, decided during
her first semester at Central that she wanted to major in social work and
transfer to a nearby university. However, she lacked familiarity with the
placement test system and with test-taking strategies:

> I wanted to get each [question] . . . right, so I took my time with
> them. So I ran out of time . . . I really didn't care cause I didn't know
> that the . . . test was what was going to count for what courses I'd be
> able to take.

She said that the advisor who helped her pick her courses did not say
much about the placement test except, "you scored fair on your reading
and your English test." This did not sound bad to Annette, and she went
along when they told her what classes to take. "They just gave those classes.
They just said, 'This is what you have to take.' " She agreed with their selection, not even realizing that she was in remedial courses for which she
would receive no college credits:

> [My teacher] told me that I scored low on the placement test, that's
> why I had to get in this . . . program for some remedial classes, to bet-
> ter my reading and my math skills, my English skills, so I could move
> on and start taking college classes. I wouldn't be able to take any col-
> lege classes until I passed, finished out of the . . . program. I was like,
> "Why didn't anyone tell me that?" I would have gone to another school
> and took the test. They had me registering and everything, and now I
> have to take these remedial classes. This is going to hold me back
> because none of this counts. So I still have two years to go 'cause none
> of these classes here even count. So I was a little upset about that
> because it was really misleading. Especially with me signing up for
> financial aid and all this, and find out your aid has to pay for all of this.

Other students had similar regrets. David said that he might have
decided to forgo college altogether if he had known that his credits were
not going to count toward anything:

> I think that a student should know in the beginning . . . that these
> classes, even though we think they're necessary and you would benefit
> from them, will not count toward graduation. The student should

know what they're getting into in the very beginning. Like I said, I don't have a lot of time to spend in school. . . . The program has helped me. . . . But if I had known from the very beginning that I wasn't going to be getting full credit for these classes, I may have thought twice about them. . . . I would have just gone on and tried to find a job. . . . I would have probably said, "Hey I don't have time for this. I've got to go."

For this student with limited funds and little time to spend in school, protecting his self-esteem actually prevented realistic career decisions. Erving Goffman (1952) described such delaying of information as an essential element of a scam. Although we do not believe this is the intention, this nonstigmatized approach necessarily prevents students from making informed decisions and anticipating negative outcomes.

## DO STUDENTS REALIZE IMPLICATIONS OF REMEDIAL COURSEWORK?

In addition to student interviews at these two community colleges, surveys were administered in many sections of six different math, English, and reading classes. Students who had formerly been enrolled in remedial classes were also surveyed. As table 4.1, panel a, shows, 610 of the 804 students surveyed had taken or were currently taking remedial courses.[1] Of these, 38.7 percent believed the classes would count toward their degree requirements, and an additional 34.6 percent were not sure. In sum, over 73 percent of students who had taken remedial courses were either unclear or wrong about the number of credits they were earning.

The results indicate that students' awareness increases over time, but only modestly. Comparing students in their first year with those in their second year and above, we find an improved accuracy over time, with 23.2 percent of first-year students correctly reporting that their credits would not count and somewhat more (29.7 percent) students beyond their first year with correct reporting (see table 4.1). The improved awareness is accompanied by a decline in the proportion of those who are not sure, whereas the proportion believing mistakenly that they do count remains constant (almost 39 percent). Despite students' improved accuracy after their first year, over 70 percent of students beyond the first year are still not aware that their remedial courses did not count toward a degree.

In the interviews, students taking multiple remedial classes seemed more confused about their situation. They were making sacrifices, improving themselves, and aiming toward a degree, and no one was telling

TABLE 4.1     Remedial Students' Perceptions of Remedial Status

| | Do Remedial Classes Count Toward Degree? | | | |
|---|---|---|---|---|
| Student Status | Percentage No | Percentage Yes | Percentage Not Sure | n (Remedial Students)[a] |
| First year | 23.2 | 38.9 | 37.9 | 280 |
| Second year or more | 29.7 | 38.5 | 31.8 | 330 |
| All remedial students | 26.7 | 38.7 | 34.6 | 610 |

*Source:* Authors' data.
[a]Analysis of students taking remedial courses (N = 610) out of sample of 804 students.

TABLE 4.2     Remedial Students' Perception of Degree Credits

| | Number Remedial | Do Remedial Classes Count Toward Degree? | | | |
|---|---|---|---|---|---|
| Student Status | Subjects | Percentage No | Percentage Yes | Percentage Not Sure | n |
| First year | 1 | 36.5 | 35.4 | 28.1 | 96 |
| | 2 | 17.2 | 45.2 | 37.6 | 93 |
| | 3 or more | 15.4 | 36.3 | 48.4 | 91 |
| Second year or more | 1 | 37.0 | 39.5 | 23.5 | 81 |
| | 2 | 32.4 | 40.3 | 27.3 | 139 |
| | 3 or more | 20.9 | 35.5 | 43.6 | 110 |
| All remedial students | | 26.7 | 38.7 | 34.6 | 610 |

*Source:* Authors' data.

them any discouraging information, even though they were taking several developmental courses. The survey data clarify students' response to this situation—students taking remedial classes in more subjects were less likely to realize that the classes would not count (see table 4.2). Even among students in their second year, those taking three or four remedial course areas were less likely to be aware than students taking one (21 percent vs. 37 percent). Although some students with correct perceptions may have dropped out, especially by second year, these findings also support the observations in our interviews. Even after the first year, students taking remedial courses in more than one area are more likely to misperceive the credit value of their courses.

TABLE 4.3    Perceived Chances of Achieving Degree Goals

| Number Remedial Subjects | Percentage "Very Likely" or "Likely" to Earn Degree | n |
| --- | --- | --- |
| 0 | 90.7 | 194 |
| 1 | 94.4 | 177 |
| 2 | 96.6 | 232 |
| 3 or more | 91.0 | 201 |
| All students | 93.3 | 804 |

*Source:* Authors' data.

We also find that students' perceived chances of degree completion do not decline with increased remediation. Our survey asked students to assess their chances of achieving their degree goals (on a five-point scale from "very likely" to "very unlikely"). We find that students' perceived likelihood does not decline significantly as they take more remedial subjects (table 4.3). Moreover, remedial students did not have lower goals. They were actually slightly more likely to indicate a bachelor's degree goal (versus associate's goal or certificate) than were nonremedial students—46.3 percent vs. 44.2 percent. Although national data indicate that the dropout rate for students with three or more remedial course areas is much higher than for those with only one (Adelman 1996, 1999), we find that students with high remedial enrollment do not in fact perceive their chances of completing their degree as lower than other students.

## IS REMEDIAL RELATED TO DEGREE COMPLETION?

If over half the students in remedial classes are uncertain or wrong about whether they are getting college credits, we must wonder whether students' reported degree plans in national survey data take adequate account of the implications of their remedial placements. What do we know about the effects of remedial coursework on various educational outcomes? Although previous researchers have examined the influence of any remedial coursework on subsequent academic success and persistence and found a negative effect, these studies have been criticized for their serious methodological flaws (O'Hear and MacDonald 1995; Boylan and Saxon 1999). Moreover, most of these studies have not examined a national sample of community college students.

However, a well-designed study using national data suggests that extensive remediation does have a negative effect on later academic success. In an

TABLE 4.4    Dropout Rate

| Number Remedial Subjects | Dropout Percentage |
|---|---|
| 0 | 31.6 |
| 1 | 28.5 |
| 2 | 35.8 |
| 3 or more | 46.3 |

*Source:* BPS.
N = 1094 (BPS).

analysis of the high school and beyond sophomore cohort, Clifford Adelman (1999, 74) found that both the type and amount of remedial coursework matter in completing a bachelor's degree, and that the percentage of students completing a bachelor's degree decreases as the number of remedial courses increases. These analyses are provocative, but they include only students at four-year colleges.

The Beginning Postsecondary Students (BPS) national longitudinal survey is perhaps the best data for examining a random sample of entering college freshmen, following them over the next five years (NCES 1996a). Compared with most prior studies of the effects of remedial course-taking, these data permit analyses of a national sample over a longer period and allow us to consider both AA and BA attainment. Many colleges offer remedial courses in reading, writing, language, and math for students lacking requisite skills, and the BPS asked students whether they were in remedial classes in each area. Because this information is self-reported, it is a conservative estimate and most likely underreports incidence of remedial course-taking.

In examining this question with the BPS data, we limit our sample to community college students. Raw statistical analyses show that compared to students taking no remedial courses, one remedial course is not associated with increased chances of dropping out, but additional ones are. Dropout rates sharply increase from about 29 percent to 36 percent, to 46 percent as one's enrollment increases from one to three or more remedial course areas (table 4.4). Similarly, one's chances of attaining a college degree decline, from about 26 percent, to 22 percent, to 15 percent as the number of remedial course areas increases (table 4.5).

These analyses do not control for student characteristics, and we are not saying that students would not be assisted by taking remedial courses. Indeed, a study that focused on students with modest remedial needs found

TABLE 4.5   Degree Attainment

| Number Remedial Subjects | Percentage Who Earned Degree |
|---|---|
| 0 | 26.6 |
| 1 | 25.5 |
| 2 | 22.3 |
| 3 or more | 15.3 |

*Source:* BPS.
N = 1094 (BPS).

that these courses have benefits (Bettinger and Long 2005). These authors find that remedial students who do not require extensive remediation are more likely to persist in college, transfer, and complete a bachelor's degree than students of similar tested ability who do not take remedial classes. However, this study is different than the present study in two key ways. First, it compares students with similar remedial needs to each other rather than considering how remedial students fare relative to all other students. Second, it examines only students with small or moderate remedial needs, omitting severely underprepared students, those most likely to need a large amount of remediation. It is exactly these kinds of students that we find have extremely poor completion rates.

Although taking one remedial course is associated with slightly better outcomes in our analyses, taking more than one is associated with severe declines in degree completion rates. For students who take remedial courses in three or more subject areas, nearly half will drop out and less than a fifth will earn any college degree within five years—not even a two-year associate's degree. These findings are consistent with Adelman's analyses (1999), which show that students taking multiple remedial courses are less likely to experience later academic success.

To better assess the importance of relative levels of remediation, we conducted multivariate logistic regression, again limiting the sample to community college students, and with earning an associate's degree or higher as our binary outcome variable. Our analysis reveals that race (being black versus white), parents' college education (bachelor's or higher attainment versus no college), and enrollment status (mostly full-time or mixed full- and part-time versus mostly part-time) significantly affect dropout. The results also confirm the negative relationship between taking remedial courses and college dropout that the tables suggest, showing that students who need remediation in three or more areas are at signifi-

TABLE 4.6    Logistic Regression

| Variable | B | Exp (B) |
|---|---|---|
| African American | .5585 | 1.748* |
| Hispanic | .1186 | 1.126* |
| Native American | .9061 | 2.4745 |
| Asian | −.2772 | .7579 |
| Female | .0717 | 1.0744 |
| Parent education: less than two years college | −.5902 | .5542 |
| Parent education: more than two years college | .2273 | 1.2552 |
| Parent education: BA or higher | −.5111 | .5998* |
| Family income | .0186 | 1.0188 |
| Financially independent household | .2337 | 1.2633 |
| Age | −.0854 | .9181 |
| Age (squared) | .0014 | 1.0014 |
| High school GPA (7 point scale) | −.2048 | .8148 |
| Expect Associate's degree or more | −.2775 | .7577 |
| One remedial subject | .1566 | 1.1695 |
| Two remedial subjects | .2389 | 1.2698 |
| Three or more remedial subjects | .8016 | 2.2290* |
| Remedial language | .7800 | 2.1815* |
| First year grades | −.0477 | .9534 |
| Full-time enrollment | −1.044 | .3519** |
| Mixed full-time and part-time enrollment | −1.9376 | .1440** |
| Average work hours per week | .0103 | 1.0104 |
| Constant | 2.6820 | |

*Source:* BPS; authors' compilations.
N = 1094 (BPS).
*p ≤ .05; **p ≤ .01
Dependent Variable = Dropout (0,1).

cantly higher risk of dropping out. Even after controlling for a host of other variables, including degree expectations, students taking remedial classes in three or more areas have more than double the odds of dropping out compared to students taking no remedial courses (table 4.6).

Because the information on remedial participation is self-reported, it is likely a conservative estimate, underreporting incidence of remedial course-work, as our analyses of actual course-taking in our local data indicates. Moreover, the dropout and disappointed degree plans associated with students reporting many remedial courses is also likely to be an underestimate.

Students who do not realize their courses are remedial may face even greater disappointment.

## CHALLENGES AND IMPLICATIONS OF REMEDIATION

We have found, then, that the problems of poor achievement and unrealistic plans in community colleges arise in part because high schools allow many students to believe that poor achievement is no impediment to attending college and attaining degrees. Community colleges are faced with the task of serving these students who arrive at their doors underprepared for college level courses, yet fully anticipating a college degree. The colleges must manage these students and their expectations. As one community college English professor aptly noted, "You have to serve your community if you're a community college."

Colleges have responded to this challenge by offering remedial courses, and more than 60 percent of beginning community college students nationwide have taken a few remedial courses (NCES 2002). As a result, many individuals enrolled in courses in a college are in fact taking noncredit high school courses. Moreover, if they take several such courses, our results indicate that they have little prospect of getting any college degree, regardless of their high plans. Therefore, one must be cautious in inferring who is a college student. Students may not realize that in critical ways they are not actually college students. Students, policy makers, and researchers need to be aware of these distinctions.

This ambiguity of defining students may be a response to the historic criticism that community colleges cool out students' ambitions. We find that community colleges have found ingenious ways to avoid conveying stigma to students who must take remedial courses. We were in fact impressed at how these community colleges were able to avoid damaging the self-confidence of students yet encourage them to improve their skills to qualify for college-level courses.

However, we discovered that this stigma-free approach has some unintended consequences. Even after two, three, or four semesters, some students remained unclear about whether remedial courses were giving them college credit and how long it would take them to get a degree. Some students had spent money and lost time taking courses they did not need and for which they did not get credit. For students with limited funds and a narrow window of time for college study, such missteps can be costly to their careers.

Our qualitative findings suggest that students' reported plans in national survey data may not take adequate account of the implications of their remedial placements, particularly on college credits, and therefore on their completion rates. Analyzing community college students in the BPS national survey, we find that taking remedial courses in three or more areas strongly predicts college dropout, even after controlling for students' degree expectations and a host of individual characteristics. Students do not anticipate the remedial influence on their chances of completing a degree.

## The Importance of Transparency

Anticipation of timetables and delays is imperative for many low-income students, who often face rigid timetables reinforced by the expectations and sacrifices of parents, spouses, and employers. In such circumstances, delays can have deleterious consequences. If the remedial system were more transparent, anticipation of delays would be easier. Students could respond by making more appropriate and realistic choices and plans so that they could attain some benefit within the allowed timetable.

Some alternative options exist that students do not generally realize. Instead of wasting time and resources taking the remedial courses required for certain types of associate's degrees, students can shift to certificate programs or to alternative associate's degrees. As noted, many community colleges offer several alternative associate's degree programs of varying difficulty (for example, AGS, AAS, AS, AA). Because degrees have different academic requirements, students who need several remedial courses for an AA will need fewer for an AAS and even fewer for an AGS. Many students do not know about the degree options available, the amount of time they must spend in remedial classes for each degree, or the proportion of students with their level of preparation who fail to complete each type of degree. Providing this information and candidly assessing students' remedial needs for each degree could help students understand their expected timetables and make more appropriate choices.

Instead, we find that students are gently led into a long-term college commitment without any indication of how little progress they are making or how long it will take to achieve their goal. We assume that community colleges are putting students in this position with the best of intentions, but the results are no less worrisome. Students are expending money and efforts, and the risk that many students will leave without a degree, and some will earn few or no college credits, is very real.

Why don't students figure out the implications of their remedial placements on their own? Several factors make this unlikely. First, most community colleges, including those that we studied, are commuter schools, and students spend little time on campus after class hours talking with other students or counselors. Second, even if they tried to meet with counselors, it would not be as easy, because guidance counselor loads are large, averaging 875 students per counselor at these community colleges. Third, even when students were aware of former students who had dropped out of college, they interpreted the dropout as the failure of an individual, not the system. Finally, simple unfamiliarity with the system may make it difficult to know what questions to ask or whether there is a question that needs to be asked.

We must also note that some students (about 15 percent) do succeed in getting a degree, despite taking remedial courses in three or more areas. This suggests that community colleges are providing disadvantaged students with a second chance to overcome environmental obstacles, just as they intended. Unfortunately, this second chance leads to a degree for only a small proportion of disadvantaged students.

For those students outside this successful minority, the BPS analyses indicate that though their failures are predictable, they are not being warned. If students had been informed, some might have made other education and career choices. If they had been informed in high school of their poor preparation, they could have chosen either to increase their efforts in high school or to take vocational courses, which can have benefits for earnings and job status (Arum and Shavit 1995; Bishop 1992; Campbell 1986; Boesel et al. 1994), and in which teachers' contacts with employers can provide access to better jobs (Rosenbaum 2001). If students had been informed of their chances for success when they first entered community college, students might have chosen certificate programs or associate's degrees with fewer academic prerequisites. They might have begun thinking about making backup plans, perhaps considering on-the-job training or skill enhancement at another kind of school in addition to their college studies.

## Striking the Right Balance

Informing students of their lowered probabilities of success may be discouraging, but withholding this information prevents them from addressing their situation proactively. College staff must find ways to convey full information yet encourage students' efforts at the same time. Practitioners must also find ways to support programs that reduce failure for at-risk remedial students. This is not an easy balance, but it is necessary to find ways to provide both information and encouragement.

The challenge of finding this balance is similar to the issues surrounding out-of-wedlock pregnancy. For years, pregnancy outside of marriage was stigmatized, and the stigma was thought to be a deterrent to pregnancy. However, when unwed pregnancy was destigmatized, the rates of such pregnancies increased because fewer women chose to get married as a means to avoid stigma. Unfortunately, this approach did nothing to provide support to those who did get pregnant. The challenge should not therefore be to merely eliminate stigma, but to get unmarried people to avoid pregnancy, without stigmatizing those who do get pregnant. Similarly, we must find ways for students to avoid remediation that move beyond the issue of stigma. Eliminating stigma will not solve students' remedial problems, just as attaching stigma will not eliminate the reality of remedial needs.

One way to strike this balance is to provide early warnings about remedial needs and their implications while providing effective procedures to address those needs. These lessons should begin in high school, when students can understand the challenges of college and prepare themselves to overcome them. Since high schools do not offer curricula aligned to the content and standards of basic college level courses, and teachers and counselors are not aware of this alignment (or lack), students' opportunities for such understanding and preparation are severely limited. If such alignment exists, and students cannot catch up academically in high school, at least they will be able to anticipate their potential remedial placement and plan accordingly.

Increased structure, dependable timetables, and short-term incentives in college may also help to guide and encourage struggling students. As we will show in chapter 6, private occupational colleges offer some of these new approaches. These colleges provide clear information, frequent mandatory counseling, programs that permit long-term planning for students, programs that reduce remedial requirements, and intervening certificates on the way to associate's degrees. These procedures keep students abreast of their degree status, make it easier to progress despite remedial needs, and offer some benefits for those who do drop out.

We conclude that nonstigmatizing counseling may resolve the old complaints about cooling out, but may also raise additional concerns about candor and deception. Reduced stigma and improved self-confidence come at the cost of deception and delay. Hiding stigma may prolong the time it takes for students to realize their situation. Information that could be easily produced is not being given to students, and students are paying the price in delayed recognition, ineffectual efforts that have a low probability of leading to their goal, and failure to take actions that may be more promising.

## Beyond Stigma

The problems of community colleges extend beyond remedial students and their misunderstanding of credits and plans, however. Table 4.4 shows that, even for those students who do not take any remedial courses, barriers to earning a degree remain. Of students without any remedial courses, nearly a third dropped out within five years of beginning college. Although these numbers are lower than the dropout rates for students in need of remediation in multiple subject areas, it is clear that remediation is not the only factor affecting degree completion at community colleges. The following chapters broaden our analysis to examine other organizational procedures in community colleges that might affect completion rates.

# CHAPTER FIVE

## STUDENT INFORMATION PROBLEMS WITH COLLEGE PROCEDURES

Overheated aspirations and hidden remedial barriers may create problems for some community college students, but these are not the only problems students face. We turn to other problematic community college assumptions. We examine student needs with respect to information and planning for college and careers, and suggest that students have a variety of problems understanding college procedures and requirements besides those related to remedial courses, often making college plans based on meager or incorrect information. To see alternative procedures, we add comparisons with a sample of occupational colleges.

Student information deficiencies have become a growing issue for community colleges in recent years because of the increasing numbers of nontraditional students and perhaps the decreasing amount of realistic information provided by high school counselors who follow a "college for all" philosophy (Rosenbaum 2001). Many of these nontraditional students—racial and ethnic minorities, low-income and low-achieving students, as well as older and part-time students—lack the familiarity with college procedures and requirements necessary for success. We examine the information and planning problems of two-year college students, the burden placed on the institutions to accommodate such student needs, and the alternative procedures some colleges have developed to address these problems.

## Information Needs and Cultural and Social Capital

As we have discussed, the revolutionary expansion of postsecondary access in the United States has meant that new kinds of students are attending college. To understand how these new students may differ from more traditional students of the past, it is helpful to go beyond ascriptive characteristics such as race and social class, and to examine the skills and behaviors students bring with them to college. With its focus on ingrained (but often unnoticed) knowledge and behaviors, sociological thinking on cultural and social capital can shed light on the nature of the problems these new students may face in college. Briefly, cultural capital refers to the knowledge and behaviors individuals use to access social resources and to gain status; social capital refers to social relationships used toward the same ends.

In considering the role of cultural capital in educational achievement and attainment, Pierre Bourdieu and Jean-Claude Passeron (1977) suggest that success in schools requires familiarity with the dominant culture. A lack of such knowledge leaves some students—especially those marginalized by the dominant culture, such as working-class and racial and ethnic minority students—at a disadvantage in the competition for academic credentials. Students who have not mastered these middle-class rules of the game will be less successful in mainstream institutions such as schools (Bourdieu 1984).

Similarly, James Coleman (1988) asserts that social capital is critical to educational success. He hypothesizes that certain relationships facilitate students' productive activity at school by creating or communicating obligations, expectations, information, and social norms. Similar to Bourdieu's thinking on cultural capital, Coleman suggests that students who come from mainstream (that is, white middle-class) families and communities also have more social capital that allows them access to institutional resources and, as a result, they are more successful in school.

Although most scholarship conceives of cultural capital in terms of knowledge and behaviors, and social capital in terms of relationships, the two concepts overlap with respect to the role of information. Indeed, Bourdieu and Loic Wacquant (1992) have suggested that cultural capital might be more appropriately termed informational capital. Moreover, Coleman (1988) and other scholars (for example, Lareau and Horvat 1999; Stanton-Salazar and Dornbusch 1995) have stressed the critical nature of information in mediating the ways that social relationships affect students' educational attainment. The types of information that scholars have suggested may be important to student success include instrumental information, for example, on coursework, careers, and social services (as we showed in chapter 3; see also Stanton-Salazar and Dornbusch 1995), as well as information on bureaucratic requirements and the behavioral demands of schools (as we showed in chapter 4; see also Lareau and Horvat 1999).

## The New College Students and Their Information Needs

Dramatic increases in college access have made a clear mark on today's student bodies. Over the last four decades, two-year colleges in particular have seen the increased campus presence of racial and ethnic minorities, low-income and low-achieving students, as well as older and part-time students. This contrasts with the students of past generations, who were mainly white, middle- and upper-class, relatively high-achievers, eighteen-to twenty-four-year-olds, attending full-time (NCES 2002).

More than just enrolling these new kinds of students, community colleges have adapted their practices to accommodate them. As noted in chapter 1, community colleges have made amazing changes in location and scheduling to accommodate students who attend part-time and must juggle many conflicting obligations. Furthermore, as described in chapter 4, community colleges have devised extensive remedial programs to address the serious academic difficulties of many new students.

Despite these remarkable adaptations, we find that many two-year college students have trouble navigating college requirements. Unfortunately, the community colleges in our sample do not appear to recognize that many of their students do not have the knowledge or skills to acquire and use information about college with enough sophistication to make realistic and achievable college plans. They see information problems primarily as a matter of providing the information, but give less attention to the quality of that information or their students' ability to use it. Because of this, a lack of appropriate and usable information appears to cloud educational planning and to discourage students.

Many of the information problems that two-year college students face would probably not have arisen among the more traditional college students of the past, given that they followed a much more restricted and traditional path to college. Today's community college students have difficulty getting information during their brief visits to campus for classes. Their time is sharply limited by competing demands from jobs, spouses, parents, and child care. In our survey, among full-time students, 30 percent of private school students and 28 percent of public school students work full-time (more than thirty-four hours per week), and about half work over twenty hours per week (50 percent at private schools and 52 percent at public schools). National data (NCES 1996a) show comparable results for community college students: 29 percent work more than thirty-four hours per week, 51 percent work more than twenty. These students do not have much time to acquire information about complex requirements, even if counseling activities were available.

## Understanding Information Problems

Even as scholars appear to agree that information is a crucial resource in educational attainment, and that some community college students may be disadvantaged in their access to useful information, few researchers have focused explicitly on the institutional structures and procedures that direct the flow of information within educational institutions. We seek to extend the literature by analyzing students' information needs in different institutional settings and do so by examining four questions related to student information problems:

1. Do students have serious information problems, and are colleges ever responsible?

2. How can college procedures improve students' information and planning?

3. Do colleges with alternative procedures affect student information, planning, and confidence in degree completion?

4. Do alternative college procedures matter for information, net of student attributes?

We use our extensive interview data to examine the first two questions; we then turn to our student survey to address the final two. We find that otherwise similar students have much better understanding of their situation in one kind of college than in another, which suggests that institutional procedures can help students obtain and apply information to enhance their success in school.

## COLLEGES' ROLE IN INFORMATION PROBLEMS AND SOLUTIONS

### 1. Do Students Have Serious Information Problems, and Are College Procedures Ever Responsible?

Colleges offer a wide range of options to students and assume that students know how to make plans that will lead to realization of their goals. Although many traditional students and some of the new students (for example, older students) may possess sufficient information or the skills to obtain and use it, some students may have difficulty with this approach. Students who did poorly in high school may not understand college course offerings and may also be reluctant to ask. Students from families with low income or education levels may not get college advice from parents who have little or no experience with postsecondary education. Such students may have significant information problems and may experience difficulty in knowing how to accomplish their educational goals. Our survey data find exactly this, that parent education and income are significantly correlated with students' reported information about college requirements.

Although academic models sometimes acknowledge that information is imperfect, our interviews suggest that imperfect is an understatement. The interviews reveal serious deficiencies in students' information at both community and occupational colleges. Many students make educational choices without considering alternatives, and they rely on meager, vague, and even incorrect, information. In particular, we find that students' selection into a given college or major appears extremely haphazard, especially when contrasted to the sophisticated information and planning processes described among students entering most four-year colleges (compare Hoxby 2004; McDonough 1997). Asked why she chose her occupational college, Tina offered a typical response: "I don't know . . . my sister was telling me her friend just graduated from [the school], and really liked it, so I called [to enroll]." With respect to her major, she continues, "Nothing really stood out, it was just something that interested me. No real, one major thing." Similarly, Becky answered that she knew about her occupational college, "Just from what my cousin told me—it's not a lot. She just said it's a good school, you can do this, this, and that. And I figured, okay, it's two years, I can graduate. So I went there." Our interviews indicate that students often do not investigate other schools, nor do they form clear ideas of how schools vary. Even when considering other colleges, they obtain paltry information about alternatives. Lorena investigated college options "just looking through a phone book, and getting all the numbers that had paralegal [programs]."

A student's choice of majors may be determined by a single high school course. In the prior example, Lorena chose a paralegal major based on one high school social studies class. Another student, Rocio, chose accounting after a single course and despite a general dislike for mathematics: "My senior year, I took a class in accounting, and I really liked it . . . and I don't really like math." These students use scant information and questionable sources, and do not actively examine alternatives or consider conflicting information (such as a bookkeeper's dislike of math). In our interview sample, both community college students and their counterparts at private occupational colleges regularly reported making college and major choices based on little and sometimes false information.

Another problem is perhaps more important. Interviews also indicate that students' informational problems once they are in college are sometimes exacerbated by college procedures. For instance, Rocio found herself in trouble because not all requirements were clear from the outset:

> Because there's certain [courses] that you *have to take*, and some, like, if you *want*. But then it ends up that you *do* need them. . . . I haven't taken my typing class because I haven't taken the test; and I couldn't take some of the classes I had to because of that. Now . . . it's like backing me up, those classes. [emphasis in original]

Another student, Leah, asked community college staff about the appropriate courses to prepare her for transfer to university, but the advisor suggested coursework that would not help.

> Leah: I took a computer course because my counselor told me to take that . . . because it would transfer. . . . But in some ways, I waste my time and money, you know.
>
> Interviewer: Because it didn't count for the transfer degree?
>
> Leah: Right . . . I told them specifically that I am interested in transferring with a science background. . . . And she was like, "Well, you can look at it in a positive way, you know, that you learned so and so," but yeah, but that wasn't my point.

Leah's poor course choices are partly related to advising practices. In her community college, much of the advising during the registration period is conducted by instructors who may not have information on programs outside their own departments. She reported, "I don't think they were trained to be counselors, like the instructors were taking turns. Because I saw my computer instructor sitting there [advising] . . . and before I knew anything, I was picking up computer classes."

Not all advising problems arise from advisors' narrow information (or self-interest), of course. Some problems come up because advising is unavailable. A student at another community college, Wanda, painted an unfortunate picture of advising practices in both academic and administrative spheres. She insisted that "if you have any problems with your financial aid, or any other problems, you can't see them [advisors] directly. . . . You have to make an appointment, and an appointment can be months from now. But you need to get that problem resolved right then."

Careful and informed advising is certainly important, but it may not be enough. Tina commented on the difference between academic advising practices at her current occupational college and her prior community college. She explained that at the community college, "You have to go to them [that is, the advisors]. Here [occupational college], they make you see the first-term advisor . . . and help you through."

Institutional practices for remediation can also create information problems for students, sometimes with serious consequences. Wanda had originally planned to be in community college for two years before taking full-time work. Because she placed into remedial classes, however, she needed to spend at least three years on her associate's degree. School staff, she noted, "kept telling me that, 'This [course] is just to help you get into 112.' . . . I didn't understand. . . . They count toward your electives, but don't count for your degree." This misunderstanding meant that Wanda must spend an extra year in school that she hadn't anticipated.

In sum, students at both types of school report using meager, vague, and even incorrect information as the basis for their educational choices, such as where to enroll and what field to study. Once in college, they also report information problems, like taking the wrong classes or misunderstanding the value of remedial coursework. Although our interview sample may not be representative of all students at these colleges, student reports indicate that college practices are sometimes responsible for impeding them from obtaining information that would guide their choices. Students fail to take the courses they need or they take courses they don't need, which delays their progress. Students mention college procedures for advising, scheduling, communicating requirements, and providing sequential offerings, which affect their capacity to fulfill their educational goals.

## 2. How Can College Procedures Improve Students' Information and Planning?

Community college administrators—including those in charge of occupational programs—report that they address students' information difficulties by providing more information. College catalogs get bigger, student handbooks are created, and additional informational meetings are provided for those who want to come. Although "piling on information" may have benefits, it assumes that students have time for additional reading and meetings, that they can understand a plethora of complex information, and that they realize that they have information problems. These assumptions may not be true for all students. Students lacking background information about college and lacking time or confidence to chase down advisors and administrators would probably face information difficulties and make costly mistakes, just as the students cited did.

Community colleges do provide counseling services, but counseling is often regarded as peripheral: offices are in out-of-the-way locations and have few staff (see chapter 7). Some counselors admit that they could not possibly handle a substantial fraction of the student body if those students were to seek out their services. Asked if more students could benefit from the services of her office, one community college counselor responded, "Absolutely, but there's just no way. There . . . [are] over 6,000 plus students . . . and . . . three full-time professional counselors, and the rest are part-time counselors that fill in the blanks." Like the health services office, the guidance office is designed to assist the few students who have the initiative to seek help.

Of course, resources are tight at most community colleges, whose public mandate is broad and expanding, even as budgets are repeatedly cut. One top administrator at a community college system included in our sample explained that, when faced with budget cuts, the colleges have progressively cut counseling staff, trying to preserve instruction. This may be due to organizational priorities toward instruction, or to funding formulas that reward classroom enrollment and ignore degree completion rates. In responding to reduced resources, community colleges may have preserved their commitment to one mandate at the expense of another. One might wonder, if colleges were forced to be more attentive to student mistakes and dropout rates, whether counseling would be given greater priority. In fact, at one community college in our sample, low retention rates were deemed a problem for enrollments. The college response was to focus on improving student information through enhanced advising. However, this was an atypical response and the effort was soon weakened by subsequent budget cuts.

The occupational colleges in our study do not face either the broad obligations of community colleges or the funding constraints imposed by external political decisions. Like community colleges, however, their mission is to develop an educated workforce. Within this sphere, occupational colleges show that an alternative approach is possible. According to administrator reports, occupational colleges address students' information difficulties by explicitly providing three forms of structure: structured programs, structured advising, and structured peer support.

*Structured Programs*    Instead of providing more information, administrators report that these occupational colleges create highly structured programs, which require little information. They specify a clear sequence of courses, which lead efficiently to student's goals. By limiting student choices and providing information targeted to students' immediate needs, students are prevented from making mistakes, which increase time, tuition, and the risks of not completing their degrees. One occupational college administrator explained how programs were explicitly designed to reduce student missteps: "We try to minimize the opportunities for students to go down the wrong path in terms of the courses they need to take. So there are a few electives and those that we have are in the general education area. . . . They all take roughly the same courses." Course options are fewer at occupational colleges, but so are students' mistakes, an issue to which we will return later.

*Structured Advising*    Instead of relying on students' initiative to contact advisors, administrators report that these occupational colleges require mandatory and frequent meetings, at least once per term (and more frequently at some colleges). Administrators recognize the necessity of such structured procedures for some students, as one explained, "We have a lot of personalized [advisory] services, and we have to because otherwise, a lot of the students . . . would be lost." Unlike the large, generic, optional information meetings at community colleges, the meetings are small, program specific, and mandatory at occupational colleges. Even students who are too passive or confused to seek out advisors must attend these meetings, where they get information about what actions and courses to take at that time. Instead of advisors being in peripheral locations, advisors are located centrally, so that students must pass through the guidance area every day on their way to classes. The centrality of advising is structured into the time and space of students' regular schedules in these colleges, and advising keeps students on track toward their goals.

*Structured Peer Support*    Although extracurricular activities and dormitories reduce dropout rates at four-year colleges, these sources of social support are limited or absent at nearly all two-year institutions (Tinto 1993). However, occupational colleges offer another form of social support. Administrators report that they create peer cohorts that progress together through the same courses and advisory meetings in each occupational program. These cohorts make it easy and cost-effective to offer required courses and frequent group advising. Moreover, peer cohorts also provide information, support, and a normative reference point for students to judge their own progress. As one administrator put it: "We give them schedules and give them the times. . . . We work the cohorts together. . . . all [these] things are helping to get them to graduation." Students can see what peers are doing and how to do it. Peer cohorts provide an informal structure to keep students on track toward their goals.

Of course, it is not surprising that occupational college personnel believe that their colleges' structured procedures should improve student information and planning. We test their assertions using our student survey data.

## 3. Do Colleges with Alternative Procedures Affect Student Information, Planning, and Confidence in Degree Completion?

If these administrator descriptions are accurate, we would expect occupational college students to have better information about college requirements, to make fewer mistakes in choosing courses, and to report increased confidence that they can complete a degree. Our survey of 4,365 students in seven community colleges and seven occupational colleges asked about the adequacy of the information students receive, the courses they take, and their confidence about achieving their degree goals. Given our interest in confidence about the degree, we limited our analyses to students who report seeking at least an associate's degree (this is also important for the sake of comparability, as community colleges tend to enroll many non-degree students). Excluding cases with missing data on the dependent variables yielded a total N of 3,698. Here we analyze whether students report different experiences in occupational colleges and community colleges.

We asked students a series of questions about their information needs, which are listed in the first three rows in table 5.1. Responses to each question were given on a five-point Likert-type scale of 1 = "strongly disagree" to 5 = "strongly agree." T-tests show that, compared with community college students, occupational college students are significantly more likely to be certain which courses they need for their degree plans (76 percent versus 65 percent, $p < .001$); more likely to agree that they know which courses give credit (80 percent versus 74 percent, $p < .001$); and more likely to agree that they have enough information about requirements and prerequisites (70 percent versus 58 percent, $p < .001$).

TABLE 5.1    Student Information and Planning

|  | Community Colleges (N = 1470) | Occupational Colleges (N = 2732) | F (p) |
|---|---|---|---|
| Agree + strongly agree: "I'm certain which courses I need for my degree plans." | 65% | 76% | 213.6 (< .001) |
| Agree + strongly agree: "I know which of my courses give credit toward my degree." | 74% | 80% | 101.6 (< .001) |
| Agree + strongly agree: "I have enough information about requirements and prerequisites." | 58% | 70% | 167.6 (< .001) |
| Respondent has taken course that does not apply toward degree | 46% | 23% | 551.3 (< .001) |
| Respondent believes or is unsure remedial course s/he took counts toward degree requirements | 32% | 8% | 1812.4 (< .001) |
| Respondent reports "much higher" confidence about earning a college degree | 28% | 41% | 5.9 (.016) |

*Source:* Authors' data.
*Note:* Two-tailed T-test.

We also asked about coursework students had completed. Table 5.1 shows that community college students are twice as likely to report having taken a course that they "later discovered would not count toward [the] degree" (46 percent versus 23 percent at occupational colleges). Moreover, as the next row in table 5.1 shows, nearly a third (32 percent) of community college students mistakenly believe that a remedial class, which they reported as having taken, would give credit toward their degree requirements, but just 8 percent of occupational college students do. Such courses will cost time and tuition and may well pose risks to students' goals. Finally, we asked students whether they felt more or less confident about their ability to complete their degree since entering their college (responses were offered on a five-point scale, with 1 = "much lower" and 5 = "much higher"). As the bottom row of table 5.1 shows, occupational college students are also significantly more likely to report much higher confidence about achieving their degree goal (41 percent versus 28 percent, p = .016). These raw statistics show that, compared to community college students, occupational college students report more information, fewer mistakes, and more improved confidence about degree completion.

## 4. Do Alternative College Procedures Matter, Net of Student Attributes?

Although these results support the contentions of occupational college administrators about college procedures helping students, it is possible that the students who choose to enroll at occupational colleges are different from their counterparts at community colleges. Multivariate analysis allows us to examine differences in student outcomes after controlling for other possible influences, including student attributes. We examine which kinds of students have more information, which kinds of students are confident about degree completion, and whether occupational colleges increase students' information and confidence about degree completion, after controlling for individual attributes. Finally, we examine whether the occupational college influence on student confidence could be explained by students' information.

Adding the three items that ask about students' information (see table 5.1) into a single scale (alpha = .86; scores range from 0 to 12, with a mean of 8.97 and a standard deviation of 2.51), we use OLS regression to explain which characteristics are associated with student reports of sufficient information on this scale. Because students in our sample are clustered within classrooms in schools, we adjust for potential correlation in the data, using Huber-White statistical techniques (that is, robust cluster commands available with Stata software), and report the resulting robust standard errors. This technique does not affect the regression coefficients, but does adjust standard errors to account for potential nonindependence of observations. Again, note that the analysis is limited to students seeking at least an associate's degree.

In table 5.2, the coefficients for the students' pre-college attributes (gender, race, age, high-school achievement, and parent education and income), show that sufficient information is significantly less common among Latino students and students entering the college more recently. At the same time, student characteristics associated with significantly higher information include older students (though the squared term indicates that the age effect is nonlinear: information increases until the mid-thirties, and then

TABLE 5.2    OLS Regression, Student Information
About College Requirements

| Covariate | b<br>Robust SE | β |
|---|---|---|
| Male | −.008 | −.002 |
| | (.084) | |
| Gender not reported | −.255 | −.024 |
| | (.191) | |
| African American | −.101 | −.017 |
| | (.122) | |
| Hispanic | −.319** | −.056 |
| | (.114) | |
| Asian or Asian American | −.039 | −.005 |
| | (.132) | |
| Other or race not reported | −.270 | −.037 |
| | (.146) | |
| Age | .177*** | .499 |
| | (.035) | |
| Age squared | −.002*** | −.436 |
| | (.001) | |
| Age not reported | −.110 | −.010 |
| | (.207) | |
| High school GPA | .211*** | .061 |
| | (.061) | |
| High school GPA not reported | .777* | .039 |
| | (.318) | |
| Parent education (truncated) | .059 | .032 |
| | (.032) | |
| Parent education not reported | −.203 | −.017 |
| | (.202) | |
| Term began at this college | −.135*** | −.091 |
| | (.025) | |
| Term began not reported | −.190 | −.011 |
| | (.308) | |
| Occupational college | .724*** | .138 |
| | (.092) | |
| Constant | 5.555 | |
| | (.566) | |
| R-squared | .044 | |
| N | 3698 | |

*Source:* Authors' data.
*p ≤ .05; **p ≤ .01; ***p ≤ .001

declines), students with better high school grades, and students whose parents have more education. These findings are generally consistent with theories of cultural and social capital, which would lead us to expect an association between socioeconomic advantage and information about college.

Despite controls for all these pre-college attributes of the student, however, we find that occupational colleges still have a significant positive effect on student information. Moreover, as the standardized ($\beta$) coefficients show, the magnitude of the occupational college influence is among the strongest of all variables in the model. Of course, one might argue that occupational college students chose their schools precisely because they had better information in the first place. Although we cannot rule out selection effects in this nonexperimental data, our interview data with occupational college students do not indicate that they had better information before enrolling in college. Moreover, as noted earlier, theories of cultural and social capital would lead us to expect that students at the occupational colleges in our sample might have had less information about college requirements initially, given their somewhat less advantaged backgrounds versus community college students.

The observed occupational college effect might work differently for students in different majors. Recall how occupational college personnel reported that structured programs, advising, and peer support were meant to improve student information. If this is true, community college programs with such characteristics might also improve student information. At most of the community colleges in our sample, students—whether in academic or occupational majors—have a great deal of leeway in selecting courses each term. Even in majors where curricula are specifically determined, courses may not be offered each term in the sequence the student needs. In one program area, however, community colleges have adopted much more structure. In response to state licensure requirements for health programs, community colleges have adopted elaborate formal procedures—most notably, structured programs and peer cohorts—that are similar to those observed at our occupational colleges.

Table 5.3 reports just the coefficient for occupational college when the same regression (that is, controlling for the same covariates used in table 5.3) is run separately on subsamples of students in the six majors with the largest enrollments in our sample. These results show a positive association between occupational colleges and information in five of the six major categories; the relationship is significant for students in four of these majors (business, accounting, computers, and electronics). In stark con-

TABLE 5.3    Comparing Students in Comparable Programs

|  | Business | Accounting | Computer | Electronics | Engineering | Health |
|---|---|---|---|---|---|---|
| b | 1.042*** | .885* | .898*** | .712** | .217 | − .966** |
| (Robust SE) | (.214) | (.376) | (.172) | (.383) | (.408) | (.320) |
| N | 722 | 284 | 865 | 435 | 365 | 317 |

*Source:* Authors' data.
\*p ≤ .05; \*\*p ≤ .01; \*\*\*p ≤ .001
*Note:* Unstandardized OLS coefficients for occupational college variable (net of controls).

trast, for students in health programs, the occupational college coefficient is significantly negative. Occupational colleges are actually associated with lower levels of information for students in health programs. This negative effect of the occupational colleges among health students may stem from the relative newness of these programs at occupational colleges or from the fact that the occupational colleges offer health degrees primarily in less regulated areas such as medical transcription and assisting. In any case, the exception here appears to prove the rule that institutional procedures can improve the quality and amount of information students receive. Moreover, it shows that community colleges can successfully adopt these procedures as well or better than occupational colleges when mandated to do so.

Finally, we examined students' confidence in their ability to complete the college degree (table 5.4). Given the frustrations students expressed in interviews, it seems plausible that better information would be associated with greater confidence. Students' confidence in their degree completion is important in itself, and one might suspect that it may be an important determinant of students' decisions to persist in college, particularly when they experience conflicting pressures. As table 5.4 shows, we find that being at an occupational college is associated with significantly higher student confidence, net of controls for students' attributes. Adding a control for the student information scale, we find that students with more information have more confidence in their degree completion (net of other background characteristics). Moreover, the size of the information effect is relatively large (as shown by the β coefficients)—in this case, the largest of all the variables. Finally, note that including student information in the model reduces the coefficient for occupational colleges by about 20 percent (from .216 to .159, though the decline is not statistically significant at the p = .05 level). This suggests that the occupational college effect on students' confidence might be partly explained by students' greater information in these colleges.

TABLE 5.4   OLS Regression, Students' Perceived Likelihood of Achieving First Degree Goal

| Covariate | b<br>Robust SE | β | b<br>Robust SE | β |
|---|---|---|---|---|
| Male | −.078** | −.046 | −.078** | −.046 |
| | (.029) | | (.028) | |
| Gender not reported | −.121 | −.034 | −.101 | −.028 |
| | (.067) | | (.066) | |
| African American | .297*** | .142 | .305*** | .146 |
| | (.041) | | (.040) | |
| Hispanic | .212*** | .108 | .237*** | .121 |
| | (.040) | | (.039) | |
| Asian or Asian American | .156*** | .057 | .160*** | .058 |
| | (.048) | | (.046) | |
| Other or race not reported | .026 | .010 | .047 | .019 |
| | (.050) | | (.049) | |
| Age | .029* | .233 | .015 | .120 |
| | (.012) | | (.012) | |
| Age squared | −.0005** | −.253 | −.0003 | −.154 |
| | (.0002) | | (.0001) | |
| Age not reported | .025 | .006 | .034 | .009 |
| | (.070) | | (.070) | |
| High school GPA | −.006 | −.005 | −.023 | −.019 |
| | (.020) | | (.020) | |
| High school GPA<br>  not reported | −.116<br>(.107) | −.017 | −.177<br>(.103) | −.026 |
| Parent education<br>  (truncated) | −.007<br>(.011) | −.011 | −.011<br>(.011) | −.018 |
| Parent education<br>  not reported | −.080<br>(.063) | −.020 | −.064<br>(.064) | −.016 |
| Term began at this college | −.010 | −.019 | .001 | .002 |
| | (.009) | | (.009) | |
| Term began not reported | −.103 | −.017 | −.088 | −.015 |
| | (.111) | | (.107) | |
| Occupational college | .216*** | .119 | .159*** | .088 |
| | (.032) | | (.031) | |
| Information | | | .078*** | .228 |
| | | | (.006) | |
| Constant | 3.55 | | 3.11 | |
| | (.191) | | (.189) | |
| R-squared | .046 | | .096 | |
| N | 3698 | | 3698 | |

Source: Authors' data.
*p ≤ .05; **p ≤ .01; ***p ≤ .001

Presumably, if community colleges provided better information, students might have greater confidence in their being able to complete their degree. In fact, among community college students in our survey sample, those students majoring in the most structured programs (that is, health) do, indeed, report the highest mean levels of confidence about completing the degree, though the differences are not statistically significant.

One may note that the amount of variance explained in these regression analyses is quite small (ranging from about .04 to .10). This indicates that many factors influence information and confidence, which our models have not explained. Although these findings explain a relatively small amount of variance, we should also be interested in whether any particular factors increase the outcomes significantly. For instance, in a simple regression on earnings in a national survey, though less than 10 percent of variance was explained, being male increased earnings by 36 percent, and going to private high school increased earnings by 10 percent (Rosenbaum 2001, 182). The limited R-squared indicates that a lot of other variation is going on that these variables didn't explain, but being a male from a private school increases one's earnings a great deal. Here we are interested specifically in whether information was improved at occupational colleges, where interviews suggested distinct procedures governing information. The finding of a statistically significant effect for occupational colleges on students' reported information offers important support for the suggestive findings of our interview analyses.

## REDUCING INFORMATION PROBLEMS: LESSONS FROM STRUCTURED PROGRAMS

Our findings suggest that two-year college students experience serious information problems, which may be impeding their college success. Alternative procedures used in occupational colleges might improve student information and planning and could serve to enhance college effectiveness.

Indeed, this study suggests that occupational colleges may provide some ideas about policy alternatives that could benefit community colleges, especially students who lack appropriate information about educational opportunities. Although community colleges provide more information, occupational colleges introduce procedures that limit the need for information, that weave mandatory advising into the space and time of students' regular schedules, and that place students in peer cohorts which provide information, support, and role models for success. Occupational college administrators report that these procedures improve students' information, reduce their mistakes, and improve their likelihood of successful degree completion; and our analyses provide support for their contentions. Similarly, when community colleges adopt these procedures—as with health programs—we find that their students' information is actually better than at occupational schools.

We must, nonetheless, be cautious about our inferences. Information and confidence are, of course, not the same as actually earning a degree. Still, one cannot avoid wondering whether the differences in students' information and confidence contribute to earlier findings that community colleges have lower degree completion rates than private two-year colleges (see chapter 1). Each kind of analysis has potential shortcomings. Our small sample of interviewed students could be unrepresentative, and occupational college administrators' reports could be distorted by self-interest. The regression analyses indicate significant associations between college type and student perceptions, but a direct causal influence is not the only possible interpretation. No single analysis is sufficient to establish causality. At the same time, the weight of multiple sources of evidence pointing in the same direction makes causality plausible and perhaps even probable.

It is important to recall that community colleges have a different mandate than occupational colleges. As a broad public resource, community colleges often encourage exploration and offer a wide range of options. It would be a radical step for these institutions to offer all three procedures described here on a large scale, especially given the resource requirements for such procedures. However, the practice of focusing budget cuts primarily on advising services should be examined, and it should be recognized that stressing unstructured choice may not serve some kinds of students. These issues deserve serious consideration and further research.

Although some may worry that such structured procedures deprive students of ample choice, our survey finds that only 19 percent of all occupational college students reported that the school does not give students enough course choices (only slightly more than the 13 percent of community college students who reported this). Indeed, the interviews suggest that, for many students, given their limited resources and time for college, completing the degree quickly and efficiently is often more important than exploration. Students report that they are happy to have clear-cut course requirements and do not complain about restricted freedom of electives. As one occupational college student explained, "It's nice . . . not having to worry about what classes to take, knowing that it's all plotted out for you." For students without information and for whom mistakes can be very costly, procedures that reduce information needs and the risk of mistakes may justify limitations on choice.

We cannot exclude the possibility that different types of students choose different types of colleges. In particular, those who value choice may be less likely to attend occupational colleges. However, students rarely mentioned this as a factor when asked why they chose their college. Indeed, it was striking that many students reported that they did not consider more than one college. But, regardless of original selection into a school, community college students clearly found themselves without enough information to make reasoned choices about how to proceed through college.

We find that students in two-year colleges have ambitious goals, but they often lack crucial information about what actions will help them to achieve their goals. Other research has shown that this problem is also true for high school students (Schneider and Stevenson 1999), and the lessons here may extend beyond colleges. High schools have increasingly emphasized choice and electives; but "shopping mall high schools" have many shortcomings (Powell, Farrar, and Cohen 1985). Extending that critique, we suggest that the problems may be especially great for disadvantaged students, but some of these problems might be reduced through alternative procedures.

# CHAPTER SIX

## THE SOCIAL PREREQUISITES OF SUCCESS

The information problems that individual community college students encounter extend beyond the obvious and involve a disjuncture that occurs when students must respond to institutional procedures. Colleges demand a certain level of social know-how, a set of skills and knowledge that help students understand school procedures and navigate these institutions. Students must know something about the paths of progress through colleges. This knowledge includes awareness of enrollment, registration, and financial aid procedures. They must also know how to initiate information gathering, acquire sound and useful advice, avoid costly mistakes, and manage conflicting demands.

Although many middle-class students have such know-how—often gleaned from family members and peers with college experience—many lower-income students, who make up a large portion of community college populations, do not. However, the community college staff members we interviewed were only vaguely aware of these information deficiencies, and often assumed that students gather the necessary social know-how from outside sources. Because these assumptions are often incorrect, these information demands of college constitute a hidden curriculum of social prerequisites that many students are not prepared for and that colleges often do not address.

### Obstacles in Community Colleges

Based on our studies in these fourteen public and private two-year colleges, we find that the implicit information requirements of community colleges present seven key obstacles for students who have little exposure to college knowledge:

- bureaucratic hurdles

- confusing choices

- student-initiated guidance

- limited counselor availability

- poor advice from staff

- slow detection of costly mistakes

- poor handling of conflicting demands

## Navigating and Reducing the Obstacles

These seven obstacles are observed at the community colleges in our study, but they are not inevitable. Just as chapter 5 showed that occupational colleges create alternative procedures to reduce the information demands, here we find that they also take steps to create procedures that reduce the need for social know-how. These practices specifically address the needs of disadvantaged students who face difficult decisions, strong competing pressures, little availability of crucial information, and large risks from even small mistakes. The many information problems students report in community colleges that pose serious obstacles to their timely degree progress are much less common in occupational colleges that use these procedures to reduce social know-how requirements. Although many community college students may only be experimenters testing whether college is appropriate (Manski 1989), these findings raise questions about whether community colleges could provide alternative procedures that would be more likely to produce successful outcomes from these experiments. Perhaps the procedures described here help explain why private colleges have much higher degree completion rates than their public counterparts. If community colleges are to serve nontraditional students, they must address this emerging issue of social know-how.

Through examination of the information requirements at public and private colleges, we expand on the sociological concept of cultural capital presented in chapter 5. Bourdieu and Passeron (1977) contend that schools have implicit requirements of certain knowledge and skills (cultural capital) that low-SES students often lack, and these hard-to-see requirements interfere with their educational attainments. Building on this research, we examine the specific procedural requirements at community colleges and their consequences for lower income students, as well as demonstrated alternatives that seem to remove cultural capital obstacles.

## DATA AND METHODS

As described in chapters 2 and 5, the sample used here and in following chapters includes fourteen two-year schools: seven public community colleges and seven private occupational colleges. They are located in and around a large midwestern city, and all offer two-year accredited programs leading to associate's degrees in similar occupational fields.

Our research includes qualitative methods, including one-hour, semi-structured interviews with students and staff, as well as an extensive review of college materials and repeatedly conducted observations at the colleges.

## SOCIAL KNOW-HOW REQUIREMENTS

As discussed in chapter 1, community colleges offer a vast array of programs for students to choose from. Although more options sometimes lead to better decisions, they can also increase the need for information and may create confusion and mistaken choices on the part of the students. Multiple options also put a strain on the institutions, making it more difficult for the colleges to coordinate offerings while allocating fixed resources. The career dean at one community college said, "It's a balancing act, and we have these external pressures on us to do 14 million things." A dean of instruction noted that part of the challenge is "knowing exactly what our role is." These multiple missions may limit community colleges' capacity to serve as an avenue of social mobility.

Certainly low-income, relatively young, minority students face many cultural barriers (Zwerling and London 1992), but choice itself can be another obstacle. Community colleges offer many program options and give students the autonomy to steer their own routes through the educational process. This can be liberating for some, but overwhelming for others. We find that many students are confused about their choices, and especially disadvantaged students who often come from public schools where counseling services are limited, and who lack the know-how they need to make the required choices. Such students also have limited time and finances, making their mistakes and delays even more costly. We find that many students are first-generation students whose parents have not attended college. In some of these cases, families may not provide financial or other support, as with Beatriz, noted in chapter 5, whose father considered college a waste of time and money. Other families provide emotional support, but not information or financial help. For example, when asked if his parents encourage college, Derrick said, "Basically it's my decision. They give me a pat on the back and say 'I'm glad you're doing it.' " However, his family could not provide financial help, so Derrick worked two part-time jobs to pay tuition and living expenses. Many students' families provide no guidance, information, or savings.

We find that these community colleges pose seven obstacles for students with little college information, and occupational colleges have devised ways to reduce their need for this type of social know-how.

## Bureaucratic Hurdles

First, bureaucratic hurdles arise from the size and complexity of community colleges. Students find their complicated class schedules and college catalogs difficult and time-consuming to understand. At a community college that serves a high poverty area, the academic support center dean notes that many students make mistakes in selecting classes on their own, and they later learn that their degree will take longer than they had anticipated.

> [Students] were constantly saying to us, "Nobody told me. I didn't know." . . . We can claim that . . . everything that they need to know we write down [somewhere]. . . . (laughs) It doesn't work that way. So they were getting frustrated, we were getting frustrated.

The college's reputation was suffering, as prospective students and their parents began asking questions. The dean of career programs noted that students want to know "how long it's going to take me" and say, "I don't wanna take a lot of unnecessary courses. I need to have a time line." He regularly heard parents ask, "This is how much money I got. How much is it going to cost? They got two years, they'd better be at the end of the road."

This was a problem at the other community colleges in our sample as well, where the issue includes transfer. A student at another urban college commented, "One of my friends went [here] and she told me, 'Don't go there because you're going to waste your time. You're going to take classes that you won't need when you transfer.' "

Students face other hurdles as well: filling out enrollment forms, registering for classes, applying for financial aid, making choices that efficiently accumulate credits toward a degree, and fitting in work and family obligations. Students must figure out how to overcome these obstacles each semester. One student complained about his grueling registration ordeal, "I went to registration at twelve and I didn't get out until seven," and became so frustrated that he didn't register the second semester and didn't return until four years later.

Even if students have the extra time and flexible scheduling required for many college procedures, information is hard to find and obtain. Students report having to search all over campus to get information about specific program requirements to learn which courses lead to their desired goals and meet requirements most quickly. Many students are not aware of the state and federal financial aid options available. Some wrongly assume they would not qualify for aid because they are working full- or part-time or because the tuition is low.

Students who apply for financial aid complain about the difficulty of the forms, and the lack of assistance at these colleges. Unfortunately, many students faced unpleasant and even hostile encounters with financial aid staff in their attempts to complete the financial aid process. Two weeks after she started, Rosa still had not finished the financial aid process. She said of the financial aid department:

> They're rude. This lady kicked me out. . . . I didn't have . . . my security card. . . . She said, "Ah, just get out of here. Just go. You don't have anything ready. Go." . . . I understand they get frustrated, but they don't have to be rude.

Corrie, who grew up in public housing and lived with friends while she put herself through school to become an occupational therapist, also faced hostility:

> The financial aid office wasn't what I expected. . . . I've had a bad experience with them. They're just very nonchalant about your funding and I feel like a lot of them don't care because it's like, "It's not me getting the money and I don't really care." And I've been yelled at a couple of times in financial aid by my counselor.

Bureaucratic hurdles continue in other domains. Because of problems with community college staff, when Lisette needed more information about transfer, she went directly to the college to which she planned to transfer to get information. Many students had similar problems getting correct information, and some, like Lisette, learned through other students or older siblings to seek information directly from the four-year colleges. Unfortunately, students who lack this know-how often found that poor information extended their time in college.

## Confusing Choices

Second, students face a confusing array of hard to understand choices because of the wide variety of programs, each having different requirements for their various degrees and certificates. Students may not even have a clear picture of their goals, which makes it harder to get good advice. Indeed, in our interviews, most students who had not chosen a major had not sought counselor advice about their course selections in their first year. In the words of one administrator, this often results in students "wandering aimlessly through the curriculum, amassing large numbers of hours but not making progress toward a degree." He believed that this explains the fact that a third of the college's students failed to meet the college's requirements for "satisfactory academic progress" (completing 75 percent of their courses) and that threatens their financial aid eligibility.

When students seek advice from community college staff, they are encouraged to explore, but the model for exploration is based on that of four-year colleges. It encourages sampling from a wide variety of unrelated courses that are highly general, does not specify clear outcomes, and may apply to some programs, but not others. Students are encouraged to sample—much like in a cafeteria, where the customer chooses from the different food groups—from five or more academic disciplines, without much regard for future career goals. Although this nondirective approach may work well for middle-class students who can afford four years of college, it presents difficulties for many nontraditional students with a shorter time frame. Exploration at some community colleges is largely confined to liberal arts courses, in which many of these students have done poorly in the past. Confusion also arises from the lack of clarity about the implications and relevance of specific choices to future careers. For students with limited resources who must obtain a marketable degree with a minimum of forgone wages or tuition dollars, this approach is problematic (Wilms 1974). Many disadvantaged students do not understand college offerings, face strong pressures to get through school quickly, and seek an efficient way to improve their occupational qualifications and get better jobs.

After students have chosen a program, choosing classes is still a daunting task. It can be difficult to schedule all the required courses in the correct order, paying attention to prerequisites and general education courses and synchronizing course schedules with work and family schedules. We encountered many students who were confused about general education requirements and the necessary prerequisites for their major courses. If students don't fulfill a course requirement, they may have to wait an entire year before the course is offered again. These mistakes can be overwhelming setbacks for students with limited resources and constrained timetables, and can lead to disappointment, frustration, and eventual dropout.

Given the complex course catalogs and class schedules and the lack of structured guidance, these mistakes are surprisingly easy to make. Even sophisticated observers could have difficulty. For example, we, as authors holding PhDs, spent many hours trying to understand some of the catalogs' labeling systems for classes and degrees, and several interviews were necessary to clarify the information. Not surprisingly, disadvantaged students rarely know what questions to ask. Due to the catalog's lack of clarity and her misunderstanding of how these classes fit into her program requirements, Annette was not aware that the remedial courses she had to take would not count toward her degree:

> Why didn't anyone tell me that? . . . They had me registering and everything. . . . This is going to hold me back. . . . So I still have two years to go 'cause none of these classes here even count. So I was a little upset about that because it was really misleading.

Apparently, Annette is not alone in her uncertainty. Our surveys find that many community college students, especially from low-income families, were uncertain of their program and degree requirements and course prerequisites.

## The Burden of Student-Initiated Assistance

Third, the burden of student-initiated guidance also raises obstacles, especially for disadvantaged students. Although community colleges make guidance available to students, the colleges require that students initiate the process of seeking out guidance. The requirements of this process for students are four-fold. First, students must be aware of what kind of help they need and when they need it. Second, they must be informed about how and where to get it. Third, they must actually go get it. Fourth, students must seek this information well in advance.

Unfortunately, these conditions do not serve at-risk and first-generation college students well. Those students whose parents have not attended college cannot easily get advice about how to succeed, what pitfalls to avoid, or how to plan their path through college. These students are left to navigate college on their own.

Often students do not even know that they need help, and thus do not take the initiative to seek it out, particularly for long-range planning. Although students know they must ask counselors or faculty to approve their course selections for any upcoming semester, they do not seek information about long-term plans. As a result, students are often left without one, and make seemingly arbitrary decisions about their classes, the direction of their education, and their career goals.

Even among those who talk with counselors, the limited knowledge first-generation students have of college and career paths often make such interactions ineffective. Students often do not understand the pathway that leads to their occupational goal, and they ask questions and gather information based on faulty assumptions. Putting the burden of initiating advice on inexperienced students leads to poorly directed college strategies, particularly when counseling assistance is focused on selecting classes, not on mapping out long-range plans. Sonia, for example, is a first-generation college student who comes from a low-income family of eight. In her interview, it was clear that her only source of career advice had been her older brother, who was in his early twenties. She was following the requirements for a math major, despite wanting to be an accountant, or possibly major in computer science. When we asked what career she was considering, Sonia told us accounting. However, in her brief meeting with a counselor, he asked only about her course interests, which led him to suggest a math major.

> Sonia: Well I was confused . . . I had to talk to a counselor. . . . He wanted to know what I was going to major in . . . I told him I liked math so I'm taking math courses. . . . So that's it.
>
> Interviewer: Did you try to go through other degrees, like accounting?
>
> Sonia: No.
>
> Interviewer: Did you tell him that you were interested in those things, too, or just math?
>
> Sonia: Just math. I figured math and accounting were maybe the same. I'd never taken accounting.

In the brief session, Sonia didn't think to mention her career interests, so she ended pursuing only one option. She has no plan for considering alternatives, should it become too difficult or uninteresting, and her courses were not chosen to provide prerequisites for other majors.

## Limited Counselor Availability

Fourth, the limited availability of counselors is a serious obstacle to getting good advice. Counselors at community colleges are typically overburdened, responsible for advising students not only about academic planning, but also about the transfer process, career exploration, part-time job placement, and personal issues. They are vastly understaffed, with typically 800 to 1,200 students per counselor for the community colleges in our sample. This can be compared with high schools where a ratio of 1:400 is common and is widely believed to be inadequate.

In fact, some administrators report that students need to schedule appointments months in advance in order to see a counselor. Counselors typically schedule thirty minutes for each appointment, and times fill up quickly, especially before registration, when counseling is needed most. One administrator highlights the need for students to plan far ahead of time: "They're going for pre-registration and they go make an appointment, and then it's October and the counselors say, 'Well, you could come in December 6th.'" Students report being too busy to see counselors, but that should not be mistaken for indifference. For instance, Dan tried to see a counselor several times, but each time, he had to schedule one far in advance, and then he either forgot or couldn't make the appointment.

None of the community colleges involved in the study required students to meet with counselors even once during their schooling. The majority of students we interviewed had not spoken with a counselor, because of the difficulties and delays entailed. Although she was conscientious about meeting the various demands on her, Lauren was completing her second semester, yet reported, "I haven't talked directly to counselors."

Even when they meet, inadequate staffing also affects students' interactions with counselors. If students do not know exactly what they need help with, then the counseling experience can be ineffective and anxiety-ridden. Rolanda described her unsuccessful experience:

> I talked to one of the counselors, but since there was a lot of people waiting, it was kind of fast. We didn't have much time to talk. Also, when you go to a counselor, many times you don't really know what you're going to talk about. You have an idea, but you don't know what

questions to ask. I think counselors should ask more questions of us. They just answer our questions then say, "OK, you can go, since you don't know what to ask." It's hard. There are things we don't know.

After her negative experience, Rolanda avoided seeking further advice from counselors. Instead, she chose classes on her own from a transfer form that she noticed on the wall outside the counselors' offices.

## Poor Advice from Staff

Fifth, poor advice is common. The complexity is so daunting that information proves to be challenging even for counselors and administrators. Students report that they often got conflicting opinions, which directed them to radically different actions. Many students report being guided into courses that were unneeded and thus a waste of their time and tuition money. Unfortunately, for students with limited resources, the time wasted and mistakes involved in figuring things out on their own can prevent them from completing their educational goals.

Even when students see a counselor, the information provided is sometimes wrong. Counselors might fail to get sufficient information about program offerings and requirements from departments, and their information is also often out of date. Some department chairs admitted that they had little communication with counselors:

> Interviewer: How much direct contact does your department have with the counselors?
>
> Department chair: Very little. . . . I would say it's pretty much just "hello" in the hallway or something. There's no real . . . contact with them, unless they have some kind of question or something, or we find out they're giving out bad info, we'll go down there from time to time to straighten them out or something.

Some administrators complain that counselors often have mistaken notions about their programs. With so many programs to understand and so many other responsibilities, counselors sometimes have difficulty keeping track of all the changes in requirements and curriculum. One department chair reports that students sometimes come to him complaining that the counseling office is giving incorrect information which appears to make their plans unachievable. This chair will send these students back down to speak with the counselors again, "I tell them . . . you know, stick to your guns and tell them, 'This is my life.' Or, don't go to them at all. Have me sign the darn registration and I'll do it!"

Other students' transfer plans are delayed due to poor and contradictory counseling from different counselors, who rarely have a long-term relationship with students. For example, Deanna spent four years at community college before she actually transferred, and though she was extremely happy with her teachers and classes, she complained about the counseling system:

> The only thing I had a problem with was the counselors weren't very helpful . . . not at all. . . . You go to them for what classes you need to take. I feel I took a lot of wasted classes. You didn't get much help. Now that I'm in a university, I realize if I would have just had a good counselor I probably would have avoided a lot of this. You had a different one every time you went. I would have graduated in the two years like I should have if I had a better counselor. . . . I feel like [students] just don't get out of there. It's a rut you can get into. . . . Counselors don't tell you what you need to do. People are walking around blindfolded. . . . They don't know what to do.

Although counselors can see students' transcripts, they often lack detailed knowledge about students, other than their grades. They also may not understand the program requirements. Because counselors' advice is often inadequate, many students get advice from even weaker sources: faculty in other programs unrelated to their own. Although students must have their registration forms signed before they can register, the form does not have to be signed by a counselor, but rather by any full-time faculty. Often, this signing takes place during extremely busy and chaotic open registration periods, which are not conducive to careful guidance. Only students who know the value of counseling, who show initiative, and who make plans in advance manage to get counselors' time. Thus, most advising is done by faculty, who have no counseling training, and who may not know the requirements for the student's particular program. Within this system, there is no assurance that the individual who signs the form can assess whether students are on track for graduation, or whether a course will transfer or even count in the student's major. Anyone can sign the registration card, and students are thus often entirely responsible for mapping out their academic progress. For students with little knowledge about the college process, this responsibility can lead to small mistakes, which can result in major setbacks.

Like many students we interviewed, Carlos's experience with his urban public high school's guidance counselors was limited to discipline problems. "[In high school] the only time you got to see a counselor was when you were in trouble. It was like that. Like, for cutting or whatever you did." So, when he first began community college, Carlos thought that a good student is one who manages to avoid seeing counselors. He did not seek out any additional help to determine what courses he should take:

> Nobody told me to go see a counselor. No. They just had that open registration. You go talk to anybody. The teachers are like, "What classes do you want? Here, go register. You've got your financial aid? Go take care of it." Things like that.

In hindsight, he realized that getting a counselor's advice would have been important "so you don't waste your time here." He thought the burden of student-initiated guidance contributed to his initial difficulties:

> Like, for example, they gave me Biology 101. This was my first semester here . . . when I was first out of high school. I didn't know anything about college. . . . I thought I was getting credit for it, but I wasn't. Now when I dropped it, I got an F because I didn't see a counselor. I didn't even know you were supposed to go see a counselor. . . . Then when I went to go retake the class, the class isn't even offered anymore. Then I find out that you don't even need the class. I saw my GPA . . . it brought me down.

This bad experience in first semester led to his decision to drop all his classes and quit altogether. He didn't return until several years had passed. Five years later, Carlos, twenty-three years old at the time of our interview, was starting his sixth semester of community college, yet had only accumulated about two semesters of college credits. Having learned the value of seeking advice the hard way, he now speaks to counselors at four-year colleges for information about transfer:

> Everything I've done was because I went to visit counselors at other schools. They helped me. They're the ones telling me what classes to take and this and that. Here, I don't know what the problem is, but they're not doing their job.

Carlos's lack of exposure to academic or career advising in high school was similar to many of the low-income students we interviewed. They lacked cultural capital regarding the value of counseling and therefore faced difficulties seeking this type of assistance in community college.

## Delayed Detection of Costly Mistakes

Sixth, students' mistakes are easy to make and hard to detect, and even a few simple mistakes can be devastating. Given the complexity of choices and the inaccessibility of guidance, students often make mistakes. An admissions counselor says that first-generation college students face many difficulties because information about the system isn't apparent. "They don't even know what type of degree they're getting. They're not aware of whether the degree they're getting is a terminal degree or not." In addition, as noted in chapter 4, students are often unaware that many of their classes are remedial and do not count toward degrees, thus incorrectly assume that they can finish a two-year associate's degree within the "promised" two years.

Although their choices are crucial, students often do not understand their situations. The risks of student error are increased because they don't know what they don't know. Many students we interviewed did not know how to distinguish between different types of degrees and different types of credits. Considerable background knowledge is required to make these distinctions, and failure to see critical distinctions can have serious repercussions. For example, many students had trouble distinguishing between credit and noncredit classes, and spent time and money on classes that didn't count toward their degree.

Students' mistakes are often not detected for some time. Many students report that they subsequently discover that they have made less progress than they expected. Denise's problems, for instance, resulted from problematic counselor advice and her own mistakes. In her second year, she realized that she could not finish the year, which was a major problem, given her financial and child-care constraints:

> I took it upon myself to be my own counselor. I took five unnecessary classes because I thought I knew everything. . . . The first counselor I had, the one that gave me those wrong classes, . . . wasted my time so I took it upon myself and I didn't go see a counselor anymore. She gave me wrong classes, but I messed up more.

Such discoveries are disappointing and may lead students to drop out of college. Although we did not interview dropouts, our respondents described struggles that led them to contemplate dropping out and reported that many of their friends did drop out in comparable circumstances.

Delays are especially harmful to disadvantaged students for several reasons. First, disadvantaged students are more likely to make decisions that prolong college beyond the minimum necessary. Often no one in their family or social circle has attended college, leaving them possibly unaware of how colleges work or even what programs are offered. In our interviews, administrators and faculty often spoke about students who lacked clear direction or goals:

> I think when a lot of students come in, they don't know what they want to do. And a lot of them, I think, are like pinballs. They're bouncing from one thing to another, you know, before they find something that they actually like.

Second, delays have direct financial costs that are particularly difficult for disadvantaged students. Community colleges make concerted efforts to remain flexible, preserve choice, and encourage exploration, and this exploration may have some benefits. But if this exploration does not lead to efficient progress, and many of the courses do not count toward a degree, then students may find their limited budget depleted before they complete their degree.

Third, delays lead to additional pressures for disadvantaged students. Although students don't always realize it, they face implicit timetables. Employers are sometimes willing to allow flexible work schedules to accommodate coursework for a limited time. Parents and spouses are typically willing to make financial and time sacrifices for a limited time. However, if a two-year associate's degree takes longer than two years, students report additional pressures to finish quickly and resume full-time jobs. For such students, the longer they take to choose their program, the greater the chance that they will run out of time, money, or support, and they will be forced to drop out of school with only an array of unrelated courses to show for their efforts. For such students, confusing choices and poor guidance creates frustration and disappointment, which may lead students to give up on the pursuit altogether.

## Poor Handling of Conflicting Demands

Seventh, colleges poorly handle conflicting outside demands. Nontraditional students usually face more numerous and more severe constraints on their time than their counterparts: parent illness, financial need, child care crises, unanticipated pregnancies, automobile breakdowns, and work obligations. Unlike young, full-time students, nontraditional students often have rigid outside commitments and crises that impinge on their studies, and some simply do not know how to balance school with other demands.

Administrators, faculty, and staff at these community colleges boasted that the variety of morning, afternoon, evening, and weekend class times allowed students to arrange their school schedule around their other outside obligations. However, though this approach clearly adds flexibility, it ironically imposes further problems. Class schedules are driven by student demand rather than planned sequencing, and course schedules change every term, thus students cannot anticipate their class schedule from semester to semester. Given the vast array of course options that community colleges offer, administrators cannot create coordinated schedules for students. Students report that the courses they need to take are often scheduled at vastly different times of day, and some are not offered for several semesters. This makes their education extremely difficult to coordinate with outside work and family commitments. Moreover, their course schedules are invariably quite different from term to term, so the work and childcare arrangements created in one semester fail to work in the next. In addition, some students find that necessary courses are already closed to additional students, conflict with other necessary courses, or are not being offered in the term originally expected. Ironically, community colleges' attempts at flexibility may delay students in finishing their degrees.

Moreover, even though these conflicts are common, community colleges do not systematically provide students with advice or assistance in handling such issues, a failure that is not limited to course selection and degree planning.

Community colleges view work as an unfortunate necessity that competes with school. One program chair described this view: "Well, in the best of all possible worlds, I think a student should not work. But, that is not an option for most of our students. . . . They have to make money." Although community college administrators are proud of their nontraditional student body, their comments about work commitments imply that the traditional student model is the ideal. When asked why students don't succeed, faculty often suggested that students need to reduce their work hours to solve the problem.

Viewing the problem as external to the college, they do not focus on institutional strategies for improving retention. Rather than helping students incorporate school and work, they merely tolerate work as an economic necessity. These community colleges help students find part-time jobs, but the jobs are often unrelated to students' area of study (compare also Grubb 1996).

Many students are in desperate need of career counseling and advice about how to explore opportunities that will best prepare them for their desired career. For example, one student sought a career in film, but didn't understand how to get experience in that industry, and received no guidance from the college on how to do so:

> I'm going to be starting at Blockbuster Video . . . because I want to . . . make movies, work in film. Blockbuster seems like a pretty good place to get some knowledge.

In fact, most community college faculty believe that students should try to minimize work hours. Working is seen as an impediment to success in school. Other than offering classes at different times and minimizing out-of-class group projects, the community colleges do little to help students manage their work and school responsibilities.

## "STRUCTURING OUT" THE NEED FOR SOCIAL KNOW-HOW AT OCCUPATIONAL COLLEGES

Given students' many problems at community colleges, it is useful to examine other options. Just as we turned to occupational colleges for alternative models in chapter 4, we do so again here, focusing on the ways these colleges "structure out" the need for much of the social know-how that the community colleges require. They have developed original procedures and processes that appear to reduce barriers to disadvantaged students with limited know-how by helping them navigate the administrative obstacles of college.

The occupational colleges in this study have found ways to transform implicit rules into explicit organizational procedures and policies. They create programs that students can easily understand, master and negotiate, even for those students who know very little about how college works. In fact, many of these occupational colleges have found that they can improve student success by making their curriculum more structured, not less. By structuring students' choices, they have found that they also reduce the likelihood that students will make mistakes in their course choices. These colleges also implement strong guidance and tight advisory relationships with their students, which facilitate completion and successful work entry.

Whereas community colleges have become overburdened with competing priorities and functions, occupational colleges continue to provide a limited number of clearly structured programs that lead disadvantaged students to a degree and a stable job in the primary labor market. They accomplish this by implementing procedures that address the seven noted problems in community colleges, which we now detail.

## Eliminating Bureaucratic Hurdles

First, occupational colleges minimize bureaucratic hurdles. Enrollment is a simple process handled mainly by one person who makes all the arrangements for a student. Every student is then assigned to a single advisor who assists in selecting courses. Information is available in one place, and students deal with one staff person, not a bureaucratic tangle of scattered offices. Furthermore, registration each term is a simple matter, and course choices are simple, with courses offered in the same time slots over the year, avoiding schedule conflicts. Students choose a package of coordinated courses, rather than individual course choices from a long menu with fluctuating and conflicting time slots.

Occupational colleges also reduce the bureaucratic hurdles to financial aid. At community colleges, obtaining financial aid is largely the responsibility of individual students and little help is provided by the college. Research has noted the low take-up rate on federal and state financial aid programs (Grubb and Tuma 1991). James Heckman (1999) speculated, using no empirical data, that it was due to students' decision not to seek aid. Our interviews with community college staff and students indicate that students do not apply because they don't know about it or they can't figure out the complex forms. In contrast, occupational colleges help students through the application process to get the best aid package possible. Admissions staff physically walk applicants to the financial aid office, where a staff person answers all questions and fills out the financial aid application with each student (and their parents, if desired). Occupational colleges treat financial aid as an integral part of the application process, and college staff explain and simplify the process. This is rarely done by the community colleges we studied or by those others studied (Orfield and Paul 1994).

## Reducing Confusing Choices

Second, though community college students face a confusing array of hard to understand course and program choices with unclear connections to future career trajectories, occupational colleges offer a clear set of course sequences aimed at efficient training for specific career goals.

Occupational colleges help students to determine from the outset what degree program best coincides with their abilities, interests, and needs. On enrolling, every student is required to sit down with an admissions counselor who will go through all the degree programs and the courses they entail, with an explanation of implications, sequences, requirements, and job outcomes. Students' achievement and goals are assessed. One student explained:

> You go through all the programs, and they evaluate you, and you take some tests. They just interview you, what you like, what you don't like . . . they get a feel for you and they tell you, you know, "We recommend this one. We think you'd be good at it."

In some cases, students are advised not to attend the college because their occupational goals do not coincide with program offerings. For students unsure of their future goals, this personal attention from a counselor familiar with all the degree possibilities can be very helpful.

Although this approach lacks the breadth of choices in community colleges, it does entail some exploration. Obviously, for these nontraditional students who often did poorly in high school, the very effort to try out college is a daring and risky exploration, and each college course is a challenge that might end their effort. In addition, though these occupational programs are far more directive than community colleges, they allow some exploration, and some redirection of career trajectory after the first semester or year. Moreover, at some occupational colleges, students who do well in the associate's program are encouraged to transfer to a bachelor's degree program in a related field.

## College-Initiated Guidance and Minimizing Student Error

Third, in contrast to the burden of student-initiated guidance, occupational colleges have actually structured out the need for students to take the initiative to see a counselor when they need assistance. Instead, the colleges take the initiative by developing systems that provide guidance without students having to ask for it. They automatically assign each student to a specific counselor who monitors their academic progress. Students must meet with this advisor each term before registering for courses, and advisors provide assistance that is specific to each student's needs.

One administrator explained the typical way that these meetings work. An advisor will sit down with the student and tell them,

> Next quarter you're going to take these classes, you have these options. . . . In this time slot, you can take this class or this class. Now, do you want to take Psych, Soc, Political Science, or History? Here is why you are taking these classes. This is required here.

In addition, the occupational colleges have registration guides that tell students exactly what courses to take each term to complete their degree in a timely manner. Although this limits course flexibility, most students appreciate the system because it helps them to complete a degree quickly and prevents them from making mistakes. According to one student,

> I think it's a good idea, a lot of people start taking classes that they don't really need and it throws them off. I think it's good . . . it's simple . . . all you have to do is follow it. There's no "Oh my god, I didn't know I had to take that class!" There's a lot of classes where you have prerequisites. But, if you go in that order you have no problem.

In our survey of almost 4,400 students, we asked, "Have you ever taken any course which you later discovered would not count toward your degree?" Whereas 45 percent of the community college students responded that this had happened to them, only 16 percent of the private occupational college students did so.

## Investing in Counselors and Eliminating Poor Advice

Fourth, though community colleges offer very few counselors, occupational colleges have invested in counseling services and job placement staff. For example, one we studied has 1,300 first-year students being advised by four academic advisors and one dean, a ratio of 260:1. Moreover, this college has five additional advisors for assisting with job placement. This provides a sharp contrast to community colleges, where counselors perform many counseling tasks, including personal, academic, and career counseling, and typically have 800:1 ratios for all these services.

Unlike community colleges, all of the occupational colleges devote substantial resources to job placement, separate from the other counseling and advising functions. Job placement offices are well staffed with low student-to-staff ratios, ranging from 90:1 to 122:1 at all these colleges. In contrast, none of these community colleges have any full-time staff devoted to job placement, and other research suggests that may be typical (Grubb 1996; Brewer and Gray 1999). Occupational colleges believe these investments are essential to their mission of helping students to complete degrees and to get good jobs.

Fifth, in contrast with community colleges, at occupational colleges, instructors communicate with advisors to exchange information about students' progress. Advisors are regularly informed about departmental requirements and faculty talk with advisors about particular students. This is a simple process given the highly explicit organization of programs.

## Quick Detection of Mistakes

Sixth, in contrast with the difficulty of detecting student mistakes at community colleges, occupational colleges require students to meet with their advisor frequently, usually every term. At one college, students must meet with their advisor three times each term.

Occupational colleges also tend to have good student information systems that keep advisors informed about students' progress or difficulties. At several, attendance is regularly taken, advisors are quickly informed of absences, and students are contacted by their advisor before the problem gets serious. After midterms, instructors notify advisors of those students who are performing poorly in class. If the student seems to be having problems, the advisor is responsible for mediating between student and teacher to find a solution to existing problems and make sure the student receives academic support. Through the scheduled interactions, students get to know their advisors on a personal basis, and thus are more likely to approach them for help even when they are not required to do so. This is a stark contrast to the more anonymous community college system of advising.

## Reducing Conflicts with Outside Demands

Seventh, occupational colleges make efforts to alleviate external pressures that increase the chances of dropping out. These schools have adapted to students' needs by compacting the school year. In one old study, Wellford Wilms (1974) estimated that proprietary schools have competitive cost-benefit ratios, despite much higher tuitions, because of their speed at getting students to a degree that raises their earnings sooner. If an associate's degree raises student wage rates, and if completing school increases student work hours each week, then getting the degree nine months earlier increases earnings in two ways.

In addition, many students face strong pressures from parents, spouses, children, and jobs to complete schooling quickly. Private occupational colleges respond to these pressures by creating year-round schooling, which leads more quickly to degrees. Several schools have reconfigured their school year to consist of year-round courses with only two one-week vacations in December and July. Students attend classes all year, and in one school, can earn an associate's degree in fifteen months.

Because disadvantaged students face many pressures and crises that may lead them to temporarily drop out and lose the benefit of work they have already put in during the term, occupational colleges reduce the cost of such discontinuities by shortening the length of the term. If outside pressures force students to suspend their studies and lose one term, it is a relatively short term, and they can resume their studies without an extended gap. In addition, prospective students don't have to wait long before a new term begins. Instead of offering classes in relatively long semesters, one school rescheduled the school year to consist of a series of five ten-week terms. Several other schools have also instituted short terms.

Moreover, unlike community colleges, which have complex class schedules in noncontinuous time slots, occupational colleges schedule two courses back-to-back that would typically be taken in a program. This blocking decreases commuting time and makes it easier for students to attend school and continue to work. Also, whereas community colleges' class schedules change from term to term, occupational colleges offer the same time schedules from one term to the next. A typical benefit is that work and child care arrangements made for one term will continue to work out in the following term.

In addition, while community colleges offer so many courses that they cannot promise to offer needed courses each term, occupational colleges plan sequences of courses for each program and make sure that every program offers the courses necessary to make progress every term. Obviously, when all students in a program are taking the same courses, this is relatively easy and economically efficient, but the commitment of these colleges goes beyond that. In several cases, a few students fell out of their cohorts' sequence in their course-taking, and the colleges offered classes with only three students, just so students could finish their degree within the promised time frame. This is expensive, but the colleges prized their promise that students can complete the degree in the customary time. In the community colleges, classes below a minimum enrollment were routinely canceled.

In contrast with community colleges' futile attempt to downplay students' outside jobs, occupational colleges essentially turn what is viewed as a negative distraction into an opportunity that can advance students' career goals. Students receive detailed guidance on how to combine their need to work with their educational goals. Occupational colleges consider work to be a valuable experience that can contribute to students' degrees, help students find relevant jobs, and convince them to take these jobs to improve their careers, even if the pay is a little less. Advisors encourage students to get jobs related to their goals:

> We tell them in the first quarter . . . try to get a job, even if you're just answering the phone, let's say, at Arthur Andersen, but you're an accounting student. One day you can say, "Here's my resume, I want to see if there's something for me here." And then you can be a clerk, you know; you've just got to move your way up.

Instead of lamenting the reality of students' need to work, occupational colleges try to guide students toward using their work to advance their career goals.

## RETHINKING COLLEGE STRUCTURES FOR NEW COLLEGE STUDENTS

We have seen that community colleges pose some serious problems for students who lack social know-how. A number of occupational colleges have found ways to address these problems. We are not arguing that community colleges cannot implement such practices. We have heard stories of community colleges that have adopted some of these practices, but have not seen detailed evidence. Although we have no idea of how common such practices are in community colleges, we suspect they are not typical, given our observations and our reading of the literature in this area. Nor are we arguing that community colleges should turn into occupational colleges. However, community colleges can better help students by borrowing several lessons from these private colleges:

1. create clear curriculum structures

2. vastly improve counseling

3. closely monitor student progress

4.  implement an information system that would quickly show signs of student difficulties

5.  alleviate conflicts with external pressures

The structure of the community colleges we studied creates a need for students to have extensive know-how about the college process. By making the implicit explicit, some occupational colleges eliminate the know-how "prerequisite" that community colleges seem to require for students' educational and career success. Most people in our society must learn to cope with bureaucratic complexities eventually, and students' ability to cope and learn from them may improve with experience. However, they may be able to adapt to complexities slowly as they proceed through college, after acquiring academic successes and developing social know-how. An individual's capacity to adapt to complexities may depend on basic skills or increased maturity. It is also possible that procedures that gradually introduce the complexities in small steps may make the complexities easier to manage, and strong advising and school supports may also make adapting easier.

The occupational college model is not for everyone. Compared to the diverse range of choices available at community colleges, the offerings of occupational colleges may be too limiting for some. For students who have the know-how to make these decisions and who do not face strong external competing pressures, community colleges may provide an inexpensive version of a four-year college education that works very well. However, community colleges do pose challenges that often require students to devote additional time (and tuition) obtaining information, puzzling among choices, exploring, and making false starts and mistakes in pursuit of a degree in this complex system. If colleges do not recognize the needs of students without social know-how, the attempts of these students may amount to nothing more than a series of unrelated credit hours and failed dreams.

# CHAPTER SEVEN

## CHARTER BUILDING AND JOB CONTACTS

Earlier chapters detailed the ways that colleges can construct institutional procedures to improve student success during college by providing accessible and useful information and minimizing complicated demands. However, student success does not end at finding advisors and choosing the correct courses. Here, and in the two chapters that follow, we address the institutional procedures that colleges use to help graduates make the transition from college to the labor market. Most students enter college to improve their job prospects (Grubb 1996), but it is not clear how college enables them to accomplish this. These chapters will describe some procedures that two-year colleges use to try to improve post-graduation employment prospects. We will show how these efforts not only can lead to acquisition of relevant jobs, but also can influence student confidence and performance during college.

The traditional college model assumes that the college plays a minor role in the labor market process: students enter the labor market as individuals with marketable credentials and skill sets they acquired in college. We explore this process, not from the individual student level, but from an institutional level, and consider the ways these colleges mediate the relationship between students and the labor market. Although some theorists contend that employers recognize college degrees as credentials that signal students' abilities or capabilities, some evidence suggests that the subbaccalaureate degrees conferred by two-year colleges are not always recognized and do not have a general charter, which the bachelor's degree does. Exploring the ways that colleges deal with this reality, we find two approaches. Community colleges tend to rely on the traditional college charter, assuming that employers recognize and value subbaccalaureate degrees. In contrast, occupational colleges seek to create new charters, forging relationships with employers and building trust in the value of their graduates.

## Institutional Theory and Traditional College Charters

Human capital theory contends that colleges train students in the skills that the labor market rewards (Becker 1975). Institutional theory, on the other hand, holds that schools have their primary influence as an institutional system with the authority to create bodies of knowledge and categories of personnel and then to designate graduates as legitimate occupants of these categories (Meyer 1977). Schools are an ideal example of highly institutionalized organizations, in which rationalized formal structures "present an acceptable account of organizational activities, and organizations gain legitimacy, stability, and resources" (Meyer and Rowan 1991, 54). Organizations' resemblance to the societally accepted form, rules, and structures of a college confers to them "social charters to define people as graduates and as therefore possessing distinctive rights and capacities in society" (Meyer 1977, 59). The charter model recognizes that employers cannot see many important skills through direct inspection. Rather, employers assume that graduates possess skills because colleges have the legitimate authority to award degrees or credentials, which represent acquired knowledge.

This foundation of legitimacy is crucial for the status-allocation process (Brint 2003). Societal members accept educational credentials as legitimate signals of enhanced value and treat graduates accordingly. Credentials operate in modern society as institutionalized rules that both are taken for granted and guide hiring decisions and behaviors (Meyer 1977, 65). Employers hire graduates because they accept the degrees as a valid representation of skills and competencies that are assumed, rather than demonstrated. Thus, in a society in which employers consider educational credentials legitimate, college graduates have, or can have, access to jobs that nongraduates cannot.

John Meyer's notion is controversial. For example, critics note distinctions in the labor market value of bachelor's degrees from different institutions. Companies recruit at certain colleges only, and research indicates different payoffs for graduates of more selective colleges, even after controlling for individual attributes (Karabel 2005; however, see Dale and Krueger 1999). However, Meyer's theory is supported by civil service rules and many company personnel policies that stipulate bachelor's degree requirements for certain jobs. In addition, organizational promotion policies define radically different job sequences for college graduates than for employees without college degrees (Rosenbaum 1984; Bills 2004). In this sense, Meyer's concept of legitimate charters is quite similar to Collins's (1979) claims that employers use credentials to allocate more educated workers to better, higher paying jobs, which may explain the customary finding that completing a degree leads to larger earnings benefits than increments of isolated credits (Jencks et al. 1979; Marcotte et al. 2005).

Similarly, economists say that academic skills are valuable human capital, and credentials are good signals. Following Gary Becker's (1975) distinction between general and firm-specific knowledge, most economists and sociologists accept the idea that bachelor's degrees represent a form of general human capital that can be applied across many labor market contexts. In addition, market signaling theory contends that colleges provide degrees that signal their graduates' qualifications (Stigler 1961; Spence 1974). In this respect, human capital, signaling, credentialist, and institutional theories agree about the employment benefit of four-year college degrees. The question of whether the possession of skills is actual or merely presumed is contested. Unlike human capital and signaling theories, theories of credentialism and institutional charters don't necessarily assume that credentials are actually valuable for productivity (Berg 1971; Bills 2004), but they posit that credentials have real consequences because employers accept bachelor's degree credentials as legitimate.

However, for educational credentials other than the bachelor's degree, legitimacy is rarely as automatic as institutional theory presumes. Research has shown that employers often mistrust the value of a high school diploma (Miller and Rosenbaum 1997; Murnane and Levy 1996; Neckerman and Kirshenman 1991). David Brown (2001) questioned the authority of credentials among employers, such as high school diplomas, technical certificates, subbaccalaureate degrees conferred by two-year colleges, and "lower-prestige" college degrees, and David Bills (1992) suggested that employers use alternate criteria to evaluate job applicants for lower-level bureaucratic jobs.

Here we apply the social charter concept to specific subbaccalaureate postsecondary contexts: community colleges and occupational colleges. Some evidence suggests that, unlike the bachelor's degree, the associate's degree does not have a general charter. Although an associate's degree conveyed an earnings advantage over a high school diploma in 1990, its benefits were significant in only three of eleven majors for men (and four for women). The bachelor's degree advantage, however, was significant in nine of eleven majors for both men and women (Grubb 1996, 95). The associate's degree may have recognition in only a few fields, so the charter may be major specific. This variation in the value of the associate's degree across fields raises the disturbing possibility that staff at these colleges may mistakenly act as if they have a recognized charter, when, in fact, they do not.

We also take a new perspective on the common view that community colleges have strongly shifted toward occupational education. Although Brint and Karabel (1989, 300–3) noted that chancellors, presidents, and deans emphasize occupational programs, they also noted "the curious lack of interest of 'career-oriented' community colleges in developing ties with local employers or studying their skill needs" (see Brint 2003, 25). They also noted that faculty resist attempts to shift to occupational education. Rather than accept administrators' statements of their colleges' missions, the present study examines occupational program staff's reports about their own behaviors on a day-to-day basis. We use the term "staff" to describe a range of faculty, administrators, and program heads—chairs, coordinators, and deans, for example—and examine the activities they actually engage in to get employers to recognize their students' value as well as how they regard these activities. We found different approaches in the two types of colleges, which suggest different models of the process.

This study supports Brint's (2003) doubts about whether community colleges' efforts have resulted in the increased legitimacy of their credentials or coordination of their programs with the needs of the labor market (Dougherty 1994). Despite the shift toward occupational programs, Brint and Karabel (1989) observed few efforts by community colleges to develop specific institutional linkages with specific employers and no consistent college-wide plan for school-employer interactions. Ironically, we find that these occupational colleges have developed legitimacy among employers and may be shaping a market niche that community colleges have neglected.

## Two-Year College Charters: Two Models

If employers cannot evaluate applicants' skills and abilities through direct inspection and do not trust all the information they receive about applicants, they must rely on authoritative information. The question is how information becomes authoritative and trusted. We look at two models that suggest two ways colleges can give authority to the information they convey about their students.

First, colleges can rely on the traditional college charter. John Meyer (1977) described four-year colleges as having social charters, that is, institutional authority to allocate graduates into personnel categories. As he noted, the amazing fact about the bachelor's degree is that its charter is widely recognized as long as the degree is awarded by an institution similar to traditional colleges. Because community colleges are designed to provide the equivalent of the first two years of a four-year degree, staff can engage in activities to emphasize this resemblance and presumably gain the resulting authority from the traditional college charter. Such activities include accreditation, the organization of departmental and administrative units, the credentials required of faculty, and the form and content of instruction.

We call the second model the charter-building model. Instead of adopting a traditional charter, colleges can build a new one. Although all colleges provide degrees that signal their graduates' qualifications (Stigler 1961; Spence 1974), it is uncertain whether nonelite colleges, whose legitimacy is more questionable, can rely solely on the standard college charter and expect employers to hire their graduates based on degrees that employers may not understand or trust. Trust is a key ingredient in the traditional college charter model. Although we agree with economists' emphasis on information, we contend that information must be trusted as authoritative, and we examine whether schools take actions to build and enhance their institutional charters to convey authoritative and trustworthy information. If colleges have non-elite status, have an unrecognized nontraditional structure, or award nontraditional degrees (that differ from traditional four-year bachelor's degrees), it is especially important for them to establish a recognized charter that gives authority to the information they convey about students. The unselective nature of these colleges makes it both more important and more challenging for them to signal to employers that graduates possess valuable qualifications.

Meyer did not consider how charters are created or sustained, but Caroline Persell and Peter Cookson's (1985) study of the relationship between prep schools and colleges provides an excellent example of the way charters are maintained and enhanced by relationship-building activities. Instead of relying on impersonal college admission procedures, elite boarding schools give their graduates distinctive forms of access to Ivy League colleges through face-to-face interactions, close social relationships, extensive exchanges of information, and negotiation between the school advisors and college admissions officers. However, even elite prep schools do not have automatic access; they must take extensive actions to maintain their charters with selective colleges. Presumably, less elite schools, such as the two-year colleges in this study, may have an even greater need to enhance their charters through relationship building between college staff and employers, but it is not certain that they can do so.

Although personal-contact influences on hiring have long been emphasized, institutional networks have recently been noted (Granovetter 1995, 162–69). In Germany and Japan, schools' institutional contacts help youths gain access to good jobs (Brinton 1993; Hamilton 1990; Osterman 1988; Rosenbaum and Kariya 1989). Some American vocational education teachers form similar ties (Rosenbaum 2001). In each case, reciprocity—a sense of obligation on which both parties can depend—makes information and transactions dependable because each party trusts that the other values their relationship and will not risk losing it for short-term gain (Coleman 1988). Unlike Coleman's examples, in which context emerges from ethnic ties (for example, El Khalili market in Cairo), such relationships may also be created if school staff convince employers that they can depend on their evaluations (Rosenbaum 2001, 248).

Extending the charter model, Takehiko Kariya and James Rosenbaum (1995) suggest that schools may build preferential access to employment (enhanced charters) by forming relationships that ensure employers a dependable supply, type, and quality of graduates. If their graduates are to gain recognition, low-status colleges cannot just provide information, they must convince employers that the information they provide about students' qualifications is dependable by creating trusted relationships through which information is conveyed. Because low-SES and minority applicants have access to good jobs through personal contacts less frequently than other students (Granovetter 1995; Lin, Ensel, and Vaughn 1981; Peterson, Spaorta, and Seidel 2000; Wegener 1991), institutional contacts may reduce this gap.

While Brint and Karabel (1989) considered transfer to bachelor's degree programs as the main source of upward mobility, we concur with Brint's reconsideration of occupational associate's degrees:

> New evidence does suggest that we were wrong to consider community college vocational education as "the bottom rung" of higher education's tracking system. Economic rewards tend to be greater for vocational students than for academic students, if they complete the

> associate's degree, and vocational students are now as likely as academic students to transfer to four-year colleges. (2003, 23)

Although transfer is a laudable goal, when 75 percent of community college students do not transfer (Dougherty 1994; Grubb 1996), "promises of upward mobility are . . . not very often realized" (Brint 2003, 25), and other goals must be considered. Subbaccalaureate colleges exist in a vague, poorly understood, position: beyond high school, yet less than four years of college. This is now a major part of higher education, with over 40 percent of new college students entering two-year institutions (Bailey 2002). Do these colleges act as if they are faithfully relying on the traditional college charter, or do they take steps to build and enhance their social charters? Are these charters enhanced through institutional contacts, and, if so, what actions are taken to initiate contacts and convince mistrustful employers that these credentials are valid representations of competence?

These results are based on interviews with program chairs, career services staff, occupational deans, and other administrators at the fourteen colleges. However, interviews with health programs are excluded from this chapter because these programs' procedures are largely determined by state licensure requirements, not college discretion. Indeed, we find that these occupational colleges initiate forms of contacts with employers that provide a new perspective on how two-year colleges can operate. Whereas earlier analysts speculated about the possibility of institutional linkages between community colleges and employers (Brewer and Gray 1999; Grubb 1996), occupational colleges report actual linkages.

Ultimately, our findings must be judged in the context of other studies. We shall repeatedly note the ways in which our findings extend two previous studies of college-employer interactions: Dominic Brewer and Maryann Gray's (1999) national survey and Grubb's (1996) research in four cities. However, beyond their economic emphasis on resource constraints, we introduce a sociological conception and describe previously unnoticed processes about the ways in which schools relate to the labor market.

## Approaches to Labor-Market Linking and Charter Building

To ask staff to talk about the college charter can lead to abstract comments unrelated to behaviors. We took another approach: studying reported behaviors. Staff views of the institution's charter is reflected in their actions, and institutions with different charters may handle the same activities in different ways.

We compare occupational chairs at community colleges with similar staff at occupational colleges. As we note later, we found that many community college staff report that they rarely initiate interactions with employers, see little benefit from such interactions, and believe that employers respond to their graduates' degrees. These practices seem to parallel those of most four-year colleges: focus on instruction and accreditation and let the degree speak for itself. To their credit, these community colleges devote much energy to maintaining accreditation, hiring competent faculty, and ensuring the transferability of their classes to four-year colleges. We found that the lack of attention given to relationships with employers may reflect the priority these institutions' place on other missions.

For colleges to have effective charters, employers must trust colleges to provide dependable evaluations. At the seven community colleges, the staff act as if employers trust their degrees to certify the quality of students. However, this is not a passive process. All the program chairs reported that they engage in many actions to make their degrees dependable, actions that show that they fit the traditional college charter. They design courses to meet the requirements of accrediting associations, and they devote much time to satisfying accreditation criteria. Much energy is spent before and during the visits of accrediting associations. The colleges and each of their programs gear up many temporary committees to address each aspect of accreditation, and these committees meet many times over one or two years before an accreditation visit. A battlefield atmosphere pervades the campus around the time of these visits, and the risk of nonaccreditation is viewed as a challenge to the charter of occupational programs. With these actions, the community colleges show their isomorphism with the institutionalized rules and formal structures that are necessary to "maximize their legitimacy" and fit the traditional college model (Meyer and Rowan 1991, 53).

In contrast, we found that at occupational colleges, where missions are more limited and where survival depends on the success of job placements, the staff reported concerted efforts to build trusted institutional relationships and to convince employers of their graduates' competence. Although both types of colleges provide similar activities (for example, employer advisory boards, career services, job placement, and occasionally reactions to labor market outcomes), they approach them in very different ways.

## Advisory Boards: The Community College Approach

To have preferential relationships with employers, colleges must be seen as providing a dependable type of graduate who meets employers' needs (Kariya and Rosenbaum 1995). Advisory boards are a way that colleges can exchange information with employers—to get information about employers' needs, to get feedback from employers about the content of their programs, and to inform employers that their graduates have dependably appropriate skills. Advisory committees provide a good example of the use of contacts with employers. The state requires each community college to convene an advisory committee before it starts a new occupational program, and some community colleges require annual meetings of advisory committees. However, what is written on paper differs substantially from what we found in reported practices.

Earlier studies have found that community colleges have infrequent, short advisory meetings, and little time is spent preparing for them. Staff use advisory boards to get general information, not to build relationships; they ask "whether there will be employment opportunities in an occupational area, not whether local employers will hire [their] graduates" (Grubb 1996, 179–80). Brewer and Gray (1999) also noted that advisory boards sometimes meet irregularly and with little purpose. Both studies blamed time and resources limitations and urged providing more of both to increase the effectiveness of such committees.

Although constraints on time and resources do limit these activities, institutional priorities of faculty and staff are also a key factor. Community colleges delegate advisory committee duties to already overburdened staff members, who tend to view such activities as a low priority. At these community colleges, nearly all the occupational program chairs—the individuals responsible for making programs effective—report that advisory committees are low on their long list of duties, and the requirement is only that the meeting take place, not that any consequences follow from the meeting.

Four-year colleges generally do not focus much effort on employer advisory boards; instead they acquire a recognized charter by performing traditional college activities (Meyer 1977). Most of the chairs of the community college programs emphasized the same activities as traditional colleges, stressing the value of the degree that they award and buttressing its value by devoting a great amount of energy to the accreditation process. The primary duties of these overburdened program chairs, who perform multiple roles, are to make sure they have adjunct faculty to cover courses and service tasks every term (a tremendous, almost full-time job), and to meet accreditation requirements, budgetary constraints, and reporting requirements. When asked about his job responsibilities, one program coordinator for a management program replied, "I identify and stock the entire staff. . . . I have to schedule classes, supervise faculty, the part-time faculty. . . . If I knew I'd have this question, I would have gotten my list of things I'm supposed to do. This is what I actually do." In addition, many also teach one or more courses, and some teach up to four classes each semester. Most reported that they devote little effort to building and maintaining relationships with employers.

There was some variation. A few program chairs, particularly those in the more applied technology programs, said that they do value the interactions, but lack organizational support and are limited by time constraints, consistent with a resource-constraint explanation.

However, this explanation is not adequate. The program chairs that reported few relationships with employers rarely expressed regrets about these limited efforts. Resources are clearly not the only issue. None of the program chairs we interviewed suggested that they would devote more time to interactions with employers or hire additional staff to do so if they were given additional resources. Most have minimal goals for these boards—they seek only to convey general information about the skills that employers look for and to provide reactions to their curriculum requirements. In one program, when a business department chair, who had taught at the school for twenty-five years, was asked where his students get jobs, he replied, "I'll be very candid with you and say I don't know." His program had not met with an advisory board in many years, and, prior to our interview, he had not thought much about it. At another community college, a career dean admitted, "We're supposed to have an advisory board. I don't know if we do . . . we have people that we call . . . but I don't know how active [the board] is."

At least one program chair in each of the three community colleges reported that the programs have advisory committees on paper, but the committees had not met in the past year or more. For example, when asked whether the department had an advisory board, a chair of a computer information systems program admitted his doubt about the need for such a meeting, saying that anecdotal information was sufficient. He added,

> [We] . . . had one a few years ago. I am now told that I will have one again. . . . An advisory council, if it's done locally, would just be five of my best friends . . . director of programming here, manager of software support there. Just go call five of my friends, and we'll have a lunch.

Furthermore, constrained time and resources cannot explain the program chairs' choice of advisory board members. Instead of selecting employers who could hire their graduates, the program chairs either ask friends or select executives from large, prominent firms, although these executives may have no say over hiring and their firms may not hire locally or at the associate's degree level. None of the seven community colleges makes an explicit effort to include executives who hire graduates on college-wide advisory boards. At the program level, half the programs (eleven of twenty-two) have advisory boards that consist mainly of employers who do not hire their students. Four program chairs (18 percent) rely mainly on friends and informal networks, and another four (18 percent) rely primarily on adjunct faculty as employer advisors. Three chairs (14 percent) admitted that they have no functioning advisory committee whatsoever.

Moreover, few colleges have procedures to monitor quality or to try to ensure it. Sometimes, even if the board exists, it is fragile, resting on the voluntary efforts of a single program chair, and furthermore may not confer any lasting charter to the program. As an administrator noted, relationships with employer advisors begin "through a very strong individual, a director, a charismatic person . . . and if that individual goes away, it can have serious impacts." Although many people noted that the maintenance of contacts often depends on single individuals, no one we interviewed suggested that this is a serious problem or reported taking steps to build broader institutional support for contacts. Indeed, many program chairs reported that they rely almost exclusively on their adjunct faculty, a self-selected, unrepresentative sample who rarely do any hiring.

Few program chairs reported that meetings of advisory boards require any preparation. The chairs reported entering these meetings with no pressing questions and did not use this time to build relationships with employers. The meetings are brief, often shorter than planned. If employers use a new software program or a new technique, that program is discussed, but such changes are rare and quickly noted. The program chairs seek general reactions to their curriculum, not to prior graduates' performances, and some reported that the information they receive is not useful. They showed little concern about the ineffectiveness of these meetings for getting detailed information about employers' needs or building relationships.

The dean of instruction at one community college was one of the few respondents to see a problem, but he did not have a vision of how to improve these committees:

> Advisory boards meetings . . . are nothing more than feed fests because nothing comes out of them. The institution doesn't ask the right questions, or the people represented around the table have no answer or clue as to how to help the college and the program grow.

Moreover, many faculty and administrators at community colleges believe that employers should not have such a direct role. They fear that employers want a curriculum that is tailored to meet their specific companies' needs, which contradicts the colleges' mission to provide a broader set of skills. The dean of a community college voiced her concerns:

> Community colleges get slammed by the Chamber [of Commerce] . . . about how we're not preparing people for the job market. . . . Well, that might be true because we're not preparing somebody to work in "Joe's" company. . . . No, I can't teach . . . somebody how to do everything at your business, so . . . you don't have to train them. [Employers must] understand what the role of the educational institution is. . . . Not everybody in the business community gets that.

## Advisory Boards: The Occupational College Approach

In contrast, all staff at these seven occupational colleges reported an interest in exchanging information and in convincing employers that their programs serve employers' specific needs. They said that they wanted their advisory boards to facilitate a systematic flow of information from employers about their hiring needs and to employers regarding the qualities that their programs' graduates possess to meet employers' needs.

These staff also believe that advisory boards create personal relationships that make information trustworthy. Unlike the community colleges in our sample, at which the responsibility to build contacts with employers usually resides on a single program chair, all the occupational colleges try to make college-wide contacts, often including college staff from several programs in advisory meetings. Administrators at all seven reported that job placement staff are present at program advisory meetings to meet recruiters and learn about their specific needs.

In all seven, the administrators reported that they solicit employers' reactions to the ways that prior graduates have met employers' needs and advanced over time. They also reported that they use employer advisory committees to learn what these employers expect from job candidates and to convince employers that the school strives to meet their needs and values their relationship. Their reports resemble Persell and Cookson's (1985) "chartering and bartering." Although the needs of the labor market and school staff will change over time, the respondents at the occupational colleges reported that they try to build enduring institutional relationships with specific employers that will give their schools a recognized charter in certain fields.

In all seven schools, the job placement administrators reported that advisory boards are one of their main job duties. They select employers that they believe can provide their graduates with jobs with good pay and opportunities for advancement. Indeed, one administrator reported avoiding a well-known Fortune 500 firm that offers only low-skilled, dead end jobs to the school's students. Although their advisory boards cannot include all employers who hire from their programs, the administrators of all seven occupational colleges reported they select ones that offer the best jobs and rotate among these employers in successive years. Unlike community colleges, occupational colleges use these meetings to learn about individual employers' specific needs, form trusted relationships between recruiters and the colleges' job placement and program staff, and ensure recruiters that the colleges can be trusted to respond to their needs. Whereas community colleges pile the tasks of advisory committees onto already overcommitted program chairs, for whom other tasks are a higher priority, occupational colleges make advisory committees the top priority for certain staff.

## Career Services: The Community College Approach

For colleges to have an effective charter, employers must recognize the value of those graduates (Kariya and Rosenbaum 1995), which requires that students present themselves effectively. Both types of colleges use career services offices to assist students with these activities, but these offices operate in different ways.

Like four-year colleges, the seven community colleges have career services offices, which inform students how to communicate their value to employers by helping them create effective résumés, conduct job searches, and develop self-presentation skills. This usually occurs through optional courses, workshops, or computer software. They provide general information (for example, the format of résumés and interviewing etiquette) and administer career-interest and aptitude tests. However, at all seven community colleges, the administrators reported that the career services office does not give specific information about which employers to visit or what skills the specific employers value. These offices post job openings on a bulletin board or computer, much like the listings in newspaper want ads. Career services staff assume that students can figure out which jobs match their qualifications or plans, perhaps a dubious assumption. We found that many students did not fully understand job qualifications. One reported that he took a job at Blockbuster because he wanted a career in the film industry. These offices, however, are not responsible for supervising students' job application process.

At the seven community colleges, administrators stressed that these offices are severely limited and serve less than 20 percent of the students. All have only a few staff. Given the recent policy mandate to serve clients on Temporary Assistance for Needy Families (TANF), the emphasis has partially shifted to community residents and jobs that do not require degrees (Jacobs and Winslow 2003; Shaw and Rab 2003). One manager of career services reported that the "ratio between students . . . and community residents using the career counselors . . . is 75 percent community, 25 percent students." Furthermore, services are student initiated at all of these community colleges. Like Grubb (1996), we found that meager resources prevent career services offices from serving many students or from collecting useful labor market information.

However, their limitations are not solely due to poor resources. These offices seem designed to be peripheral. Just as health services offices serve only sick students, career services offices serve only the few students who realize they need the services, ignoring those who do not realize it. The administrators reported that many students may not know about these offices because they are not widely promoted. At all seven community colleges, these offices are also spatially peripheral—usually located in a hard-to-find part of the campus. At one college, the office is on the third floor, around the bend and down a dark hall. At another, it is poorly marked with only one small sign that is hard to see. As one career counselor noted,

> We are really tucked away here. The action . . . is all at the other end of campus: the classroom buildings, the library, the bookstore. The students are not here, and on top of it all, we're here on the third floor, in the corner, behind the financial aid office and health services. . . . We're just not in a high-traffic area. . . . If we were located somewhere else . . . we'd never be able to handle the flow.

Even faculty members do not always understand what these offices do. When asked how students get information about jobs, the program chairs at several community colleges said, "the career office must do that," and they referred students to it. However, visiting these career service offices, we learned that they lack any information about the local labor market. They provide general information about styles of résumés, interviewing, and career-interest inventories, but they do not provide job information or placement.

## Career Services: The Occupational College Approach

In contrast, at all seven occupational colleges, job placement is considered a central function of career services. Some are in fact named "Job Placement Office." All are located in high-traffic areas. All but one are visible from the main entrance, and students are required to use them (except by special petition). At these occupational colleges, staff help every student craft a résumé. They know the employers' specific needs as well as which skills and experiences each occupational program provides to meet these needs. Although community colleges give a few students general advice on preparing résumés (including software for creating an attractive layout), occupational college staff meet with each student and tell them what local employers in their field want to see on a résumé, which of their courses and skills meet the employers' needs, and how to present these skills and courses on a résumé and in interviews. They also supervise the job application process for every student. If a student fails to get a job offer, the staff will sometimes ask employers how the student did in an interview to understand the student's interviewing skills and to gain a better understanding of the employer's needs.

These job placement staff meet with each student and use their knowledge of individual students to match them with employers' particular needs. This process is beneficial to students, employers, and colleges. The job placement staff at all seven occupational colleges reported that a student's poor presentation can harm the college's reputation, a concern never mentioned at community colleges. Several of the occupational colleges try to direct student-employer contacts in ways that will ensure access to their students in the long run. As one respondent noted,

> We [normally try] to build a relationship with [an employer] to build more in-roads for our graduates. . . . It is great to work with this company, you always know that they'll have these positions available, so let's try to impress them with this group of candidates that we send them. Then . . . they come back again, or next time, they just automatically fax the position to us.

When this job placement director was asked how the job placement staff figure out which students will impress certain companies, she replied,

> We know each student well, so it'd be a good fit. Like this student, they really have good communication skills, they have a good GPA, they seemed motivated when we met them, I really think that for this position, they're a good candidate. This company has a really good chance of liking this candidate.

When asked what happens if they send a student who does not meet the employers' needs, she explained that employers sometimes understand, but sometimes they refuse to hire any future students.

The community colleges cannot prevent students from sending out poor résumés for inappropriate jobs. However, the occupational colleges control the job application process and believe that it reduces the chances that any student will make a serious mistake that will harm the school's legitimacy.

## Job Placement: The Community College Approach

In contrast with their extensive accreditation efforts, community colleges devote little effort to job placement. No centralized full-time job placement function exists for graduates, and offices that do some job placement usually focus on part-time work for enrolled students (often in low-skilled jobs). Contract education and workforce development appear to be exceptions. Like 90 percent of community colleges (Dougherty and Bakia 2000), all those in our study offer contract education, but it is usually available only to a firm's employees and has little impact on other programs, as Grubb (1996) noted. Similarly, two of our community colleges have workforce-development offices to provide job training and job placement services (Jacobs and Winslow 2003; Mazzeo, Rab, and Eachus 2003; Shaw and Rab 2003). However, they emphasize community residents more than students, and most jobs appear to be unskilled, requiring specific short-term training. At both colleges, with enrollments of more than 8,000, these offices have a single professional staff person and two clerical staff to serve students and community residents. If these offices increased in size, focused on college students, and aimed at appropriate jobs, they might be able to create institutional linkages for the colleges' graduates. As it is, both contract education and workforce development seem to divert resources from more traditionally enrolled students, including low-income students.

Some heads of programs (nine of twenty-two, or 41 percent) reported that they actively help some students get jobs, but none said that this is a formal duty, and it is often haphazard. Our findings resemble those of a national survey that found 39.4 percent of faculty reporting they often provide assistance to students who seek employment, 39 percent reporting they had time to develop or maintain contacts with employers, and most believing that "other people in this college have responsibility for developing links" (Brewer and Gray 1999, 405). Similarly, Grubb (1996, 180) found that "the majority of instructors seem to do little placement" and attributed this to the shortage of time among overburdened faculty.

At all seven community colleges, almost every chair reported that job placement is not a formal responsibility, and though some do help a few students, for most it is a low priority. In this respect, these community colleges differ from university graduate schools (for example, business and engineering schools) with active job placement offices, but resemble doctoral programs, which use faculty member contacts rather than placement staff.

Many program chairs admit that they do not have time for anything beyond teaching and staffing duties, regardless of their job descriptions. However, constraints on resources are not the only limitation. The community college chairs reported that they respond to employers' telephone calls if they are not too busy. However, most do not see this as a valuable use of their time—they handle the calls quickly, and few reported using calls to build relationships or initiating calls to employers for a student. Most department chairs do not view job placement as part of their duties, some emphatically deny that it is, and several expressed resentment at employers' requests for names of qualified students. They think that it is inappropriate to be asked to be "employment agencies" or "headhunters," because doing so interferes with what they consider their primary goal of providing degrees. The comments of one program chair captured this view:

> I've got mixed feelings about dealing with a lot of employers and just feeding people to them. . . . They expect you to be a free headhunter. . . . I don't have the kind of time that I can interview all my students and find someone that's appropriate for that particular job. . . . Sometimes I'll just . . . give the employers a list of students that I think might qualify and let them deal with it. Other times, I may not respond.

## Job Placement: The Occupational College Approach

In contrast, all the occupational colleges devote much energy to job placement. One college has seven full-time professional and three support staff serving 608 graduating students, and another has six full-time professional and two support staff serving 705 graduating students. A large college has twenty-six full-time staff serving 3,083 students (119 students per staff person). Three colleges have one full-time professional and one or two clerical staff members who are solely responsible for job placement, serving ninety to 122 graduating students. Every one of these occupational colleges has full-time professional staff and clerical support staff who are solely responsible for job placement, with ratios ranging from sixty to 122 students per staff person.

The same kinds of employer requests that are sometimes resented at community colleges are actively encouraged at occupational colleges. At all of these occupational colleges, staff engage in many activities to build relationships with employers. Three occupational colleges call the office career services, and the others call it job placement, yet all these offices provide both student advising and job placement. The job placement staff engage mainly in relationship-building activities, which create a charter for the schools' relevant programs as dependable providers of skills that recruiters value. They actively initiate contacts, create a responsive procedure, provide information and applicants who are appropriate to particular employers, and develop trusted personal relationships with recruiters in several ways.

First, they initiate contacts. At all these occupational colleges, placement staff make contact with employers. They attend meetings of the Chamber of Commerce, telephone employers, visit workplaces, and make contacts at job fairs. As one placement director reported, "You'll pretty much always find [one of our] placement coordinators at [Chamber of Commerce] events."

Second, they strengthen relationships through systematic responsiveness. All these occupational colleges stress that they respond quickly to employers' requests and tailor their recommendations to employers' specific needs. The placement staff at three colleges emphasized their responsiveness:

> Employers ... [are] repeat customers. ... We don't charge any fees. We're really fast ... and as soon as the job request comes through, we know exactly what résumés to send in. So it's very fast. We get lots of students who tell us, "the calls [from employers] are so many."
>
> Some companies just love us ... [they] just call up and say, "This new accountant position opened up. Can you get me 10 résumés in

10 minutes," and we can. . . . They'll have three interviews set up with three graduates from the accounting program tomorrow. So, some companies are just like, "Oh, my gosh, I found the way to recruit." We're just one of their regular methods.

Our response to employers is critical; the rapidity with which we can respond to a job lead gives us a real edge. . . . Community colleges . . . they're still snail-mailing. . . . We get a lead, [and] we respond immediately.

Third, these occupational colleges convey appropriate information. Although none of the community colleges oversee the job application process, the job placement staff at the occupational colleges assess employers' needs, systematically organize and package information on applicants, and send out appropriate résumés in response to job openings. When employers send them a job description, the placement staff send out appropriate résumés that meet the job qualifications, as the staff at two colleges reported:

Placement dean: [Our job is] to make sure that . . . their paperwork is fine [and] their résumés meet all the [employers'] standards, to make sure their résumés get sent out every time there's a lead. . . . So we have like a tickler file of each major who's seeking [a job]. The jobs come in, and we code them by major, and then we take the résumés and fax them.

Placement staff: They'll give us a job description. We'll enter it into our database. From there, all the coordinators can see which position is available, and then they can refer people who seem like a good fit, . . . if they want them in quicker . . . [we respond] within the hour.

Instead of just bulletin board postings, the job placement staff help recruiters do their job by channeling appropriate and timely information.

Finally, the job placement staff develop personal relationships with recruiters and promise them appropriate and trusted information. The occupational college staff work to build relationships. Occupational colleges require job placement staff to meet recruiters and learn their specific needs in advisory board meetings and to continue to build these relationships, as the placement directors at two occupational colleges reported:

We talk one on one with companies . . . about what they're looking for in candidates . . . so then we can [select and] coach our candidates.

> We usually work one on one [with recruiters], and so . . . we try and
> keep it very simple. . . . They only work with Chris, and . . . when this
> company calls, they always get Chris.

At all seven occupational colleges, job placement staff work personally
with recruiters. They meet in advisory meetings, where they ask employers about their specific needs. They show their schools' commitment to serving employers' needs and to sustaining the relationship by initiating calls
to ask employers if they are satisfied with the graduates' performance. Of
course, these calls also help them learn about further openings.

On this last dimension, we found some variation. The relationship is
stronger and more specialized at the larger colleges. At the three largest
occupational colleges, the job placement staff learn about employers' specific needs by working with employers in a few occupational fields, and they
get to know employers' needs, even technical details. All job placement staff
create personal relationships based on reciprocity of mutual benefit between
schools and recruiters, the kind of mutual obligation that creates social
capital (Coleman 1988). When they know an employer's particular needs,
they can select students who are a good fit for the employer and inform
the employer of desirable personal attributes that are difficult to assess in
job interviews. Even when they do not specialize, they make it clear that
their job is to satisfy employers, so employers can trust that they seek to
form lasting relationships, and their recommendations will be dependable.
All seven occupational colleges reported that they have long-term relationships with some employers.

## Responding to Labor-Market Outcomes:
## Differences Between College Types

Perhaps the best indication of the difference between the two types of colleges lies in their reactions to students' labor-market outcomes. The community colleges are not involved in students' transition to the labor market.
Students are expected to find their own jobs. When asked about the jobs
that students take, the chair of a department of computer information
systems said,

> I was afraid you were going to ask me these questions. . . . You know
> that old song by Tom Lehr about Werner Von Braun [the Nazi rocket
> scientist who shifted his expertise to work for the United States after
> World War II]. . . . "I shoot 'em up. I don't know where they come

down." My job is to shoot 'em up [out of college], not where they come
down [what jobs they get]. In theory, a student that does not go on to
a four-year degree is going to get a beginning job, probably with some
business, probably a small office, where they use computers. . . . But you
know, this is only hearsay-type stuff. I don't know how to collect the
data for this.

None of the community colleges that we studied has anyone specifically
in charge of deciding where students will land in the labor market or even
anyone who knows what jobs the students get or whether they get jobs.
Like the colleges Grubb studied (1996), those in our sample do not themselves collect systematic information on graduates' jobs, and thus do not
have systematic information on the graduates' outcomes. Although data is
collected at the state level, it is incomplete. We found no indication that
the information gets back to programs in these colleges in any useful form.
Even if programs did receive this information, they would have difficulty
finding the time and resources to respond. Chairs would have to do it, and
they already spend most of their time scrambling to find adjunct faculty
to cover next term's courses. The state provides no additional resources for
responding to this information.

These community colleges see their main responsibility as conferring
credits and degrees and the accompanying skills that the degrees represent. Even if some program chairs informally learn that their graduates
with associate's degrees fail to get appropriate jobs, their charter conceptions are challenged, but they still do not initiate actions in the labor market. Some chairs of business and accounting programs reported that local
employers do not value the associate's degree, but that the chairs nonetheless do not try to convince employers of its value or to use their advisory
committees to improve placements. Instead, they assume that the labor market will respond to another degree. The chairs of the business programs at
five community colleges mentioned that they encourage associate's degree
students to get a different credential: a bachelor's degree or a one-year certificate. As they shift their emphasis to another charter and de-emphasize
their associate's degree, they ignore the needs of the students who remain
in these programs.

In the very same fields, these occupational colleges strive to find or
"create" a labor market demand for their associate's degrees. All seven
occupational colleges collect follow-up information on graduates, and
every placement office provided us with actual placement rates. They
reported that 90 to 97 percent of their graduates obtained jobs, mostly in

relevant fields. Although these claims rise and fall with the economy, they have remained above 85 percent for many years. Despite our initial skepticism, our interviews with college staff and our observations of job placement activities persuaded us that such claims were probably true for at least five of the occupational colleges. We have detailed job placement listings for two of these colleges (including the college with the most minority students), and these listings support their claims. Moreover, all staff support the claims and describe activities that seem likely to be effective. We also interviewed higher level staff who had retired from three of these colleges and had no continuing connection. They not only verified the claim, but also spontaneously mentioned it as a major gratification of their job. Although skepticism is appropriate, the extensive procedures used by these colleges makes the 90 percent job placement rate seem plausible, perhaps even likely.

However, our contention is about their efforts at placing students in jobs, not their effectiveness. The staff identify and contact local employers in relevant fields, try to convince them to try their students, and carefully select especially good students to confirm their promises to new employers, so that employers will return with more job offers the next year. They try to convince employers that any student who earns a degree has the skills that employers need. Staff reported that sometimes they can convince employers to give preference to their graduates. In the same fields (for example, business and accounting) in which the staff of community colleges shift to a different credential, the staff at occupational colleges try to increase the demand for their associate's credential.

## BUILDING A CHARTER OR RELYING ON THE CREDENTIAL

Although previous research has described the shift toward occupational education in the nation's community colleges (Brint and Karabel 1989; Dougherty 1994), it noted some curious ways in which the transformation was incomplete (Brint 2003). Extending these observations, we have described two different approaches to labor-market entry and have posed theoretical dilemmas in practical terms. By examining the approaches of exemplary occupational colleges, community colleges may discover new approaches that they can use to help students enter the labor market.

Like Meyer's (1977) model, these community colleges act as if they have a traditional college charter, striving primarily to meet the demands of accreditation so that they can confer accredited degrees and fit the traditional college model (Meyer and Rowan 1991, 55). They believe that additional actions are unnecessary for the labor market to recognize the value of their graduates.

While Meyer (1977) de-emphasized agency and did not indicate how charters could be constructed, we have discovered actions that low-status private occupational colleges take to try to build charters in certain occupational fields. Although these colleges offer accredited degrees (as do community colleges), they also spend much time and energy in activities that they believe create trustworthy institutional relationships with employers and provide access to employers' job networks for all their students. We could not ascertain if they are correct, but they clearly believe that charter enhancement via relationship-building is a way that low-status colleges can improve their graduates' success in getting employment.

Unlike personal contacts, institutional linkages have rarely been studied (Granovetter 1995). Some faculty members at community colleges have personal contacts with employers; however, their personal contacts are not a formal responsibility and are not systematically used for institutional purposes. This situation is reminiscent of a study of high schools, which found that high school vocational teachers' personal contacts with employers are not recognized by the institution, do not extend beyond the students who are known by a particular teacher and certainly not to other programs, and, according to teachers, would not persist if the teacher departed (Rosenbaum 2001). Indeed, high school teachers' personal contacts do not have the same charter-building qualities for the institution as the contacts we observed in these occupational colleges.

In contrast, at all seven occupational colleges, the institutional linkages represent a formal institutional responsibility of certain personnel for helping students make the transition to the labor market. Furthermore, although the community colleges rely on individual faculty for job connections, construe the job search as an individual student process, and largely leave students to their own devices in searching for jobs, the occupational colleges supervise the job application process of all students at every stage and actively manage their contacts with the labor market.

While personal and family contacts help advantaged youths (Granovetter 1995), charters help students from all backgrounds (Meyer 1977). The administrators of the seven occupational colleges reported providing job help to all students, including their many low-income or minority students, just as the charters of prep schools benefit the schools' low-income students (Persell and Cookson 1985). The occupational colleges' high job placement rates of over 90 percent include a large number of low-income and minority students. At these colleges, the hiring process is controlled by institutional processes, thus may be less affected by individual students' mistakes or social backgrounds (Deil-Amen and Rosenbaum 2003). Although disadvantaged youths rarely have access to job networks and are avoided by employers (Moss and Tilly 2000; Neckerman and Kirschenman 1991), these administrators asserted that the colleges' charter-building activities may overcome employers' preconceptions, providing all students with access to jobs.

We cannot prove the generalizability of the community colleges in this study, yet we have noted many comparisons of our findings with prior studies. For instance, if some community colleges build strong contacts with employers, they would differ from those in our sample, but they would also differ from those in prior studies (Grubb 1996), including most of Brewer and Gray's (1999) national sample. Our study replicated Grubb's findings that advisory boards, career services, and job placement are weak, not active, and poorly connected to labor markets. Like Grubb, we found modest job placement efforts, poor information about labor-market outcomes, and career advisors who "admitted virtual ignorance about employment opportunities" (Grubb 1996, 183). Are we being too rosy about the strong job placement activities at these private colleges? The Community College Research Center did interviews at one for-profit college, and recommended many aspects, including job placement, to be tried at community colleges (Bailey, Badway, and Gumport 2002). We have presented a more detailed analysis of these issues.

We must note that some of the differences in institutional priorities may be related to the colleges' different sources of funding. Community colleges receive funding from local and state taxes if they remain accredited, so great institutional efforts are devoted to accreditation. However, the seven occupational colleges we studied also devote great effort to accreditation. Although both types of colleges report occupational goals, job placement may be more important to the private colleges because they depend on federal student loans, which are contingent on loan default rates of less than 25 percent (which probably reflects graduates' earnings). In addition, students' perceptions of the success of job placements may be important in both types of colleges, but are fundamental to occupational colleges that get funds from students by promising job outcomes.

Although sources of funding explain some differences, they do not explain the way in which colleges seek to build their legitimacy. It is remarkable that occupational colleges' descriptions match the sociological model of charter building that Persell and Cookson (1985) saw in elite prep schools, though they provide it to disadvantaged students. These colleges provide information about students' skills, and also try to build a charter they hope employers will trust to provide dependable information and a dependable supply, type, and quality of students.

Although staff reports of these different models can be distorted, it is hard to dismiss some findings: the central locations of job placement offices, the required use of career advisory offices, and the carefully developed job placement model. If this model is a fiction, it is a highly detailed one. We saw no evidence to contradict these accounts and much evidence to support them. None of the seven community colleges employ any staff whose primary responsibility is to place students in jobs, but all seven occupational colleges have several full-time job placement staff, serving sixty to 122 students per staff member. These differences reflect different resources, but also different conceptions about how college can relate to the labor market.

The unique conceptions of community colleges are evident in their staff's actions. Even when chairs of programs spend time inviting employers to advisory meetings, they often choose prominent employers who enhance their programs' perceived legitimacy, not necessarily ones who hire their students. Even when they spend time in advisory board meetings, they often do not use this time to build relationships with employers. Even when they answer employers' telephone calls, they give low priority to these calls and even resent them. Even when they provide career services, the peripheral location of these services at all these public colleges suggests that other processes are at work besides constraints on resources. Even when the State of Illinois collects information on employment outcomes of previous graduates, the data is incomplete, program heads we interviewed do not get the information, and no resources or procedures are made available for using these results.

We have reported processes, and do not attempt to systematically measure the outcomes—such as completion rates, labor-market outcomes, or employers' reactions—of the two charter approaches. We do have some indications that occupational colleges are successful in building solid employer relationships and placing students in jobs, but systematic research on the job outcomes of occupational college students is needed to test this. Community college staff in this study view charters as an attained status, arising from conformity to institutional forms and practices like Meyer's (1977) charter. In contrast, the occupational college staff view charters as requiring ongoing processes. These are two conflicting models of legitimacy, and their effectiveness may depend on institutional and external conditions. The charter concept helps identify previously ignored issues that may have practical consequences. If the charter-building approach is indeed found more appropriate for non-elite colleges and nontraditional programs, community colleges might consider investing more resources in career services and employer relations. This could be done by shifting some focus away from the extensive accreditation process. If this is not feasible, community colleges could more efficiently utilize the resources currently allocated for career services. Rather than investing time and resources with prominent employers who have no intentions of hiring their graduates, the colleges could build relationships with smaller companies that can and would offer useful information and job prospects. In some cases, local chambers of commerce might assist with such efforts. Small changes such as this would not require extensive resources and could have a positive impact on the labor market experiences of graduates.

## APPENDIX: JOB PLACEMENT, THE STUDENT EXPERIENCE*

Job placement is a major task for any institution, but it is especially challenging for the types of colleges in our study. These colleges are non-elite institutions offering non-elite (that is, associate's) degrees to disadvantaged, low achieving students who often lack relevant labor market experience. Yet these colleges propose to help these students climb the economic ladder. For students who attend college directly after high school, the hope is often to obtain better jobs than their parents or siblings. For students who attend college after working for years in unskilled jobs, the hope is to obtain better jobs than they had in the past.

It is important to grasp the magnitude of the task that these colleges undertake, and to understand how they accomplish it. Job training programs attempt a similar effort and are often unsuccessful (Martin and Grubb 2001; Heckman, LaLonde, and Smith 1999; LaLonde 1995). How do these colleges integrate the various procedures that we have described in other chapters to accomplish these goals? We have presented an analytic framework to understand the ways that colleges handle career services and job placement; this appendix describes how services are presented to students throughout their college careers and how colleges prepare, package, and place students.

---

*This appendix section was written by Julie Redline and James E. Rosenbaum.

To do so, we compare two very different career service models that guide students through the job search, focusing on student-centered activities rather than the employer relationships we addressed earlier.

The descriptions of student experiences are based on interviews with administrators and career services staff at several community colleges and at one occupational college in our sample. This occupational college was chosen as a focus because it has the most comprehensive and coherent career system in our sample. Other occupational colleges in our sample incorporate some of the same procedures, but this one provides an example of a highly developed job placement program with many diverse elements. Describing the placement procedures at this institution helps clarify and expand the student experience at a college that offers extensive job placement services and can serve as an ideal type.

## Community Colleges: Passive Career Development

As noted, career services offices at the community colleges in our sample provide no job placement and little job search assistance. Community college career services staff report that job search is an easy task that students can undertake on their own and does not require much attention, time, or energy from the college office. One career services director said, "None of the job search stuff is all that [difficult], it's not rocket science. . . . Teaching them how to use the internet is as difficult as it gets." Others echoed this opinion, emphasizing the importance of career decision making rather than job searching. This assumption that job searching is not difficult is translated into institutional goals that avoid job search services, and focus instead on career development. Career services staff specifically point out that their offices are not meant to place students in jobs; their goals are rather to help students discover their interests and choose career paths.

This goal drives the timetables and activities of these colleges. Throughout students' college years, career office activities, such as counseling or workshops, focus on career assessment. This continues until students near graduation, and at no point during the college career does this office's emphasis switch to job search or practical preparation for job search activities. The only job search assistance comes at the very end, when students realize that they need a job. These offices post unscreened job openings on bulletin boards, and provide lists of general job search Internet sites as well as a few small optional workshops on résumé preparation and interviewing skills. Very few students participate in these workshops, primarily because most students are not aware of them and those who are do not understand their possible benefits. Because job search is considered an easy task, the community colleges take few steps to reach out to students, their services are optional, and their facilities are often hard to find.

## The Occupational College: An Ongoing Active Job Search

Job placement at the private occupational college highlighted here differs in nearly every respect from the community college programs. Placement is a dominant theme, and programs for students are highly planned. Participation in job preparation and search activities is compulsory, beginning at the outset and continuing through many stages until graduation, and even afterward.

The job placement process begins at enrollment. Students are expected to declare a major when they enroll, and those who are unsure are counseled on the spot. Undecided students meet with placement staff to discuss possible fields of study and to decide on an occupational program and career path. At these meetings, students begin to plan for their futures. They learn about career options, earning potentials, likely job conditions, and employment outlooks. Students who do not encounter placement staff during enrollment first meet them at orientation, during which the staff introduce students to the services available and register them with the placement office.

Shortly after orientation, each student is assigned to a placement coordinator who assists them throughout their college careers. This coordinator regularly initiates meetings with students to discuss progress and plans, part-time jobs and internships, and later to develop résumés and interviewing skills. Coordinators whom we interviewed referred to this as a mentoring relationship. Most placement coordinators have worked in the field for which they advise (for example computer, health, business), and can offer students concrete and detailed advice about their employment futures.

Throughout college, placement staff repeatedly reach out to students regardless of whether students visit the office regularly. Staff visit classes several times each year, making presentations to students about the options and services available, and recruiting them to participate. Coordinators report that they sometimes use class rosters and systematically call students to encourage participation in job placement activities.

Even if they do not keep up-to-date with the placement office, students are nonetheless guided toward job preparation and placement through their courses and other college experiences. The director of job placement explained, "We have to get them into the mode of professional business.

How to act, how to talk, how to think, how to be." All courses are designed to teach students communication skills, regularly assigning class presentations and group projects. Students develop these skills through frequent class presentations as well as a school-wide "casual professional" dress code. The vice president of student services explained that these presentation skills are taught from the beginning because they must be developed over time; she stressed that students typically cannot wait until the actual job search to begin working on these skills.

Required courses also help students in acquiring job search skills. While career workshops are optional and rarely attended in community colleges, they are mandatory and credit-granting at this private occupational college, which offers a required professional development course for all majors. In it, students learn how to write résumés and cover letters, how to answer interview questions, and how to dress for interviews, as well as more minute details such as choosing the correct salad fork at a professional lunch and leaving appropriate messages on an answering machine. Job fairs are optional, but are strongly encouraged and regularly held. They present an opportunity for employers to make themselves known to students, both to recruit for part-time jobs and internships as well as to begin long-term relationships that might lead to jobs after graduation.

During their final semester, those few students who have largely avoided the job placement office are forced to confront it just before graduation. The placement staff man a table that students must visit when picking up their cap and gown for graduation. In addition, all students are required to fill out forms indicating their placement status, and these forms are given to placement staff after graduation. The placement staff use this information to contact each graduate individually as a final form of recruitment.

As a result of this ongoing process, every student at the college has multiple contacts with the job placement staff throughout the course of their college careers. Unlike community colleges, at which students may spend their entire college career exploring multiple options, and where career services staff encourage and focus on such exploration, this occupational college compels students to declare a specific occupational goal at the outset and to execute a careful plan by which to achieve their goal through ongoing job search preparation throughout their college career.

Job placement activities continue during the job search. When students are ready to begin, whether during college or after graduation, placement coordinators take an increasingly active role. All students are required to work with coordinators to revise and refine their résumés and practice mock interviews. (Only by special petition can students be exempted from this requirement—for instance, if they already have appropriate jobs.) Placement coordinators then send students' résumés to employers, many of whom have worked with the college for years and have requested résumés for a particular job opening. The college continues its close involvement in the job search process even after sending the résumé; the job placement staff specifically omit students' contact information from the résumé so that employers contact the placement office first, which then arranges interviews for students. This gives the college leverage in making sure that students respond appropriately and strengthens the college's relationship with employers. Critics might consider such an approach patronizing, but staff justify it on the grounds that students do not always understand how to respond and that the college has a vested interest in maintaining strong positive ties with employers.

Placement coordinators work with students on a regular basis until they find desired employment. Incentives encouraging efficient placement go beyond the coordinator's personal commitment. The college offers a placement guarantee to students that if they are not placed in a job within 180 days, the college will offer them free tuition to pursue another applied associate's degree.

The final stage occurs after the actual hire. The college's job placement staff continue their efforts, conducting follow-ups with both employers and students. After the student's initial interview, the placement coordinators contact the company to obtain details about the interview—both about how the student performed and what can be improved in the future. Later, at given intervals throughout the year following the student's employment, coordinators continue to monitor the success of the placement, surveying both employers and students. These follow-ups are essential for serving the placed student, but they are also important for maintaining strong relationships with employers and gathering inside information that can be used in placing future graduates.

The programs at the private occupational colleges in our sample differ greatly from the community college model. This alternate approach incorporates different assumptions and goals, as well as different timetables and services. We do not present outcomes of these two models and cannot conclusively argue the merit of one over the other, but seek to explain the primary differences between them. The placement-oriented goals and the comprehensive student services offered, in conjunction with the employer relationships described earlier, lead us to believe that the private occupational model may more effectively serve hard-to-place individuals and demanding employers. We find four areas in which the private occupational college model differs from the community college model:

1.  While community colleges assume that job searching is a straightforward and student-initiated activity, the private college assumes that getting a job is complex, and requires a planned campaign and institutional intervention.

2.  While the goal of community colleges is career development, mainly in the form of career counseling, the private college's goal is job placement.

3.  While the community colleges emphasize exploring career interests throughout students' college careers, the private college encourages quick career decisions and focuses on job preparation and searching over the following years.

4.  While community colleges offer passive job posting services that are optional and largely invisible, the private college offers active, mandatory, and unavoidable training and placement services.

# CHAPTER EIGHT

## LABOR-MARKET LINKING AMONG FACULTY

A s described, colleges engage in a range of institutional charter-building activities to improve their graduates' employment prospects and seamlessly usher them into relevant and high-quality jobs. Beyond these, however, individual staff can also engage in activities to build and maintain relationships with prospective employers.

Research has found that teachers and employers are largely suspicious of each other and reluctant to leave their respective domains to interact with the other (Lortie 1975; Useem 1986). We examine an important class of exceptions: two-year college faculty who go beyond formal job duties to interact with employers in order to facilitate students' labor market transitions. Using data from a sample of forty-one faculty members, who also serve as department chairs, at both community colleges and occupational colleges, we examine five questions:

- Which instructors develop linkages with employers?
- What actions do they take?
- Why do they take these actions?
- In what institutional contexts do they do so?
- What factors encourage or discourage their actions?

The interviews with department chairs allow us to understand both the various levels and types of activities that they engage in, as well as the institutional environments that facilitate or impede their behaviors.

## Previous Research: Need for Links in the Subbaccalaureate Labor Market

Despite great enthusiasm among some scholars about the contention of a correspondence between social relations of school and workplace, research has produced little evidence to indicate how this correspondence might take place. Indeed, several empirical studies observe that the two parties do not have much to do with each other (Lortie 1975; Useem 1986). Dan Lortie (1975) notes that the teaching role is characterized by being contained within classrooms, with no expectation of responsibilities outside the school. Studying school staff and employers, Elizabeth Useem (1986) finds great suspicion of each toward the other, and reluctance to trust each other or to interact. Yet education policy makers consistently call for practices that enhance the relevance of education to employment. Unfortunately, the responses have generally been small-scale programs, and studies indicate serious deficiencies in many of the reforms that have been attempted (Grubb 1995, 1996; Stern et al. 1995; Hughes 1998). A great deal of uncertainty therefore remains with regard to the specific behaviors and practices that support relationships between education and employers.

The relationships between two-year college instructors and mid-level employers are becoming increasingly important as the demand for subbaccalaureate labor grows. Students at these colleges have a growing need for information about and referrals to quality jobs; similarly, employers are demanding information about students and colleges, as well as trusted connections to potential employees. In his 1996 book, *Working in the Middle*, Grubb emphasizes the centrality of "mid-skilled" labor to the U.S. economy, noting that the subbaccalaureate labor market includes over three-fifths of all workers (2). Further, he notes that in the immediate future, the highest job-growth rates are projected for subbaccalaureate positions like technicians and support staff, especially in areas such as health and information technology (4). As such, two-year colleges play a critical role in the nation's workforce development and can provide a particularly rich source of data on education-employment connections.

If the benefits of subbaccalaureate education—for both employers and employees—are to be realized in the labor market, it is important that students find work in the fields they have studied (Grubb 1996). Finding such work requires good information, which, Grubb asserts, is especially hard to come by in the subbaccalaureate labor market. Given such imperfect information, Grubb (1996) identifies colleges' institutional relationships with employers as a critical component in the labor market success of their students.

School contacts with employers serve the critical function of conveying information between employers and students (that is, prospective employees). Signaling theory (Spence 1974) provides the most direct discussion of the role of school staff in this process, positing that faculty can serve as authoritative sources of information on the level of the students' knowledge and skills necessary for employment (Rosenbaum et al. 1990). Although colleges' credentials are intended to signal students' competencies, employers want more details about applicants, and faculty-employer relationships may influence the kinds of information that can be conveyed about students, especially where the content of the students' credentials is unclear to employers.

Despite their critical role providing trusted information between students and employers, Grubb (1996, 4) cites the "sluggish responsiveness of many educational institutions to shifting [labor market] demand" as a major hurdle that community colleges need to overcome in order to enhance their graduates' labor market outcomes. Dougherty (1994, 67) arrives at the same conclusion, arguing that "the community college indeed dances to the rhythms of the labor market, but it rarely keeps very good time." The implication is that community colleges are, to some extent, missing the mark in supporting their students' labor market success.

Although Grubb's and Dougherty's analyses focus on the institution, Brewer and Gray (1999) examine college-employer relationships at the individual level with their study of labor-market linking activities by community college faculty. The authors' systematic analysis of the type and extent of employer linkages, however, yields anything but systematic results. On the contrary, Dominic Brewer and Maryann Gray conclude that linking activities "were often ad hoc and informal in nature" (415). Bailey, Badway, and Gumport (2002, 34–35) echo this sentiment in their analysis of public and private colleges, calling job placement at community colleges a "haphazard process . . . based on a case by case system of individual faculty or staff using employment relationships for the students in their programs."

On the other hand, Grubb and Brewer and Gray do identify institutional barriers to community colleges' links to labor markets. Among other obstacles, the authors point to a lack of resources and institutional support for linking activities, as well as departmental or programmatic isolation within colleges that impedes the flow of information. Grubb optimistically asserts that linkages can be improved (173), yet Brewer and Gray note the general weakness of conceptual foundations and lack of empirical evidence for how linking actually occurs (414). This fact may underlie Grubb's insistence that "there is no substitute for individual community colleges examining the practices linking them to employers" (173). Despite a focus on institutions, however, these authors have not identified standard practices that might support college-employer linkages in a variety of institutional settings.

## EXAMINING THE PROCESS OF LINKING: NEW APPROACHES

Although Grubb (1996) and Brewer and Gray (1999) correctly describe and diagnose many of the problems related to two-year college labor-market connections, and they offer some solutions, their analysis remains at the aggregate level. Even Brewer and Gray and Thomas Bailey and his colleagues, who use interviews and case studies as part of their analyses, present findings that speak primarily of colleges and instructors on average. This analytical approach is certainly useful, but it fails to shed light on the processes by which two-year college faculty actually make and maintain labor market connections, or the variation within the averages. We know very little about how or why some faculty manage to overcome institutional barriers and attend to relationships with employers. As such, those linkages that do exist are inevitably viewed as random, the serendipitous result of particular individuals acting in specific contexts. Previous research has said little about how colleges might adjust their own practices to better support labor-market linking.

We draw on extensive qualitative data to examine in depth the processes at work in two-year college faculty members' connections with employers. These data are used to parse out the diverse behaviors and practices that make up the aggregate approach of two-year college faculty to labor-market linking. While Bailey and his colleagues choose to focus on averages, and conclude that "the quality of these relationships varies across programs" (35), we try to determine which programs are marked by what qualities, and how and why instructors are able to capitalize on contextual supports or overcome obstacles to develop labor market ties. We find that certain institutional factors appear to inhibit labor-market linking activities and the exchange of information between students and employers, while other institutional factors can support this process. In addition, we describe how these relationships vary by occupational field. In identifying the common characteristics of instructors, programs, and institutions that emerge as patterns in what might otherwise appear to be ad hoc or haphazard practices, these findings may inform educators and policy makers

TABLE 8.1    Description of Program Chair Interview Sample

| Program | Community Colleges | Occupational Colleges | Total |
|---|---|---|---|
| Business and management | 6 | 3 | 9 |
| Health | 5 | 2 | 7 |
| Computer | 5 | 2 | 7 |
| Electronics and engineering technology | 2 | 4 | 6 |
| Design (CAD, architecture, etc.) | 2 | 2 | 4 |
| Accounting | 3 | 0 | 3 |
| Paralegal–court reporter | 0 | 2 | 2 |
| Office administration–secretarial | 2 | 0 | 2 |
| Environmental technology | 1 | 0 | 1 |
| Total | 26 | 15 | 41 |

*Source:* Author's data.

about the elements that promote colleges' labor market linkages and, ultimately, help students to succeed.

## ANALYTIC APPROACH

We focus on program coordinators and department heads who also serve as instructors, maximizing comparability among respondents' actual job duties. At the same time, we allow for the greatest degree of comparability with past research, which has looked primarily at the role of instructors in creating and maintaining labor market linkages. The subsample includes forty-one program chairs from five public and five private colleges (we were unable to interview faculty at four of the fourteen colleges in the broader sample). All of these program chairs are also faculty with teaching responsibilities. Most have no explicit responsibilities for interacting with employers. They do, however, bear primary responsibility for the well-being of their programs, especially given that many other faculty are adjunct, only responsible for teaching isolated courses, but not for program duties. This responsibility may prompt some to initiate additional actions not formally required. The sample is not intended to be representative of two-year college faculty, more generally, or even of occupational program faculty. Nevertheless, these individuals offer a rich source of information on the processes that underlie faculty-employer contacts, given their positions in career-oriented programs. Table 8.1 describes the program chair interview sample.[1]

The individual program chair is the unit of analysis. After coding for the particular linking activities of each individual, as well as the intensity of their involvement in linking activities, each program chair was rated as low, medium, or high in linking activity compared to the other chairs in the sample. We briefly explain each level, using a typical case for each. For the sake of consistency, the examples are all from the same occupational field, computer information systems (CIS), and community colleges.

## Low Linking Activity

The only linking activity Mr. Jones (all names are pseudonyms) described in the interview is his personal interaction with colleagues in the computer information systems (CIS) field. He reported, however, that he doesn't often use these contacts to get students jobs. He explained, "People who are looking for students usually go to the four-year schools first. If they don't find somebody there, they'll try to find somebody in-house who could be promoted into that. They don't often come here. Or if they do, they come here with unrealistic expectations." As noted in chapter 7, this is the program chair who said his department's advisory committee "[would] just be five of my best friends . . . and we'll have a lunch somewhere." Mr. Jones expressed some suspicion about the value of contacts with employers, and his actions reflected this ambiguity.

## Medium Linking Activity

Ms. Mark is the CIS chair at a different community college. She described her work with the department's advisory committee explicitly in terms of their usefulness as a potential source of jobs for students. She also noted that adjunct faculty in her department, who continued to work in the field, sometimes had job opportunities from their places of employment, and that "they share that with me." She continued, "And I do get a lot of calls from companies in the district that they're looking for help-desk people, support people, whatever." Note that she engaged in several different types of labor-market linking, but she most often received information from contacts who approach her, rather than taking the initiative herself to foster contacts. This passive-active distinction often separates individuals coded as medium versus those coded as high for linking activities.

## High Linking Activity

Like Ms. Mark, Ms. Lewis spoke of adjunct faculty as an important source of information about jobs and the labor market. Rather than waiting for them to come to her, however, she reported making efforts to stay in constant communication with them. In addition to finding faculty with industry experience to teach courses, she explained, "I see my job as not only hiring these people, but also going out to industry, and not just having a meeting yearly with the new advisory committee, [but] actively being out there and seeing what they want." She also conducted surveys of her program's graduates to see how they have fared in the labor market, as well as surveys of employers who have hired her students to assess whether they were meeting employer expectations.

## INSTITUTIONAL STRUCTURES AND PRACTICES

Earlier studies have appropriately emphasized faculty's modest average involvement with employers. We examine the nature of linkages that are forged, with special focus on institutional contexts. Several key issues are addressed. As the literature indicates, there is, indeed, a certain ad hoc element to faculty efforts to make labor market connections. But faculty behaviors appear to be more patterned and more nuanced than surveys indicate. Indeed, qualitative evidence reveals that certain institutional structures and practices may contribute to the level of faculty effort directed toward building and maintaining links with potential employers. These include both structures and practices of the college itself, as well as the infrastructures of professions with which programs are associated.

### Resource Constraints

Beyond a particular instructor or program in question, colleges themselves can play an important role in fostering as well as hindering faculty labor market linkages through their own institutional structures and practices. Perhaps the most commonly cited institutional barrier to instructors reaching out to employers is the resource constraint that so many educational institutions face (compare Grubb 1996). Instructors in our sample, too, reported that resource constraints—especially on time—prohibit, or at least inhibit, linking activity. On the other hand, fiscal constraints do not appear to be as problematic: All but one of those faculty members who sought reimbursement for linking activities (for example, participating in professional meetings, invited talks) reported that funds were readily available. It should be noted that they sought small amounts of funds, and it is possible that some faculty would not seek financial support for linking activities because they believe it would be a fruitless endeavor. Or, perhaps more important, if financial resources were more available, more administrators and support staff could be hired and faculty would be less pressed for time. Indeed, hiring new faculty (which could, for example, be handled with the help of human resources administrators) and paperwork (which could be handled with the help of clerical support staff) were two of the time burdens that department chairs mentioned most frequently.

## Part-Time Faculty

A similar result of institutional resource constraints that we observed at most of the colleges in our sample is the trend away from hiring full-time, tenure-track faculty in favor of part-time and adjunct instructors. Interestingly, this trend appears to support employer linkages on the one hand, yet impede them on the other. Among computer-oriented programs in particular—such as computer information systems (CIS), information technology (IT), and network specialist—chairs frequently cited adjuncts' experience in the field as a source of labor market connections that could benefit entire programs and individual students alike. Chairs explained how they may update curricula based on input from faculty working in the field. Respondents also reported that individual students sometimes get jobs directly through such connections. Still, not all program chairs viewed such adjunct involvement as beneficial. Certainly, as one IT chair phrased it, "part-time faculty enhance the program because they're out there doing what it is that they're teaching." On the other hand, a CIS chair lamented that "the loss of four full-time teachers is a major loss to the department. . . . I can't improve my program with part-timers." Only two program chairs, both at community colleges, were explicitly negative about part-timers and adjuncts. In both cases, the chairs felt that the time required for finding and hiring faculty impinged on their other activities, including making employer contacts. The CIS instructor just cited also reported that high turn-over among part-time and adjunct faculty resulted in curricular discontinuity.

## Division of Labor within Bureaucracy

A final category of institutional supports and obstacles is bureaucratic. The division of labor within the colleges often assigns contact with employers to a specific person or unit. Most prominently in our broader sample of college staff, representatives of career services offices were likely to report making employer contacts as a contractual obligation. Similarly, department and program chairs often named a specific person—usually the coordinator of internship or externship programs—as the person formally charged with forging employer linkages within their departments. The benefit of this type of division of labor is that contacts are institutionalized and more likely to be sustained, despite staff turnover or changes in local job markets.

On the other hand, bureaucratic structures tend to isolate departments and individuals with specific functions. In the presence of career services and internship coordination structures, faculty can easily dismiss their own potential role in connecting with the labor market, as such connections are formally defined as someone else's job. In fact, of the twelve instructors coded as low for linking activities, six suggested career services as the appropriate place for making connections with employers; four of these instructors offered this as a response when we asked them specifically for their own linking activities. Even so, among these instructors, their level of faith in the function of career services varied widely. An office administration technology chair was enthusiastic: "I always try to connect [students] with career services." A CIS chair was more blasé: "I assume that [students] will go to, at some time, the . . . job placement office." This evidence should by no means be interpreted to mean that career services offices are not useful to institutions or students. Rather, it is only noted that the presence of such offices may discourage some faculty from considering it to be their obligation or in their interest to work on employer linkages.

## DIFFERENCES ACROSS COLLEGE TYPES

Although the institutional issues identified to this point applied more or less equally to all of the colleges in the sample, some institutional factors affected faculty linking activities differently at community and occupational colleges. The most prominent difference between the community colleges and their occupational counterparts was the nature of faculty interactions with career services and advisory committees. The CIS chair cited, who "assumed" students will eventually find their way to career services is somewhat typical for the community college faculty, in that he did not appear to know exactly what services are provided (for example, "job placement," as he called the office, is not offered); nor does he consider it his business to know. At the occupational colleges in our sample, bureaucratic division did result in a few program chairs citing career services or internship coordinators as the people in charge of making contacts with the job market. Nevertheless, these individuals were aware of precisely who could provide a student with information on jobs or internships, as well as the nature of the services these individuals or offices could offer.

With respect to advisory committees, community college program chairs report a wide range of involvement: from the CIS chair cited earlier, who had no interaction with the group, and who would be satisfied with a committee of "five friends having lunch," to a management chair who considered the committee her primary connection to the corporate world, meeting with them frequently, and relying heavily on their input in devising the curriculum. In contrast, the program chairs from occupational colleges were more uniform in reporting frequent and meaningful involvement with their advisory committees. Indeed, one of the least active program chairs among the occupational college faculty continued to meet frequently with his advisory committee (between two and four times each year).

Moreover, because the occupational colleges are private institutions, applying the information garnered from labor market linkages to enhance the curriculum is usually a much more streamlined process than at the community colleges in our sample. Community college faculty describe cumbersome and bureaucratic processes of curricular innovation. "You gotta jump through a lot of hoops," one business chair said, in a statement typical of the community college faculty. A business chair at an occupational college described a very different process, typical of his counterparts at the occupational schools: "We move so quickly—with almost no bureaucracy—that if I want to make a change, we make it."

These differences come, perhaps, as no surprise. As explained in earlier chapters, the two institutions have very different histories and mandates. Community colleges have traditionally emphasized general education and transfer to four-year colleges, whereas occupational colleges have emphasized more specific workforce training. Indeed, the interview data show that the faculty at the two college types articulate very different institutional or departmental missions. Community college faculty discussed their mission as broad and holistic, using terms such as *developmental*, and *life-long learning*. As one community college department chair explained, "with our mission, really, you've got to serve everybody's needs. That's the function of a community college, [to] deal with all the different needs." In contrast, occupational college faculty saw their school's mission as more narrow, focusing on career preparation and entry into suitable skilled jobs. They used terms such as *applied* and *career-oriented* to describe their missions. As one chair succinctly put it, "our mission is to serve students, so that they [have] an opportunity to be successful in a career."

The different institutional contexts, respectively, suggest that instructors at the private schools might be more apt to engage in higher levels of linking activity. Table 8.2 offers some—though by no means overwhelming—

TABLE 8.2    Level of Linking Activity by College Type

| Level of Linking | Community Colleges | Occupational Colleges |
|---|---|---|
| Low | 35% | 20% |
| | (9) | (3) |
| Medium | 19% | 20% |
| | (5) | (3) |
| High | 46% | 60% |
| | (12) | (9) |
| Total N | 26 | 15 |

*Source:* Author's data.
Actual N appears in parentheses.

support for that contention. Less than half (46 percent) of community college instructors were coded as engaging in high levels of linking activity, and about a third were coded as low on linking. At the occupational colleges, 60 percent of instructors were found to engage in high levels of linking, while just 20 percent were at the low end. It is worthy of note that coding was conducted without explicit information on the respondent's department or college, but this information was, nonetheless, often revealed in the transcript. It is also important to recognize that despite institutional environments that offer little support for them, nearly half of community college instructors still manage to engage in a good number of linking activities.

## INDIVIDUAL FACTORS

In open coding of the interview data, two related themes emerged that suggested patterns of involvement at the individual level: affiliation with a traditional profession and the notion of work as a calling.

In sociology, professions are defined as exclusive fields that both create abstract knowledge and apply it to particular cases (Abbott 1988; Perlstadt 1998). Classic examples of traditional professions include medicine and law. Their exclusivity is a result of both high educational qualifications and endorsement requirements that are stipulated and controlled by a governing body, usually a professional association (Perlstadt 1998). Such regulation of membership leads to shared knowledge and activities, which could be considered a shared professional culture. Accordingly, faculty reports suggest that the characteristics of professions that are especially pertinent

to faculty labor market linkages include the rules and regulations governing membership and established membership networks.

The chair of a physical therapy assistant program at a public college
offered her explanation of the situation: "As faculty, we're responsible for
maintaining currency in our field. . . . You read the publications, you read
the journals, go to professional development course work. We attend state
and international meetings . . . and so we keep up with those kinds of
things." Professional associations foster both social and work-related interactions among members. Asked how students get jobs, an architecture
instructor hinted at the importance of such organizations: "Well, you tie into
the *network*, the *architectural community*" [author's emphasis]. Echoing this
language, the chair of occupational therapy (OT) at one community college
noted that employers prefer to deal with the department directly, rather
than contacting the college's career services office: "They would call the program. The *OT community* is not that large" [author's emphasis].

As a point of contrast, instructors in fields that lack a distinct professional
culture also feel compelled to stay abreast of developments in their occupational area. Yet in the absence of formal associations, shared culture, or professional requirements, their energies may yield fewer concrete linkages
with employers. For example, instructors in CIS, business, and secretarial
departments mentioned reading trade publications to stay abreast of their
respective fields. Such endeavors almost certainly ensure that instructors
have some appropriate information on labor markets to share with their students; but such broad information is only one useful aspect of linkages.
Reading industry publications would not normally translate into actual contact with potential employers or sharing of specific information about a student or a job.

Interestingly, the implications of college program association with a
profession are important for instructors in both an individual sense and a
structural sense. With respect to the individual instructor, membership in
a profession leads to personal identification with that profession; and at the
same time, membership fosters activity with colleagues in the profession.
The chair of the paralegal program at a private college offered a rich explanation of the relationship:

> I do a lot of networking. I'm very involved in the [county] bar associa-
> tion. . . . I go to some [city] bar association committee meetings. I try
> and network with attorneys whenever I can. I mean, those are employ-
> ers. Those are employers for paralegals. I'm on the publications board
> for the [county] bar association. . . . I'm on the labor and employment

committee for [the bar association], I'm also on [several bar association committees] . . . so I try and meet as many lawyers as I can, consistent with my academic load.

Asked whether such activities are part of his job description, this program chair hesitated: "I don't know how to answer that question. I really don't know. I mean, it's something I feel I need to do if I'm going to publicize the program." This instructor certainly appeared motivated by a personal sense of responsibility to the program in his charge. Moreover, he clearly identified himself with the legal profession. Asked about adapting the paralegal curriculum to suit the needs of the legal profession, he said, "I know how lawyers work. I've been one; I am one."

In sum, the program chair's personal identification with the legal profession was bolstered by professional structures that encourage collegiality and enforce membership rules. Both personal and structural aspects foster and sustain the instructor's links to potential employers. An accounting instructor, who was also the chair of the business department at a community college, offered a similar example. He described himself as "intimately involved" with accounting firms in the city. "I keep an active communication with managers and partners," he continued, "because we're members of the American Accounting Association." Again, asked if this was part of his formal job description, he responded, "I consider that my responsibility, however, I don't think that is part of my formal responsibilities in terms of my contract." Still, he also noted that "the goal is to prepare people to take the CPA exam," so participation in the formal professional association (which determines exam content) is reinforced beyond personal identification with the broader profession.

Given the small size of the faculty interview sample it is difficult to detect distinct patterning of labor-market linking by program. Even when combined into groups of related departments, our sample includes four or fewer respondents from most fields. Table 8.3 displays data from the four programs with the most respondents: business, computers, electronics engineering, and health. It is interesting to note, as table 8.3 shows, that chairs of health programs—which are marked by relatively strict rules for employment, including certification—show overwhelmingly high levels of linking activity (86 percent were coded as high linkers, and none were coded low). Instructors in business and computer fields—which are not governed by professional associations—show relatively low levels of linking (only about 30 percent coded high in linking, and over 40 percent coded low in each case).

TABLE 8.3    Level of Linking Activity by Program Type

| Level of Linking | Business | Computer | Electronics or Engineering | Health | Others |
|---|---|---|---|---|---|
| Low | 44% | 43% | 33% | 0 | 25% |
|  | (4) | (3) | (2) |  | (3) |
| Medium | 22% | 29% | 17% | 14% | 25% |
|  | (2) | (2) | (1) | (1) | (3) |
| High | 33% | 29% | 50% | 86% | 50% |
|  | (3) | (2) | (3) | (6) | (6) |
| Total N | 9 | 7 | 6 | 7 | 12 |

*Source:* Author's data.
Actual N appears in parentheses.

## OVERCOMING BARRIERS TO LABOR-MARKET LINKING

As noted, the small size and geographic homogeneity of the faculty inter-view sample limit the extent to which the findings of this study might be generalizable. Future research should include larger numbers of respon-dents from each type of college and each instructional program. Such research could include surveys as well as interviews as data sources. Still, the identification of institutional contexts that might support or inhibit labor-market linking among two-year college faculty is useful in that it combines both the individual and institutional perspectives that have been the focus of separate bodies of research in the past.

Institutional factors that appear to inhibit labor-market linking activities include resource constraints (especially time) and discontinuities related to the high rates of turnover among part-time and adjunct faculty. On the other hand, such nontenured instructors can also be a source of labor mar-ket linkages because they are often still working in the field that they teach. The isolation of career functions, such as placement and internship coordi-nation, encourages some faculty members to conclude that linking with labor markets is someone else's job. As a matter of fact, very few faculty members cited linking with the labor market as a formal duty. Trends were somewhat different between the two college types, however. With their explicit career education mission, occupational colleges appear to support somewhat higher levels of linking activities than community colleges. Individual involvement in professional associations is another factor that may pattern faculty linking activity, though our data in this respect is only suggestive. Identification with a profession, as well as rules and regulations governing membership appear to enhance linking both in an individual and a structural sense.

These results suggest potential steps for improving faculty-employer linkages at two-year colleges. For instance, our interview data suggest that the benefits of relying on adjunct faculty may be more mixed than is usually thought, and the presumed benefits of adjuncts' personal contacts must be compared with the sacrifices in program continuity as well as linking activities by program chairs (whose time is consumed by the continual need to recruit new adjunct faculty). Likewise, the benefits of separate career services offices may be offset somewhat by the fact that they may lead some faculty members to conclude that labor market links are not something that students need from them. In all of the community colleges we studied, top administrators have emphasized occupational preparation, much like the top administrators in prior studies (Brint and Karabel 1989). However, our analyses have found many examples where the enthusiastic words of community college presidents are not accompanied by corresponding actions of occupational program chairs. Attention to the institutional issues discussed here might help to align the two parties' attitudes and behaviors.

The meager success of many school-work reforms and the mutual suspicions of teachers and employers indicate the difficulties of labor-market linking endeavors. This study helps us to understand the linkages through elaboration of the processes by which two-year college faculty are able to utilize institutional supports and overcome institutional barriers to develop relationships with employers that may benefit their students in the labor market. By systematically examining which instructors help foster employer connections, and in what settings, we offer insight into the conditions that support education-employment reforms. We next examine the influence of such linking activities on student behaviors and attainment at college.

# CHAPTER NINE

## EDUCATIONAL OUTCOMES
## OF LABOR-MARKET LINKING

Although labor-market linking has obvious benefits on outcomes after graduation, here we examine whether such linking can improve outcomes during college. First, using student survey data from the fourteen colleges discussed earlier, we determine how student effort and confidence in college are influenced by their perceptions of the usefulness of college and teacher contacts in securing employment. Next, using national data, we determine whether job placement services are similarly associated with timely completion of the associate's degree.

As noted, systematic information about school-employer contacts can be difficult to obtain because these linkages often rely on informal arrangements between individual teachers and employers (Brewer and Gray 1999). Moreover, many of the best national longitudinal studies of students (NELS and NLSY, for example) and the best studies of employers (Neckerman and Kirschenman 1991; Holzer 1996; Moss and Tilly 2001) offer poor information about the use of such contacts for placing students in appropriate jobs. Although the value of school-employer linkages has most often been considered in terms of employment and wages after graduation (labor market outcomes), if employer contacts can help students get good jobs, they might also have benefits for student motivation in school.

Previous research has danced around the issue of student motivation without directly addressing the ways that institutional structures—specifically those that foster employer contacts—may affect students and encourage them to excel academically and graduate on time. Laurence Steinberg (1996) emphasizes that motivation may be enhanced by students' perceptions of curriculum relevance, but does not consider what institutional actions might stimulate those perceptions and he has nothing to say about employer contacts. Vincent Tinto's (1993) model of student integration—which is arguably the dominant theoretical model in research on postsecondary attainment—suggests that students' persistence through college is influenced by factors that integrate the student into the college community, for example, extracurricular activities and living on campus (neither of which are common in non-residential two-year colleges). He does not, however, examine labor market contacts or other incentives that might encourage the student to complete the degree to gain potential rewards after graduation. Even some reforms that consider the motivating influence of careers focus only on adding career content to instruction, not on employer contacts that could provide concrete incentives (Kemple and Scott-Clayton 2004; Stern et al. 1995). In contrast, other nations operate differently. Stephen Hamilton and Klaus Hurrelman (1994) describe the ways that apprenticeship connections provide incentives that motivate German students and suggest that motivation could be increased in American colleges with more transparent connections between school and the labor market.

Relatively few scholars have considered the effects of school-employer linkages on students who are still in school. Furthermore, all of this work has been in high schools rather than in colleges. Studies of high-school academies combining academic and vocational curricula have focused on achievement, attendance, and drop-out (Kemple and Scott-Clayton, 2004; Stern et al. 1995). They have not examined school or instructor labor-market linkages as a potential factor influencing positive outcomes for students, even though some academies may have such relationships.

Other studies of secondary schools find that many students believe that high school is irrelevant (Steinberg 1996; Stinchcombe 1965; Rosenbaum 2001), and reformers call for practices that enhance the relevance of education to employment. However, few of these analyses look outside the school's walls (Hamilton 1990; Rosenbaum 2001). It is difficult to expect students to exert effort in school if there is no ostensible material payoff on graduation. Most observers assume that students have some reason to be motivated in school, and implicitly assume that subsequent societal institutions will reward students' school efforts. This is probably true for high-school students aspiring to selective colleges, but may not be so for students aspiring to jobs, given that employers' hiring criteria and earnings are often unrelated to student effort or achievement, at least at the high school level (Bishop 1989; Rosenbaum 2001).

High school reformers may ignore employer contacts because they want all high school graduates to attend college. Nonetheless, it is hard to explain why college reforms also fail to consider employer contacts. Like the high school career academies, college level reforms also tend to emphasize instructional practices that integrate occupational content into the curriculum (Grubb 1996; Perin 2001), but little is said about forging actual linkages to employers. However, given the many occupational students who say that getting a job is a primary reason for entering college, college-employer contacts might bolster incentives and convince students that their college efforts will have payoffs.

## IMPACT ON EFFORT, CONFIDENCE, AND DEGREE COMPLETION

Before trying to understand differences in student motivation and completion, however, it is important to note that motivation is only part of the equation. Two-year colleges have historically catered to students who might otherwise be unable to attend college, whether because of past achievement or current obligations outside school (Dougherty 1994). We find, as noted earlier, few differences in students at the two college types in these respects, and that those differences do not indicate systematic advantage in one group. For example, whereas community college students reported working slightly more hours per week, occupational college students were more likely to have dependent children. Table 9.1 displays descriptive statistics of our local survey sample.

Despite enrolling apparently similar students, the differences in degree-completion rates eight years after entry at the two types of colleges are striking(see table 1.1). Of course, students may have difficulty perceiving eight-year completion rates, so a shorter time frame may be pertinent for student perceptions. Among first-time beginners in postsecondary education, just 26 percent of community college students (and just 11 percent of African Americans in this group) finish the associate's degree in five years (Bailey et al. 2003). At private two-year colleges, three-year completion rates are much higher, ranging from about 35 to 50 percent for the same students, depending on the type of college (Bailey, Badway and Gumport 2002; Futures Project 2000). Although community colleges enroll more part-time students than private colleges, five years would allow for a student to register at less than 50 percent of full-time and still complete the two-year degree if he or she were on track.

TABLE 9.1    Sample Means for "College to Careers" Student Survey

| | All Degree Seekers | | Community College Degree Seekers | | Occupational College Degree Seekers | |
|---|---|---|---|---|---|---|
| | Mean | SD | Mean | SD | Mean | SD |
| Effort versus high school | 4.295 | .810 | 4.200 | .853 | 4.338 | .787 |
| Confidence regarding degree | 4.102 | .848 | 3.930 | .892 | 4.177 | .816 |
| Female | .522 | .500 | .550 | .498 | .509 | .500 |
| Gender not reported | .062 | .240 | .052 | .224 | .066 | .247 |
| African American | .212 | .409 | .131 | .338 | .248 | .432 |
| Hispanic | .245 | .430 | .196 | .398 | .266 | .442 |
| Asian or Asian American | .113 | .316 | .148 | .355 | .097 | .296 |
| Race other or not reported | .130 | .336 | .128 | .334 | .131 | .337 |
| Age | 24.10 | 6.82 | 24.51 | 7.41 | 23.92 | 6.54 |
| Age not reported | .050 | .217 | .040 | .196 | .054 | .226 |
| High school GPA (four-point scale) | 2.677 | .713 | 2.721 | .714 | 2.657 | .712 |
| High school GPA not reported | .014 | .116 | .016 | .124 | .013 | .111 |
| Parent education (truncated)[a] | 2.670 | 1.366 | 2.908 | 1.455 | 2.565 | 1.311 |
| Took any remedial | .420 | .494 | .721 | .449 | .287 | .452 |
| Occupational college | .693 | .461 | — | — | — | — |
| Agrees college contacts could help get good job | 3.610 | .986 | 3.221 | .959 | 3.783 | .947 |
| Agrees teacher contacts could help get good job | 3.28 | .988 | 3.111 | .987 | 3.359 | .979 |
| Job placement | .619 | .486 | .560 | .497 | .646 | .478 |
| N | 3,328 | | 1,023 | | 2,305 | |

*Source:* Authors' data.
*Note:* All colleges are located in a single metropolitan area in Illinois.
[a] Parent education: 2 = high school graduate, 3 = some college.

Using our student survey from the fourteen colleges, analyses limit the sample to students who report at least an associate's as their degree goal (N = 3,328). A great diversity of students attend these colleges, but we focus on those in comparable programs preparing for similarly accredited degrees in the same group of occupational majors, and thus are likely to be studying students with similar goals in the two types of colleges.

The following analyses examine whether the promise of job placement and students' perceptions of college-employer contacts are related to students' reported changes in school effort and confidence about obtaining a college degree. We coded a college as offering job placement if the career-services staff member interviewed reported that the college offered placement or if college materials made such claims (or both). Faculty reports of offering placement were alone not enough to consider a college as offering placement, given that instructors would presumably only offer such help to a few students from their own program, and most students could thus not anticipate with any certainty that they would benefit from such help. In measuring student reactions to contacts, we use students' responses to two items: "My teachers' contacts could help me get a good job"; and "My college's contacts could help me get a good job" (responses on a five-point Likert scale: 1 = "strongly disagree" and 5 = "strongly agree").

Using OLS regression, we examined two time-variant outcomes: students' reported changes in effort in college compared with high school; and students' reported changes in confidence about obtaining the college degree since beginning at their present college. The effort variable is perhaps more problematic for inferring a college effect on student behavior because it measures change since high school, and many factors could have influenced students in that time. Still, the validity of the measure is supported in that the data show a significant negative correlation between this reported effort and students' high school grades, and a positive correlation between reported effort and college grades. Moreover, because both outcomes measure change since prior schooling experiences (for effort) and since entering the college (for degree confidence), we hope to control for unobserved student characteristics that could influence effort and confidence and might also have impacted students' selection into the different schools.

Because students in our sample are clustered within classrooms in schools, adjusting for potential correlation in the data is necessary. Toward this end, we used Huber-White statistical techniques (using the robust cluster commands available with Stata software) and report the resulting robust standard errors in the tables that follow. The adjustment does not affect the regression coefficients, but adjusts standard errors to account for potential non-independence of observations. Note that we ran the same models as ordered logistic regressions, given the ordered categorical nature of the dependent variables. The direction and significance of coefficients were virtually identical to the OLS analyses, which we present here for greater ease of discussion and interpretation.

Our first analysis examined the determinants of students' effort at college. Students were asked, "Compared to when I was in high school, my effort now is [insert response]." Responses ranged from "much lower"(1) to "much higher" (5) on a five-point scale. Table 9.2 reports the influence of a host of variables on students' reported change in effort at college. Following the lead of prior research on college completion, we control for several student-level independent variables: gender, race, age, high-school achievement, and parent education. Given the patterns identified in our qualitative analyses, we also control for college type (that is, public community college or private occupational college). In addition to using a time-variant dependent variable to help control for unobserved heterogeneity, we also run a final model including school fixed effects in order to estimate the influence of students' perceptions of job contacts even among students who have selected into the same school.

As the baseline model (table 9.2, model 1)—without linking variables—shows, gender significantly predicts effort changes, with females showing greater increases in effort than males. Black and Latino students report significantly greater effort increases than their white counterparts (the reference category). The effects of age are significant and nonlinear, with the positive influence of age peaking at about forty-four years before declining (as the coefficient for age-squared shows). High school grades are negatively associated with increased effort, which makes sense, given that those students with high achievement in the past are likely to have exerted a great deal of effort during high school. Finally, private colleges are significantly associated with reported effort increases. As model 2 shows, however, this private college influence is greatly diminished (from b = .138, p = .000, in model 1 to b = .070, p = .045, in model 2) when the linking variables—job placement and students' perceptions of college and teacher contacts—are included in the model. Placement, and specifically student perceptions of contacts, shows strong and significant influences on students' reported effort. Inclusion in the model of the linking variables also reduces the racial effects seen in the baseline model to levels that are no longer statistically significant. This may indicate that African American and Latino students' reported effort changes are related to their perception of the usefulness of linkages, or that the institutions where linkages are most available and apparent to students also somehow support these minority students' effort increases.

Next, we asked students to gauge changes in their confidence about obtaining a college degree. Students were asked, "Compared to when I first

TABLE 9.2   OLS Regression, Change in Effort and Confidence, on Variables

| Covariate | Model 1 Effort Versus High School Coef. (Robust SE) | β | Model 2 Effort Versus High School Coef. (Robust SE) | β | Model 3 Confidence Regarding Degree Coef. (Robust SE) | β | Model 4 Confidence Regarding Degree Coef. (Robust SE) | β |
|---|---|---|---|---|---|---|---|---|
| Female | .103*** (.029) | .064 | .094*** (.029) | .058 | .090** (.031) | .053 | .079** (.031) | .047 |
| Gender not reported | -.060 (.066) | -.017 | -.052 (.065) | -.015 | -.131 (.071) | -.037 | -.124 (.070) | -.035 |
| African American | .096* (.039) | .048 | .051 (.040) | .026 | .287*** (.043) | .139 | .238*** (.045) | .115 |
| Hispanic | .098* (.039) | .052 | .078 (.040) | .042 | .229*** (.042) | .116 | .210*** (.044) | .107 |
| Asian or Asian American | -.049 (.051) | -.019 | -.070 (.051) | -.028 | .151** (.050) | .056 | .127** (.050) | .047 |
| Race other or not reported | -.008 (.049) | -.003 | -.021 (.048) | -.009 | .034 (.053) | .013 | .022 (.053) | .009 |
| Age | .045*** (.011) | .383 | .049*** (.011) | .410 | .032** (.012) | .259 | .037** (.012) | .297 |
| Age-squared | -.0005** (.0002) | -.271 | -.0006*** (.0002) | -.294 | -.0005** (.0002) | -.264 | -.0006** (.0002) | -.296 |

| | b | β | b | β | b | β | b | β |
|---|---|---|---|---|---|---|---|---|
| Age not reported | −.026 | −.007 | .004 | .0009 | .023 | .006 | .064 | .016 |
| | (.074) | | (.072) | | (.075) | | (.073) | |
| High school GPA | −.244** | −.215 | −.242*** | −.213 | −.001 | −.001 | .001 | .001 |
| | (.021) | | (.020) | | (.022) | | (.021) | |
| High school GPA not reported | .090 | .013 | .083 | .012 | −.200 | −.027 | −.210 | −.029 |
| | (.101) | | (.102) | | (.120) | | (.123) | |
| Parent education | .003 | .005 | .004 | .007 | −.005 | −.007 | −.004 | −.007 |
| | (.011) | | (.011) | | (.012) | | (.011) | |
| Took any remedial | .058 | .035 | .040 | .024 | .033 | .019 | .010 | .006 |
| | (.031) | | (.031) | | (.032) | | (.031) | |
| Occupational college | .138*** | .079 | .070* | .040 | .219*** | .119 | .126*** | .068 |
| | (.035) | | (.035) | | (.036) | | (.036) | |
| Agrees college contacts could help get good job | — | — | .085*** | .104 | — | — | .114*** | .133 |
| | | | (.018) | | | | (.019) | |
| Agrees teacher contacts could help get good job | — | — | .042* | .052 | — | — | .069*** | .080 |
| | | | (.016) | | | | (.019) | |
| Job placement | — | — | .084** | .051 | — | — | .089** | .051 |
| | | | (.031) | | | | (.032) | |
| Constant | 3.96*** | | 3.48*** | | 3.33*** | | 2.65*** | |
| | (.176) | | (.192) | | (.196) | | (.206) | |
| R-squared | .080 | | .100 | | .046 | | .081 | |

*Source:* Authors' data.

N = 3,328; *p ≤ .05; **p ≤ .01; ***p ≤ .001.

entered this college, my confidence about getting a degree is now [insert response]." As before, responses ranged from "much lower" (1) to "much higher" (5) on a five-point scale. The question is worded to indicate perceived change since entering the current college, which may mitigate problems of sorting of different types of students across school types if it occurs.

Here we find that females and minorities report somewhat greater increases in confidence than males or white students (the reference categories; table 9.2, model 3). The effects of age are again nonlinear, here dropping off at about thirty-two years. Occupational colleges are also associated with strong increases in students' confidence. Adding the job placement dummy and students' perceptions about teacher and school contacts into the regression (model 4), we find that all three types of labor market links are also associated with increased student confidence about the degree. Moreover, the linking variables again reduce the impact of the private colleges by about half (that is, versus the baseline, model 3).

As job placement and the contact variables account for a large part of the influence of private colleges on student outcomes, it may be useful to examine the community college and occupational college samples separately to determine if these labor-market linking variables function differently in the different college settings. As we discussed in the prior chapter, the occupational colleges in our sample focus solely on occupational preparation, while the community colleges have a much broader public mandate. Furthermore, research on proprietary colleges has shown that their connections to the labor market are critical to their reputation and success in drawing students (Bailey, Badway, and Gumport 2002; Deil-Amen and Rosenbaum 2004; Grubb 1996).

To determine the extent to which the promise of job placement and the perception of the usefulness of college and teacher contacts might function differently among students at the two college types, we ran the same model on the split sample, analyzing students at occupational and community colleges separately. Interestingly, as shown in table 9.3, students' perceptions that school and teacher contacts could be useful in securing employment are actually associated with slightly greater improvements in effort among community college students than among their counterparts at the occupational colleges. For confidence about completing a college degree, the effect of contacts is similar across college types. The influence of job placement services is more mixed, showing positive associations with effort among community college students and with confidence among occupational college students. These results are somewhat different for the private and public colleges but do not imply that labor market linkages function in drastically

TABLE 9.3    OLS Regression, Change in Effort and Confidence, College Types[a]

| | Effort Versus High School | | Confidence Regarding Degree | |
|---|---|---|---|---|
| | Community Colleges | Occupational Colleges | Community Colleges | Occupational Colleges |
| Linking covariate | Coef. (Robust SE) | Coef. (Robust SE) | Coef. (Robust SE) | Coef. (Robust SE) |
| Agrees college contacts could help get good job | .091** (.034) | .081*** (.020) | .107** (.037) | .117*** (.023) |
| Agrees teacher contacts could help get good job | .067* (.033) | .034[+] (.020) | .076* (.036) | .071*** (.022) |
| Job placement | .125* (.059) | .067[+] (.037) | .081 (.063) | .106** (.039) |
| N | 1,023 | 2,305 | 1,023 | 2,305 |

*Source:* Authors' data.
N = 3,328; [+]p ≤ .10; *p ≤ .05; **p ≤ .01; ***p ≤ .001.
[a]Full model includes student and institutional variables; full table available on request.

different ways across college types. Indeed, both occupational and community college students respond positively to perceived college labor-market linkages.

Finally, to estimate the influence of the contact variables on student effort and confidence among students at the same school, we run a school fixed-effects model. Holding constant all the same individual-level variables as reported in table 9.2, but omitting the school-level variables for college type and job placement, table 9.4 shows that among students at the same school, reported effort and confidence about obtaining the degree are still boosted by perceptions of the benefits of teacher and college contacts.

Of course, many students in two-year colleges hope to transfer to four-year colleges. This is true even for many of the occupational students in our sample. It may be assumed that labor-market contacts would be less of an incentive for students with bachelor's degree plans. We repeated the analyses, however, restricting the sample solely to students with BA plans or higher. These analyses (available on request) yield a very similar pattern of results, with one exception. Even for students with BA plans, job placement and perceived college contacts are associated with increased student effort

TABLE 9.4    School Fixed-Effects Model: OLS Regression Coefficients, Student Perceptions of School and Teacher Contacts[a]

| Covariate | Effort versus High School | | Confidence Regarding Degree | |
|---|---|---|---|---|
| | Coef. (Robust SE) | β | Coef. (Robust SE) | β |
| Agrees college contacts could help get good job | .091*** (.018) | .111 | .124*** (.019) | .144 |
| Agrees teacher contacts could help get good job | .041** (.017) | .050 | .071*** (.019) | .083 |

*Source:* Authors' data.
N = 3,328; *p ≤ .05; **p ≤ .01; ***p ≤ .001.
[a]Full model includes student variables; job placement is institutional and therefore not included; full table available on request.

and confidence about earning a degree; but perceived teacher contacts are not associated with these outcomes.

Although it is possible that students who perceive teachers or college contacts may differ in unmeasured ways (perhaps seeking out such contacts), we have conducted extensive analyses of student characteristics that might influence the outcomes of interest here and have been unable to detect any such differences. In addition to the individual-level variables included in our models, we also examined whether a host of other variables affected our results. Among these were measures of student attitudes toward the value of schooling for employment (compare Steinberg 1996; Rosenbaum 2001) and student reasons for selecting their college, with job placement included among response options. Given that none of these variables affected our major findings, and in the interests of parsimony, we have not retained them for these analyses.

In chapter 8, we found that some teachers and colleges have strong contacts with employers, which they report using to help graduates get jobs and to make curricula relevant to the workplace. Here, these analyses indicate that students respond to such contacts to reap their potential benefits and gain greater confidence on completing their degrees. Granted that unobserved heterogeneity among students may conceivably explain some portion of these effects, we would be surprised if these linkages had no impact. Indeed, anyone hearing students' statements would have difficulty doubting the effect contacts have on some.

An illustrative example of how contacts may serve to improve student behaviors and attitudes comes from an information technology major interviewed at one of our occupational colleges:

> If you're ever feeling down, I mean, there have been times when I've been kinda depressed between my job, the economy . . . spending all this money for school, and actually had an instructor say, "Come here," take us into a lab, go to a website and say, "what's your specialty?" type it in, and on the website it's showing the baseline salary and the requirements they need for it. He's like, "This is what you're working for." You know, that makes you feel good! [laughs] So, it's nice . . . by the time that you graduate, you'll have a very full working knowledge of exactly what the industry's looking for, because they [the teachers] are coming from the industry . . . so they know exactly what, you know, the jobs they're looking for. That is so helpful. It really is.

## JOB-PLACEMENT SERVICES AND DEGREE ATTAINMENT IN NATIONAL DATA

The importance of effort and confidence to degree attainment aside, it is important to examine whether colleges' links to labor markets will ultimately pay off in terms of actual attainment of the associate's degree. As in chapter 3, we turn to the Beginning Postsecondary Students Longitudinal Study (BPS), this time to test whether institutional efforts to link students with labor markets actually improve timely college degree completion. These data also allow us to see whether the processes suggested by our local cross-sectional findings are evident in a national sample.

For these analyses, we limit our sample to include only students at two-year colleges, who report a degree goal of at least an associate's (with information on the dependent variable N = 921). This way, our BPS sample is comparable to our local sample, and our results are not affected by those students, especially prevalent at community colleges, who enroll for a few courses with no intention of completing a degree.

Because BPS provides only limited data on institutional characteristics, we must rely on the Integrated Postsecondary Education Data System (IPEDS; NCES 1996b) for data on labor-market linking procedures that occur at the institutional level. IPEDS is a yearly survey of all postsecondary institutions in the United States. For these analyses, we used institutional case identifiers to integrate IPEDS 1996 institutional data with the BPS student data for the same year.

TABLE 9.5   Descriptive Statistics for BPS-IPEDS Sample

| | Two-Year Degree Seekers | | Two-Year Public | | Two-Year Private | |
|---|---|---|---|---|---|---|
| | Mean | SE | Mean | SE | Mean | SE |
| Attained degree by 1998 | .106 | .013 | .084 | .013 | .419 | .044 |
| Female | .521 | .025 | .513 | .026 | .640 | .040 |
| African American | .123 | .017 | .121 | .018 | .152 | .033 |
| Hispanic | .128 | .017 | .123 | .019 | .196 | .036 |
| Asian or Asian American | .062 | .014 | .062 | .015 | .054 | .018 |
| Race other or not reported | .008 | .003 | .008 | .003 | .014 | .006 |
| Age | 21.15 | .264 | 21.06 | .278 | 22.35 | .749 |
| High school GPA (7-point scale) | 5.37 | .110 | 5.37 | .114 | 5.25 | .157 |
| High school GPA missing (did not take SAT or ACT) | .577 | .027 | .567 | .028 | .715 | .038 |
| Parent education (truncated)[a] | 3.510 | .061 | 3.529 | .066 | 3.257 | .100 |
| Parent education not reported | .114 | .016 | .113 | .017 | .130 | .026 |
| Took any remedial | .231 | .020 | .239 | .021 | .127 | .031 |
| No report of remedial | .087 | .014 | .085 | .015 | .114 | .029 |
| Private college | .066 | .006 | | | | |
| Enrolled mostly full-time 1996 to 1998 | .396 | .026 | .369 | .028 | .777 | .037 |
| Job placement available | .864 | .024 | .859 | .026 | .933 | .016 |
| Unweighted N | 1,252 | | 861 | | 391 | |

*Source:* Authors' estimates based on BPS and IPEDS.
Estimates are weighted unless otherwise noted.
[a] Parent education: 3 = both parents high school, 4 = higher parent some college.

Given the complex sampling strategy of the BPS study design (NCES 1996a), these analyses employ the survey commands available in Stata 9.0 software (including the panel weights, strata, and primary sampling unit, as well as subpopulation commands). Table 9.5 reports weighted means for the effective sample.

The dependent variable in the BPS-IPEDS analysis is timely attainment of the associate's degree at the institution where the student first enrolled—that is, a dichotomous variable for whether the student earned at least an associate's degree at the institution where he or she enrolled during the 1995–1996 school year by the end of the 1997–1998 school year. The explanatory variables included in the BPS-IPEDS analysis are as close to our local model as possible, given the data at hand. The student character-istics included in the BPS-IPEDS model are the same, though it should be noted that nearly two-thirds of students lack data on high-school achieve-ment. This low response rate results from the fact that the BPS variable was obtained through student reports of their high school grades when they took standardized college entrance exams (SAT, ACT), which many students bound for two-year colleges do not take. Given that we are con-cerned with timely degree completion, we added controls for student enroll-ment status (mostly full-time, with always part-time or a mixture of full- and part-time as the reference category) and whether the student took any remedial courses (which may also provide an added control—beyond high school grades—for prior achievement). Finally, IPEDS does not provide data on school-employer contacts, per se. It does, however, ask whether institutions provide job-placement services for their graduates. We used this dichotomous variable to test the association between such services and student attainment.

In contrast to our local findings, the analysis presented in table 9.6, model 1, reveals that job placement services, though positive in direction, have no statistically significant effect on degree attainment. Perhaps sur-prisingly, none of the student characteristics included in the model have significant associations with attainment either. One possible explanation for this is that a few key predictors of attainment are perhaps not measured well: the variable for high-school achievement comes from student reports on the SAT or ACT, and parent education is reported in truncated form, without any distinction between college attendance and college degree completion. Another is that, because we are examining only two-year col-lege students, the range of variation on most variables is likely to be some-what compressed. Unsurprisingly, table 9.6 shows that students enrolled full-time are more likely to complete the degree by the end of 1998. Private colleges are also associated with increased likelihood of degree completion. This finding parallels the positive effect of the occupational colleges found in our local sample.

Given our qualitative findings (chapters 7 and 8, in particular), as well as prior research that has shown the importance of job placement to propri-etary two-year colleges (Bailey, Badway, and Gumport 2002; Deil-Amen and Rosenbaum 2004; Grubb 1996), we question whether placement ser-vices might operate differently in private and public colleges. We split the sample to analyze students at private and public colleges separately (table 9.6, models 2 and 3). Here we see that, indeed, job placement services

TABLE 9.6  Weighted Logistic Regression, 1998 Associate's Degree Completion

| | Model 1 All Degree Seekers | | Model 2 Public Colleges | | Model 3 Private Colleges | |
|---|---|---|---|---|---|---|
| Covariate | Coef. (SE) | Odds Ratio | Coef. (SE) | Odds Ratio | Coef. (SE) | Odds Ratio |
| Female | .129 | 1.14 | .218 | 1.24 | −.263 | .768 |
| | (.297) | | (.354) | | (.374) | |
| African American | −.120 | .886 | .043 | 1.04 | −1.206 | .299 |
| | (.462) | | (.539) | | (.748) | |
| Hispanic | −.634 | .531 | −.726 | .484 | −.123 | .885 |
| | (.390) | | (.536) | | (.518) | |
| Asian or Asian American | −.834 | .434 | −.451 | .637 | −1.741* | .175 |
| | (1.087) | | (1.224) | | (.728) | |
| Race other– not reported | −1.294 | .274 | — | — | −1.038 | .354 |
| | (.711) | | | | (1.024) | |
| Age | −.062 | .940 | −.053 | .948 | −.459** | .632 |
| | (.094) | | (.154) | | (.167) | |
| Age-squared | .0007 | 1.00 | .0003 | 1.00 | .008** | 1.01 |
| | (.001) | | (.002) | | (.003) | |
| High school GPA | .043 | 1.04 | .055 | 1.06 | −.173 | .841 |
| | (.166) | | (.178) | | (.228) | |
| High school GPA missing (did not take SAT or ACT) | −.588 | .555 | −.710 | .492 | .177 | 1.19 |
| | (.329) | | (.388) | | (.397) | |
| Parent education | .008 | 1.01 | −.020 | .980 | .201 | 1.22 |
| | (.108) | | (.129) | | (.167) | |
| Parent education not reported | −.742 | .476 | −.717 | .488 | −.348 | .706 |
| | (.911) | | (1.172) | | (.717) | |
| Took any remedial | −.263 | .769 | −.200 | .819 | −.938* | .392 |
| | (.371) | | (.442) | | (.446) | |
| No report of remedial | .614 | 1.85 | .967 | 2.63 | −2.933*** | .053 |
| | (.514) | | (.545) | | (.770) | |
| Enrollment mostly full-time | 1.205*** | 3.34 | 1.261*** | 3.53 | .714 | 2.04 |
| | (.321) | | (.363) | | (.467) | |
| Occupational major (fall 1995) | .358 | 1.43 | .244 | 1.28 | .722 | 2.06 |
| | (.316) | | (.350) | | (.484) | |
| Private college | 1.822*** | | — | — | — | — |
| | (.265) | 6.18 | | | | |
| Job placement available | .343 | 1.41 | .277 | 1.32 | 1.215* | 3.37 |
| | (.497) | | (.533) | | (.602) | |
| Constant | −2.43 | | −2.38 | | 4.11 | |
| | (1.73) | | (2.52) | | (2.58) | |
| Unweighted N | 1,252 | | 861 | | 391 | |

*Source:* NCES 1996a.
*p ≤ .05; **p ≤ .01; ***p ≤ .001.

have a significant positive effect on degree attainment among students at private colleges, but not at public colleges.

There are at least two potential explanations for the differing impact of job placement in the two college contexts. First, students who plan to transfer into four-year programs (more common in community colleges) may be less motivated by job placement subsequent to earning the associate's degree. However, even when we restrict our local analyses to students with bachelor's degree goals, job placement and college contacts positively influence effort and confidence. (A corresponding analysis of the national data yields no effect of job placement, but the number of observations in that group is only about 300.) Second, job placement may be qualitatively different in the two types of college. Our interview data (see chapters 7 and 8) reveal that many community college officials refer to job placement services when, in fact, the college offers only career counseling. Although vocational interest tests and general career advice certainly have value, our local data show that students are motivated by the instrumental value of contacts that can link them to specific good jobs—something career counselors in our sample of community colleges reported they do not do. Based on our interviews, we suspect that the job placement survey response at community colleges rarely involves links to specific jobs. In any case, as practiced, job placement clearly has different effects on students in public and private colleges nationally.

It may also be useful to examine the specific impact of placement on those students whom our analyses show to be influenced by it. For this, we calculated the marginal effects of the availability of job-placement services on several different types of students at the private colleges in the BPS sample. In order to do this, we set student characteristics equal to values of empirical and/or policy interest (for example, the typical or modal student, the at-risk student) and then calculated the change in probability of completing the degree for each student type, first, at a college without placement services, then at a college with placement services. For the typical student in this group, the predicted probability of 1998 completion of the associate's degree is about 34 percent at a college without job placement. (A typical student is defined as a white female, age twenty-one, whose parents have some college, and who earned a B average in high school, taking no remedial at college, attending full-time, and studying in an occupational major.) At a college with job placement, the same student's predicted probability of degree completion jumps to 63 percent—almost double. For an underrepresented minority student with otherwise the same characteristics, the predicted probability for her to finish the degree jumps from 19 percent to

FIGURE 9.1    Marginal Effects of Job Placement at Private Colleges—
Predicted Probability of 1998 Degree Completion for
Selected Student Types

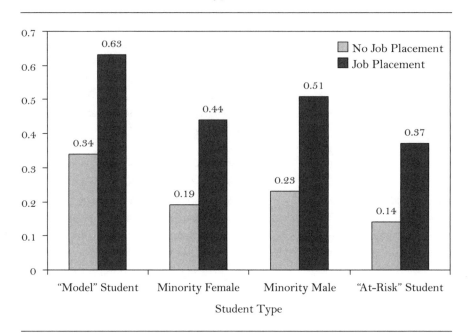

*Source:* Authors' compilation.

44 percent, going from a college without job placement to one with it (see
figure 9.1). For a minority male (otherwise the same), the probability of completion also more than doubles, from 23 percent to 51 percent. Perhaps most
strikingly, for an at-risk student—here, an underrepresented minority
whose parents did not finish high school, who had a C-minus high-school
GPA, and who took at least one remedial course at college—the predicted
probability of finishing the associate's degree in a timely manner is
increased almost three-fold by attending a college with job-placement services (moving from 14 percent to 37 percent). Job placement has strong
effects on degree completion for all groups, and proportionally stronger
effects for more disadvantaged groups.

## IMPLICATIONS OF LINKING EFFECTS

We have examined school-employer linkages at two levels. First, we analyzed students' perceptions of labor market contacts and how these percep-

tions, along with the promise of job placement, are related to reported student effort and confidence in degree completion. Second, we tested whether and to what extent job-placement services are associated with timely degree completion. We discovered that students' perceptions of college and teacher linkages significantly predict students' increased efforts at school and confidence about degree completion. In our local sample, students' perceptions of linkages account for part of the influence of the occupational colleges, pointing to institutional practices that support positive student outcomes. Using national data, we find that job-placement services—which serve the same purpose as contacts identified in our local data, especially at the occupational colleges in our sample—are also associated with increased likelihood of timely degree attainment at private colleges. Finally, we see that the marginal effects of job placement on students at private two-year colleges are fairly impressive, doubling the predicted probability of attainment for typical students, and almost tripling it for at-risk students.

Despite the scope of our analyses here, some problems in interpretation remain. First, we cannot be certain whether students' perception of the usefulness of contacts precedes their changes in effort and confidence at college. That is to say, we cannot rule out reverse causality. We have, however, attempted to address this endogeneity problem by controlling for time-invariant student characteristics and examining dependent variables measuring a change since the student began at college. Moreover, we have identified a similar pattern of influence using national data, which shows that job-placement services have a significant and positive effect on timely degree attainment for students at private colleges. Taken together, our local findings and the results from the national data suggest that when schools offer clear links to employment upon graduation, students may be more likely to attain the associate's degree.

A second potential problem with these analyses is that other aspects of private college structures may account for our findings in both the local and national data. Because private colleges tend to offer fewer programs and more structured curricula than community colleges (see chapters 1 and 5, as well as Person, Rosenbaum, and Deil-Amen 2006), the effects of such features are difficult to separate from the effects of labor-market linking. Indeed, focus, structure, and linking are all part of the occupational colleges' mission to provide career-oriented education. Although we cannot be certain that it is the only influence, private colleges' extensive investment in job placement and the strong relationship between student views of placement and contacts and important precursors to attainment, like effort and confidence, suggest that job placement may be especially important.

Given that our local occupational colleges represent ideal types, it is possible that the influence of job placement depends upon how it is implemented. It is noteworthy, however, that job placement retains a strong influence in the national sample of all private colleges. Even without resolving this issue, students' responses to placement and contacts at both college types—showing bolstered commitment to college in the face of frustrations—reinforces our central contention that transparency in the school-to-work transition supports student success.

These results point to potential procedures for improving college program effectiveness. Our analyses indicate that career services that involve actual job placement are most helpful to students' college outcomes. Although colleges often try to improve student motivation and persistence through instructional techniques and special services, these findings suggest that college and faculty linkages to employers, especially those that lead to actual placement in jobs, may also be powerful influences. It is unlikely that community colleges could or should adopt large-scale job placement initiatives, but our findings indicate that attention to placement might be worthwhile for some students. In particular, students in occupational programs—who often cite getting a good job as their primary reason for attending college—may be motivated by placement. Moreover, given that our BPS analyses show bigger impacts for more disadvantaged students, community colleges could adopt limited placement programs for students most in need. Such programs would not only bolster community colleges commitment to equity, but might even improve attainment among some of the hardest to reach students.

# CHAPTER TEN

## TO TEACH OR NOT TO TEACH "SOCIAL SKILLS"?

Along with institutional procedures, instructional activities are also part of the equation in fostering student success. The first part of this book describes ways that college procedures help students during college, and the second half describes ways that college procedures can enhance graduates' transition to employment. However, labor market success does not depend solely on institutional charters and employer links. Students also need subtle soft skills to find, secure, and maintain jobs. Traditional college procedures assume that college students already possess such skills, yet many two-year college students come from disadvantaged backgrounds and often have not been exposed to the behavioral codes and social cues necessary to succeed in the professional world. Besides helping students to catch up academically, colleges can also help many students catch up socially, providing them with direct guidance about how to dress, speak, and interact in job interviews and in the professional workplace. In many cases, if colleges do not provide this soft-skill training, the benefits of the academic education that they offer may be lost in the labor market.

Here we explore the mandatory teaching of professional social skills, a different form of college procedure that can help two-year college students overcome culturally specific professional barriers and achieve their goals. We find that community colleges assume that students possess, or are aware of, the kind of professional social skills that employers expect, whereas occupational college procedures provide mandatory training in such skills. These institutional procedures represent a dimension of instruction particularly relevant to colleges' occupational programs, in which students are explicitly trained for a specific role in the labor market.

Given the overwhelming evidence that employers strongly emphasize social skills (Baxter and Young 1982; Cappelli 1992; Cappelli and Rogovsky 1993; U.S. Census Bureau 1994; Murnane and Levy 1996; Rosenbaum 2001; SCANS 1991), it is unfortunate that research has not examined if and how social skills are handled in schools and colleges. It is imperative that research attend to these issues. These results are not intended to be definitive, but instead to provide initial findings on the topic and contribute to further research.

## The Need for Soft-Skill Training

Many of the students we interviewed reported that the soft-skill training gleaned through college courses and experiences was essential in preparing them for the labor market. Ron Gonzalez is one such student. In high school, Ron was a gang member and a "hip-hop b-boy." He gave schoolwork little attention, took six years to finish high school, and was a few feet away from getting shot, or as he says, "popped," by gun fire from an opposing gang in his neighborhood. One of his closest friends did not survive the attack. Ron's father works as a supervisor at a factory. Ron explained that the pay is decent, but

> you look at the workers though, and it's a hot-ass factory. I mean, I work there in the summertime and it's hell. . . . All the kids that like drop out go work over there, you know. They go there to work, and this is like a nasty job. That's why I decided, nah . . . they're working there, you know, but not me. If I get my degree, I'll be just at my computer doing my stuff, . . . No sweat. I'm in my own chair, you know. Nobody to scream at you.

At his family's urging, Ron was just about to join the Navy when he decided to use his artistic graffiti skills and apply them to a two-year degree in information technology with a specialization in web design. However, his style of clothing, "G-clothes"—dickies, bandanas, hair nets, goggles and Adidas—clashed with the dress code at the occupational college he had decided to attend. "A lot of these were typical styles, you know that I was around. In my school, everyone was a b-boy, and in the streets." He described the transition to what he calls "casual 24-7" as a "big time . . . dramatic change." He actually felt extremely uncomfortable at first. Wearing collared shirts and slacks was so foreign to him that he thought he looked "stupid" dressed in them on the first day of college:

> So you know what's kinda cool? The first day I came to school I felt like uncomfortable, you know. I said, "ugh." I felt like a "ugh." I felt bad, you know, "Look how I look! I look all stupid, you know." I didn't like it. After a while you get used to it, and then you feel good, you know. And I can even walk around the street, you know, you don't get harassed by police or bangers. It's straight. . . . Like in a way, now I understand it, you know now. When I started going up for job interviews, you know, when I sign up for jobs, applications, and I say [the name of my college], they look at it, "Oh." They know that we dress up. . . . I think that's probably a good reason they make us do it, and I understand. It's pretty cool.

Ron is just one of the many students whose college taught them the expectations of the workplace culture of the professional support fields into which they hoped to enter. These students also learned how to present themselves in an interview, manage themselves at a lunch or dinner interview, talk about their talents and strengths, make effective speeches and presentations, work together as team members, and communicate effectively with clients and customers. Broadly defined, these examples can be considered the social skills appropriate for success in a professional work environment. Ann Swidler (1986) describes culture as a "tool kit for constructing strategies of action," and we contend that teaching students about occupationally relevant social skills and expectations is a project in expanding their cultural repertoire, thereby increasing their options for the economic mobility that they seek through schooling.[1]

Past economic and sociological research has found that noncognitive skills and behaviors are important predictors of labor market outcomes (Barrick and Mount 1991; Bishop 1987; Bowles and Gintis 2002; Duncan and Dunifon 1997; England and Farkas 1986; Farkas 1996; Farkas, England, and Barton 1988; Filer 1981; Heckman and Rubinstein 2001; Jencks et al. 1979; Rosenbaum 2001). A survey of 4,000 private employers by the National Center on the Educational Quality in the Workforce (NCEQW 1994) and a more intensive local study by Roslyn Mickelson and Matthew Walker (1997) find that employers place even more weight on noncognitive behaviors than on cognitive skills. These noncognitive attributes range from basic attendance, cooperativeness, and attitudes, to facility with social interaction, participation, leadership, effort, and preparation (Rosenbaum 2001, 173). Such behaviors play a critical role in employers' evaluations of job candidates, and the "wrong" noncognitive displays can be particularly harmful for black and Latino job seekers (Heckman and Lochner 2000; Holzer 1996; Kirschenman and Neckerman 1991; Moss and Tilly 2001).

Although Samuel Bowles and Herbert Gintis (1976) and F. L. Pincus (1980) have warned of the oppressive consequences of teaching social skills in school, alternate theories suggest the opposite: a lack of familiarity with the dominant culture can be an obstacle to upward mobility (Bourdieu 1984). Such a view would suggest that the teaching of social skills could be a mechanism to assist low-income students in their attempts at economic mobility. Harold Garfinkel (1967) alerts us to the power of taken-for-granted perspectives on reality, noting that when one violates norms based on common-sense assumptions about shared understandings, others are likely to take offense. Likewise, employers who interview students who fail to conform to the performance norms and expectations of professional culture will not be impressed, even if these individuals are otherwise attractive applicants. The lack of specific culturally relevant social skills may be an important barrier to the upward mobility of low-income students attempting to secure semiprofessional support jobs after completing sub-baccalaureate degrees.

We examine the approach to teaching social skills in community colleges and private occupational colleges. We find that nearly all faculty in occupational programs at both types of colleges believe that employers in these fields require certain social skills (what this chapter calls professional service skills, because these workplaces are controlled by individuals with professional training). However, while we present here three reasons why the community colleges in the study neither demand nor teach these social skills, we find that the private occupational colleges make these skills an explicit part of their curriculum and teach many kinds of social skills. These findings suggest that the way that schools teach and cultivate social skills can further expand our understanding of how schools shape students' opportunities in the labor market. This chapter outlines some of the reasons for the differences in social skill training across college types, and it suggests speculations about their implications for social mobility. Ironically, in contrast with the Bowles and Gintis view, these findings raise the disturbing possibility that community colleges may be actively contributing to the social reproduction of inequality by avoiding instruction in the cultural competencies and social skills required in today's workplace.

## THE TEACHING OF CULTURAL CAPITAL

Bowles and Gintis (1976) have certainly colored our thinking about the teaching of social skills in schools. Their now famous correspondence principle opened our eyes to the possibility that our schools function to channel students differentially into a highly stratified class system structured by the social relations of economic production. Such a perspective implies an intentional and conspiratorial relationship between educators and employers to "match" educational curriculum to meet employers' labor market needs. The teaching of class-specific social skills, the reinforcement of class-based behavioral norms, and the rewarding of class-appropriate personality traits were presented as the main tools applied to accomplish this task. In short, this perspective proposes that teaching students social skills in schools is an oppressive process.

In contrast, Bourdieu emphasizes that a primary mechanism of social reproduction is students' lack of familiarity with the dominant culture that schools reward. Schools require and reward the cultural resources of upper-class students, leaving lower-class students at a disadvantage in the competition for academic credentials. Bourdieu notes that the failure of schools to teach these cultural competencies preserves the relative advantage of the upper classes over the lower classes in meeting implicit cultural capital requirements, which simply reproduces existing inequalities (Bourdieu and Passeron 1977; Bourdieu 1984). In short, his work implies that explicitly teaching cultural competencies in school could potentially enhance lower-class students' chances for academic success.

Bourdieu and others have discussed the relevance of these cultural capital issues for students' academic success (Bernstein 1990; Bourdieu 1984, 1992; Bourdieu and Passeron 1977; DiMaggio 1982; Lamont and Lareau 1988). However, Bourdieu does acknowledge that even if students acquire the same technical and academic credentials, their possession of cultural capital also determines their opportunities for success after graduation (Bourdieu and Passeron 1977). We extend Bourdieu's ideas one step to consider how they may also apply to cultural capital requirements of students' aspired occupations. If the acquisition of cultural competencies promotes relative advantages in the classroom and the lack of such competencies results in disadvantages, could such processes also play a role as students enter the workforce? More specifically, can community colleges address students' lack of familiarity with the professional culture that is required in today's workplace environment?

We examine how two kinds of colleges approach the teaching of cultural capital, that is, professionally relevant social skills. Bourdieu stresses the knowledge of elite culture, and more specifically, the relationship between elite culture and the system of culturally based rewards in school. Academic success is often judged on the basis of exclusionary, culturally biased signals that are often irrelevant to the hard skills demanded in the labor market. These high-status cultural signals are arbitrary in the sense that they are functionally detached from economic productivity (Bourdieu 1984). Michelle Lamont and Annette Lareau (1988) describe cultural capital as "institutionalized, [that is], widely shared, high status cultural signals (attitudes, preferences, formal knowledge, behaviors, goals, and credentials) used for social and cultural exclusion" (156).

Our focus is not elite culture, but rather a culture that is more relevant to the demands of today's workplace—professional culture. Broadly defined, professional culture includes the norms, expectations, behaviors, styles of dress, and communication patterns that pervade workplaces dominated by health, technology, business, and other professionals. Given the exclusionary quality of cultural capital, students from lower social classes, whose experiences do not prepare them to act appropriately at any given moment according to the norms of professional culture, are likely to be at a disadvantage in the competition for jobs.

Several authors have examined the importance of social skills in employers' interactions with entry-level job applicants and workers (Rosenbaum 2001; Bills 2004). Sociologically, successful upward movement in a status hierarchy involves much more than a mere acquisition of technical skills, it involves familiarization with the norms, expectations, and social networks in occupational cultures. These social skills may be related to acceptance and ability to work and interact in the workplace culture as Bowles and Gintis acknowledge:

> Individuals who have attained a certain educational level tend to . . . adjust their aspirations and self-concepts accordingly, while acquiring manners of speech and demeanor more or less socially acceptable and appropriate to their level. (1976, 141)

However, most research has neglected the question of the extent to which educational institutions actually teach or even guide lower SES students toward such alternative dispositions. This topic is in need of attention, given that Bourdieu acknowledges that by *not* teaching cultural capital, schools make it "difficult to break the circle in which cultural capital is added to cultural capital" (Bourdieu and Passeron 1977, 493).

Unlike Bowles and Gintis (1976), who portray schools as reproducing the existing class structure through their correspondence with the needs of the labor market, we consider correspondence between education and the labor market to be an asset in increasing opportunities for social mobility. In fact, a lack of correspondence between community colleges and employers may actually leave students ill-prepared for opportunities to advance in the labor market.

## DATA AND METHODS

We use interview data from students, various administrators, faculty, career services and job placement staff, program coordinators, deans, and departmental chairs in fourteen two-year colleges.[2] Interviews were coded using a grounded theory approach.

Although we did not systematically observe classrooms, interviews allowed us to discover aspects of an issue that is poorly understood and largely ignored in existing research. Moreover, staff's outright denial of teaching work habits or social skills leads us to doubt that we would have seen such instruction if we had observed classrooms. Furthermore, instructors report that administrators actually prevent instructors from enforcing behavioral rules about attendance, so it is unlikely that instructors explicitly apply such rules in their classrooms. Teaching of soft skills and related social norms may sometimes occur in community college classrooms, but staff statements indicate that it was not incorporated systematically and explicitly into instructional practice or into the wider institutional agenda.

## WORKPLACE SOCIAL SKILLS ACROSS COLLEGE TYPE

The community colleges and occupational colleges in our sample teach the same technical skills required in each occupational field, and also agree that workplaces require social skills and cultural knowledge. The interviews found a consensus among faculty and career services staff that students often lack important professionally relevant social skills. However, as we will note, there is a marked difference in the ways that community colleges and occupational colleges respond to this belief. Community colleges do not teach these professionally relevant skills. Occupational colleges, on the other hand, devote great effort to teaching them.

Nearly all of the community college occupational program chairs interviewed (twenty-five of twenty-eight) and nearly three-quarters of the community college counselors and career services staff interviewed (ten of fourteen) believe that many students lacked the soft skills that employers require. For example, when a community college counselor was asked, "How informed are students . . . usually about the job market that they're going into?" she replied, "They're not informed. Are you kidding me? No. Very few have a real clue as to what's going on." More specifically, the chair of the executive secretarial program at a community college noted students' lack of familiarity with office culture:

> Some people have had no exposure to offices. It just sounds like a good field to go into but they have no concept of, well, how should you dress in the office, how should you look, you know, what should your appearance be and so on. What about the way that you speak? "Yeah." "Nah." You know, answering the phone and saying "Bye-bye" at the end of the conversation. So individuals need to have more of that kind of an education. And there's no course . . . that they've had in high school that covers things like that, which is kind of interesting.

Such statements mirror the sentiments of those at the occupational colleges. For example, the director of placement at one of the occupational colleges gave several examples of the types of "mistakes" she typically saw students making in their job search, "just not dressing professionally, not putting their resume on resume paper, showing up way too early or too late for an interview."

Several of the faculty and staff at both types of college recognized how the norms of some students' cultural background actually contradict the norms of professional culture. The same director of placement observed that some students have trouble presenting themselves effectively:

> Maybe just learning about how to package themselves—talk about accomplishments that they did in a concise way. . . . We deal with a lot of different cultures and types of people and I think that there are different barriers, like some people really—I think it's almost a cultural thing—do not want to talk about themselves. They don't want to brag, for lack of a better word. And then we have to coach them a lot on, you know, "This is your moment to talk about what you know and what you've done." They want to just kind of be quiet and, "Oh I should talk about that?" That type of thing.

This type of observation was more prevalent among staff at the occupational colleges, perhaps because job placement services were less available at the community colleges, affording their staff and faculty fewer opportunities to witness such culturally relevant nuances.[3]

## TEACHING SOCIAL SKILLS AS A COLLEGE FUNCTION

Although staff at both types of colleges agreed that students often lack professionally appropriate skills, the colleges respond to this need differently. Those interviewed at the community colleges were more likely to believe that their job is to provide academic instruction, and did not teach employment-related social skills. The occupational colleges, on the other hand, favored an employment-centered model that emphasizes preparing students for better employment options and includes social skills development.

### Community Colleges: Academic-Centered Institutions

In many cases, the comprehensive community college grew out of the more traditional junior college model, which was primarily designed to provide the equivalent of the first two years of a university education. Occupational programs were added onto that traditional liberal arts transfer function in recent decades and still exist within an institution that favors the traditional educational model, where legitimacy is garnered through adherence to a traditional form (Brint and Karabel 1991). In short, the legacy of community colleges defines its role as an academic institution. We find that these community colleges, like the four-year colleges on which their institutional structure is based, lack strong college-wide linkages to employers and rarely establish relationships with employers, a finding that coincides with those of other researchers (Brewer and Gray 1999; Grubb 1996).

Among the community colleges' top-level administrators we interviewed, little concern was expressed about the need to teach social skills, the value of social skills in the labor market, and the priority that should be given to employers' demand for social skills. At the faculty level, most occupational program faculty believed that social skills are necessary and valued by employers and that many of the students need to improve in these areas, but they admitted that the curriculum does not prioritize these skills. The chair of one community college's administrative assistant major articulated this dilemma:

> I go out and visit the employers and I ask them "what do you need?"
> And it is really many times, the human relations skills . . . and students

not only get the hard skills but the soft skills as well. And, they do say, that is what the students need. They need to know how to work on a team, they need to know how to cooperate. They need to know how to work the telephone, how to talk on the phone, first impressions. All these things that are so important. Today I don't think we are doing enough teaching them. We're just taking it for granted, saying "Well, people know it." And they don't.

However, even though many occupational program faculty at the community colleges were aware of employers' demand for social skills, they gave three general reasons why social skills are not effectively taught: lack of recognition of the problem and support to remedy it among administrators; faculty's view that the direct teaching of social skills is outside the college's mission; and a definition of social skills as an innate personality attribute, rather than learned.

*Administrators Downplay or Fail to Recognize the Problem of Social Skills*   Some administrators did not regard such qualities as skills that can and should be taught in college. As a result, few high-level administrators support teaching social skills. For instance, the vice president of the community college just discussed disputed the idea that employers value these social skills. She believed community colleges should focus mainly on technical job skills and on providing students with a general knowledge base. It is clear from her comments that she does not view social skills as playing a pivotal role in acquiring and succeeding in entry-level positions:

> You know how employers say, "Give me somebody who can think, I'll teach them the job skills." It isn't true. In the real world, I mean. Because what they really want is both. But at the point of entry, the gatekeeper is really skills, until you get to a higher level. . . . They need to have a knowledge base. And I think that employers, when they say, "Give me someone with people skills, I'll train them," they're assuming, without even saying it, that there is that fundamental knowledge base. That's our job. And so we can't skip over that.

Even when some faculty make efforts to teach social skills, their efforts are often rendered ineffective. The lack of administrative support reduces the impact of individual faculty members' efforts to incorporate the teaching of social skills into their classes. When efforts are made, these attempts are often limited in scope and uneven in quality. Faculty reported that some individuals try to implement a few requirements, but each faculty member emphasized different rules, and other faculty required none. As a result, students considered these teachers and their requirements idiosyncratic, and they were usually indifferent about complying. These instructors did not have ways to systematically encourage a social skills focus, though we did learn of distinct nonsystematic advice-giving sessions, role-playing, and mock job situation exercises that some instructors used periodically in their classes.

Even when some faculty demand social skills, they do not believe they have the authority to demand such behaviors from students. Indeed, the lack of systematic administrative support leaves faculty relatively powerless to demand social behaviors from students. A lack of authority is usually hard to document, but it becomes explicit in the unusual cases when a faculty member attempts to enforce a policy about social behavior. Although none of these community colleges had any formal college-wide policies about attendance or punctuality, individual teachers were free to impose such policies but had difficulty implementing them. Only 4 percent of the faculty interviewed ever attempted to enforce an attendance policy, and those who did found resistance and lack of support. For example, at one community college, a professor tried to penalize students for coming to class late by locking the door fifteen minutes after class began. Students complained, and reported in interviews that they saw no rationale for this rule other than the personal idiosyncrasies of the instructor. Administrators caved to students' complaints and forced the professor to abolish the policy. This incident was well known by other faculty and was cited in explaining why they did not make such requirements.

Lacking authority to require social skills through behavioral policies, most instructors try to transmit social skills through didactic instruction rather than demanding that students practice these social skills in their classes. For example, a few instructors admitted in their interviews that they revert to vague assertions about the importance of attendance, and tolerate students who ignore their advice. A teacher at a community college gave us his account of how he handled attendance in his class:

> I don't have any attendance policy in my classes. I don't have any tardiness policy in my classes. I just give, "If you want to be successful in this class, there's a direct correlation between success and punctuality and attendance. And it's across the board." Just make them aware.

This teacher considered students who did not conform to his attendance philosophy lazy, lacking effort, having bad habits, or unconcerned with their success in college. However, students may feel that they can pass the class requirements without good attendance or punctuality given that these are not components of the final grade. The teacher never explicitly communicated to students how class requirements might be connected to success in the real world.

*Many Faculty See Social Skills as Outside the Mission of Colleges*    Although many community college faculty reported that social skills are important for students to learn, they do not see the teaching of these social skills as "something that colleges do." Several did say that these behavioral attributes are skills they hope students will learn or otherwise pick up (like osmosis), but not skills that colleges can teach.

Most of the faculty interviewed (more than two-thirds) believe that traditional college courses will somehow transmit necessary social skills. In addition to a lack of behavioral policies, community colleges also lacked mechanisms to ensure that students develop other kinds of professionally relevant social skills and "higher-order" thinking, which are often rewarded by employers. Over three-quarters of the faculty and administrators interviewed thought that students would pick up the cognitive and noncognitive social skills necessary to succeed in life and on the job through the general education curriculum. Although some of these cognitive skills are part of the implicit agenda in some classes and among some instructors, there is no systematic attempt to ensure that students are able to acquire professionally relevant independent and critical thinking, problem-solving, teamwork, and communication skills through the curriculum. Students are taught writing and speech skills, but are not encouraged to develop such skills in a way that is directly relevant to particular work settings. Such curricula is presented to students as necessary for developing general competencies, not specific occupational competencies. Students therefore often fail to see the need for such skill development. For example, they are taught how to make presentations in speech classes, but are rarely exposed to messages about how best to interact with customers, clients, or co-workers. The limited patchwork attempts that some occupational faculty make to convey these messages reveal students' lack of knowledge about the need for such social skills. For example, one business department chair reported:

> [In] the more advanced class, like Intermediate Accounting, I'll bring it up there. You know, the fact that your people-handling skills and

stuff is very important as an accountant. A lot of students are surprised at that. They think accountants, they don't need a personality. I say, "It makes a world of difference, you know, because you *are* dealing with people in . . . other departments. Or if you're a public accountant, you've gotta be able to get along with people."

Some faculty believed that social skills cannot be taught but that oral communication skills and a disciplined organized approach to work are instead largely a matter of personality. Some thought it is innate, some that it comes from early childhood socialization, and some that it is taught in elementary or high school. In short, faculty believed that by the time students get to college, they have either learned it or they have not, and it is not something college can teach. As one faculty member reported,

Well, some people just innately have better skills. . . . Some people, it seems like instantly you like them, and then others are really, you know, they're just stand-offish and . . . some are really a little abrasive.

In sum, there are several reasons why the importance of social skills is acknowledged yet not taught in the community colleges in our study. A key component is the failure of administrators and faculty to identify the teaching of such skills as central to the agenda of the college.

*The Exception to the Rule: Community Colleges Teach Social Skills in Health Programs* Social skills are emphasized and systematically taught with many different strategies in community colleges' health programs. For example, one physical therapy assistant program chair described their required orientation course "What does your dress say about you?" An interview with the chair of radiography at another college is a good example of the multiple and systematic methods used in the health programs to enhance students' professionally relevant social skills:

We don't accept any late assignments. We penalize late assignments. We don't offer make-up tests without a penalty. Handouts are passed out at the beginning of class to those who are there and then put away and those who come in late have to get copies from somebody else. Quizzes are given within the first five minutes. . . . We just finished a trust walk last week where we blindfold students . . . and we role-play you're the patient and I'm the radiographer. I blindfold you in the classroom. Then I lead you around the hallway, down the stairs, into the cafeteria just using verbal instructions, and then I have to sit you down in the cafeteria. I make you sit there for five minutes. I don't talk to you. Then I bring you back to the classroom and then we reverse roles. And that's to let the person know how much they have to trust somebody when they don't know them and to know how long five minutes sitting alone really is, and what it's like to be disoriented. We have students, second semester freshmen, they take turns operating a wheelchair. . . . They come in at eight in the morning, get in the wheelchair, and they cannot get out of the wheelchair until three in the afternoon. They wheel themselves down to the classroom, they wheel themselves in the bathroom. They participate in everything that's going on that day, but they just have to get themselves around to get an experience of what that's like. And all told, we have about thirty strategies that are program-wide, not just course-wide, that the faculty has decided are program things we want you to learn no matter what course it is or who's teaching the class. They are mandatory parts of the course and no matter who's teaching it, must do. . . . And some are designed for critical thinking; others are designed for affective enhancement.

Most of the other health programs we studied engaged in similar practices. The ability of the health programs to implement such practices broadly, across all classes, rests partially on the fact that most of these health programs have limited enrollments and additional admissions criteria. Students who gain admission to the programs' courses were less likely to resist such behavioral requirements due to the high demand and limited supply of such classes. Furthermore, students tended to see any policy linked to their relevant professions as legitimate, unlike students in general education classes, who may not see clear links between classroom content and later jobs. It is noteworthy that the idea that social skills are an innate personality attribute, rather than learned behavior, was much less prevalent in the interviews with health program staff.

In these health programs, such skills were most often discussed as professional skills rather than personal skills, and attempts were made to incorporate the cultivation of such skills into the curriculum. Another radiography chair asserted this idea when asked about work habits and social skills:

We have a lot of strategies within the curriculum that are designed to address just those issues. As opposed to the technical abilities, we also want them to be compassionate and to act professional and to be punctual and those things form major cornerstones of what we do here.

Professional associations reinforce students' need to learn such skills. They are emphasized in the licensing exams and the clinical experiences that are so central to students' training and entry into the profession. Professional licensing criteria serve as an alternate and positive external authority to offset the fact that community college administrators do not prioritize social skills. The tight relationships between community college health programs and professional associations and clinical settings lends weight to instructors' emphasis on social skill development.

## Occupational Colleges: Incorporating Employment-Centered Missions

In contrast to community college program staff more generally, nearly all of the staff and faculty at the occupational colleges recognized that students might need assistance to develop the social skills so often critical to job success. They do not construe it as merely a personal issue. They also accept responsibility for educating students about the necessity of these skills and assisting them in developing the appropriate behaviors. Both administrators and faculty agreed across the board that teaching career-relevant social skills was a necessary component of their education. In fact, such a task was considered central to each occupational college's mission. By following the lead of the employment world, these colleges have become deeply committed to teaching students any skills that will give them an advantage in the labor market. The teaching of the skills appears across the institution; it is present in classrooms, college-wide policies, and career and job placement services.

The dean of an occupational college articulates how they package social skills in their curricula and mission:

> I always tell students the hiring equation is relatively simple: it's one-third communication skills, one-third interpersonal skills, and one-third technical skills. You don't even get to walk in the front door if your communication skills aren't good, because they're going to throw your resume away. . . . You don't teach somebody communication skills by putting in an extra English class. You don't teach them to work in a team by another psych class. You build it into the teaching and learning process so that it's cross curriculum, rather than a string.

These priorities filter down into the daily life of the classroom in occupational colleges. In stark contrast to community college faculty, nearly all occupational faculty talked about encouraging particular communication styles in the classroom. They try to help students become more comfortable with what will be expected of them in the workplace. They described the need to inform students about behaviors that might seem common sense for middle-class people familiar with such norms. Often, when students do not conform to professional norms, college staff are surprised, and deliberately instruct students about what seem to be the most basic social rules.

Because occupational colleges explicitly focus on employer needs and expectations, faculty members are given the authority and institutional support to incorporate career-relevant social skills into the content of their classes. They report that having social skills as a stated component of the school's curriculum is especially important for minority and low-SES students, who are sometimes not aware of basic social skills in the workplace. In addition to what happens in the classroom, career services and job placement staff are officially designated to prepare students in this area. The director of job placement at one occupational college gives an example of teaching students about the social culture of answering machines:

> We even just have to deal with the fact that they've never had an answering machine. . . . I promise it's not expensive, but it is almost impossible to have a job search without having a way to leave messages . . . or that they have to change their message because it's got rap music on in the background. . . . You would never think something so basic, but, boy, it can be an impediment.

The professional social skills that occupational colleges teach are reflected in the colleges' policies and in the integration of personal, social, and self-presentational skills into curricular requirements. Professional skills include knowledge about conduct and appearance considered critical in the workplace. Some social skills might be considered arbitrary, such as dress code and appearance, but they are often commonly expected. Other skills are more clearly essential, such as communication, cooperation, and punctuality. All reflect norms of professional culture; that is, they represent common ideas on appropriate behavior in professional work settings.

Explicit policy about social behaviors is a way that several of these occupational colleges try to incorporate social skills. An administrator at an occupational college provided an example of their punctuality and the attendance policy.

> At fifteen minutes late, they are marked absent. They are encouraged to stay in class but they are absent. If you are absent six times, you automatically fail the course. If you are tardy three times, that is the equivalent of one absence, and programs have the right to decrease the number of absences at which point the student fails. The medical assisting and HIT (health information technology) teachers have recently discussed lowering it to four absences and then you fail. And the institution supports allowing the program to do anything that is more than what the institution requires.

Teachers in occupational colleges consider these policies attempts to foster strong work habits among students, and stress this rationale by telling students that excessive absences or tardiness at work will not be accepted. Because teaching these social skills is considered legitimate throughout the college, especially by top-level administrators, individual faculty are supported in their attempts to enforce them as college-wide policies. College staff, in a sense, present a united front to persuade students of the need to develop such skills.

Although attendance and punctuality may be dismissed as subordinate socialization (Bowles and Gintis 1976), all occupational colleges also taught students to think independently and critically, solve problems, communicate effectively, work with others, and present themselves well physically, orally, and in writing. These colleges require courses that are specifically designed to nurture and develop these skills. At one, the description of a class called Critical Thinking and Problem Solving reads:

> This course helps students master the fundamentals of effective problem solving and apply them to a range of practical problems. Major areas of subject matter and activity include problem-solving methodologies, research strategies, logical reasoning, critical analysis of information and cooperative learning.

At another occupational college, a group dynamics course emphasizes communication, critical thinking, and group process techniques, and students "examine the elements of successful teams and small decision-making groups." Within the various programs, professional social skills are built into the program requirements and evaluation process. For example, the medical assisting program at one college teaches students the most basic presentation skills involved in talking on the phone with clients:

> The students have a clinical evaluation tool, it's a checklist. And at the end of each course, they are to have done so many mastery demonstrations of each procedure. Answering the phone, transcribing a letter, giving injections, drawing blood, whatever it is. So that by the time they've graduated, their tool is built in, and they have mastered all of those skills. . . . We do mock patients calling on the phone, so that they demonstrate those kinds of skills.

The rationale for developing these skills, namely the idea that such social skills will be rewarded in the workplace, is explicitly stated. Faculty, administrators, and staff draw from their frequent contact with employers to convince students of the need to develop these skills.

In addition, dress codes and rules of appropriate appearance are formally implemented at occupational colleges. If colleges do not have a policy about what to wear routinely, they often require students to conform to a strict dress code while attending job fairs and interacting with potential employers. A dean of general education at one occupational college put it this way:

> The reason we have a dress code is we are preparing you to go to the work place. And it's a battle, a constant battle. "I'm not in class, I'm in the lab." You still can't wear jeans. You can't dye your hair purple. You can't have a pierced nose. You can't have twenty-seven earrings. . . . What is acceptable in a casual, social situation is not acceptable in a business situation. So we try to teach them that division.

Both community colleges and occupational colleges conduct job fairs where students can get an overview of the job market and meet employers. Although community colleges rarely instruct students about how to dress or act, occupational colleges tell students what to wear and arrange both real and mock interview sessions between students and employers. Such opportunities are provided to all students, not just the few who seek out specific additional help, which is the case in community colleges. Occupational college administrators point out that social skills are no substitute for the technical skills students must have, but are almost as important for getting a good job and advancing in the future.

## TEACHING SOCIAL SKILLS: ANOTHER LEVEL OF PREPARING FOR THE LABOR MARKET

An occupational college administrator echoed the sentiments we encountered with Ron early in this chapter.

> If I would have known [this college] was available when I was younger, I would have considered it for business [instead of a liberal arts college].... I think we hit a market, first generation primarily, people that want to make a career. Bottom line is, the ultimate goal for everybody [both types of college] is to get a job, regardless of what major you choose, you do want to graduate from school and be employed, make a living.... I think, ultimately the goals are the same. It's just the way they're taught.

Ron's struggles led him to decide on education as a way out of the type of manual jobs his father and friends hold. Like Ron, most of the low-income, first-generation, and minority students in community colleges and occupational colleges need these degrees to lead them into better job prospects. They are often relatively disconnected from the people who live and work in more professional settings. Their hope is that college can somehow serve as a bridge into more desirable labor market positions.

Our study moves beyond the idea of colleges as credentialing institutions. As we have attempted to show here, community colleges and occupational colleges take very different approaches to the challenge of preparing students in applied occupational programs for labor market success. Outside their health programs, community colleges have few formal mechanisms for explicitly teaching students the professionally relevant social skills that are likely to enhance their opportunities for success in the occupations they strive to enter. Teaching such skills is not seen as a primary function of colleges or even an acceptable purpose for educators, a view that probably comes from the traditional university model.

Occupational colleges, however, are explicit in their attempts to align their actions directly with students' employment needs. Because they see work-relevant social skills as critical to employment success, occupational colleges have developed mechanisms for systematically helping students develop them.

If Bowles and Gintis are correct, occupational colleges are doing their students a disservice by socializing them into subordinate positions within a capitalist labor market. If Bourdieu is correct, community colleges are doing their students a disservice by withholding critical culturally based knowledge, the lack of which may serve as a barrier to upward mobility for students from lower income backgrounds.

Critics of Bourdieu's emphasis on cultural capital tend to define culture narrowly, as the high culture activities and appreciations of the elite. Perhaps a broader definition that recognizes the exclusionary power of professional culture should be incorporated into our understanding of the importance of cultural capital in the transmission of privilege. Such a consideration speaks to the ways in which our postsecondary educational institutions may be limiting social mobility, not by teaching subordinate skills, but by not teaching the social skills that may facilitate access to higher occupational positions and opportunities. It is noteworthy that most of the occupational faculty interviewed (at both types of colleges) believe that such skills are required and that many students lack them. This suggests that, unless students are somehow able to learn them on their own, community college students will face serious obstacles in the labor market and that occupational college students of the same background will not.

We have identified a pedagogical problem in occupational teaching that is usually not considered in academic settings. These findings indicate the need for further research on how and when to teach social skills. The pedagogy of teaching social skills is unclear, and research is needed to identify best practices. One current barrier is that teaching social skills is largely voluntary. Because most institutions do not offer such courses and do not require teachers to incorporate them into coursework, the degree and type of such instruction varies widely. This also means that it is sometimes difficult even to identify who teaches social skills, let alone the methods that they use. However, the occupational colleges in this study have found ways to build these skills into the curriculum in a standardized way. Much can be learned from their approaches.

As Bourdieu suggested, schools tend to require and reward particular skills without teaching them. This insight may be especially relevant to the requirements of the labor market as well. This research extends Bourdieu's ideas about the content of instructional practices, and how they affect students' transition into (or back into) the labor market. This aspect of Bourdieu's work has not been applied to particular institutional settings, and particularly not to community college contexts. Further research could continue to identify and evaluate methods of social skills instruction to add to the body of pedagogical literature. Fields heavily circumscribed by the licensing requirements of professional associations (for example, various health occupations) may be fruitful arenas in which to examine how these skills are systematically taught and evaluated.

In addition, it should be noted that social skills are not only a concern of occupational fields; rather, such noncognitive competencies can benefit students in academic programs as well. These students also must enter the job market after graduation, and social skills can be just as important to them as they are to occupational students. Despite the focus of this chapter on instruction in two-year occupational programs, these findings are not confined to specific groups or fields, that is, they can readily and aptly be applied to many types of educational institutions.

# CHAPTER ELEVEN

## CONCLUSION: ORGANIZATIONAL PROCEDURES TO REDUCE STUDENT PROBLEMS

In only a little over one generation, American society has shifted to "college for all" policies. Despite changing their admissions requirements and enrolling new groups of students, however, community colleges still use traditional procedures designed for traditional college students. Thus, though poor degree completion rates are blamed on students' academic and financial limitations, we found community college procedures that may also contribute to student problems. The occupational colleges we studied use, as we discovered, alternative procedures, not based on traditional assumptions about students and which reduce students' problems, even among nontraditional students with academic and financial limitations.

## AN ALTERNATIVE INSTITUTIONAL MODEL: REDUCING MISTAKES, INCREASING SUCCESS

Society often hurts disadvantaged youth (and struggling adults) by offering dreams without directions for how to attain them. Although community colleges often warm-up students' plans, just as often they do not provide adequate information about requirements or dependable pathways to graduation. Occupational colleges, on the other hand, devise procedures that reduce students' mistakes and increase their success.

Of course, because they serve a broader range of students and purposes, community colleges cannot totally emulate occupational colleges. However, they might learn some lessons from occupational colleges, particularly for their occupational programs, which are the focus of our study. Ironically, though community colleges are usually blamed for posing barriers to students, we have found the opposite—these colleges offer many options, but they do not facilitate their attainment. Their efforts to create boundless opportunity are laudable, but climbing to the top of the educational ladder should not be blindly adopted as the only goal. Colleges must also consider realistic options on which students can depend, and devise plans to serve the many students who now leave community colleges with no degree and too few credits. We contend that a close examination of organizational procedures may help these colleges better understand why so many students face disappointments, and to identify alternative procedures that might help them better accomplish their goals.

Comparing these two kinds of colleges has allowed us to uncover features we might not have noticed and has identified alternatives we might not have imagined. The comparison showed how student incentives, behaviors, services, support, and guidance procedures differ across organizations.

One must be cautious about inferring causality. Nonetheless, a detailed understanding of procedures sometimes leads to compelling causal inferences, even as it helps us understand the paths by which an outcome may occur. When students experience more information problems with complex procedures than with simple ones, or when they express more confidence about job payoffs in colleges where they perceive useful employer contacts, causal inferences are hard to avoid.

As we have seen, schools are more than classrooms, and implement procedures other than instruction. The procedures influence whether students persist and progress in college and make effective transitions from college to careers. Colleges need to consider whether their procedures match student needs, especially those of nontraditional students.

## REDUCING SOCIAL PREREQUISITES FOR COLLEGE

Community college procedures are premised on many assumptions about student capabilities and attributes, which we find are not always true. Students are assumed to possess well-developed plans, yet we found many students whose plans are vague or unrealistic. Students are assumed to be highly motivated, yet we found student efforts to be highly dependent on contextual factors. Students are assumed to be able to make informed choices, know their capabilities and preferences, know the full range of college and career alternatives, and weigh the costs and benefits associated with college, yet our analyses show that many of them have great difficulty with such choices. We find that many students have poor information about remedial courses, course requirements, realistic timetables, degree options, and job payoffs. In addition, though students are assumed to possess the social skills and job-search skills to get appropriate jobs, faculty report that many of their students do not.

The community colleges we studied use procedures that assume that students already have certain social prerequisites—plans, motivation, information, social skills, and job-search skills. In contrast, the occupational colleges in our study use procedures not based on these assumptions. The community colleges blame student failures on individuals' deficiencies, but the occupational colleges use procedures that make these social prerequisites less necessary. In effect, community colleges make students responsible for their success or failure, but occupational colleges shift the responsibility to the institution, devising procedures to help students succeed even if they lack the traditional social prerequisites.

1.  While community colleges assume that students can make effective plans on their own, occupational colleges give students a package deal plan for attaining an explicit educational and career goal in a clear timeframe.

2.  While community colleges assume that students are motivated, occupational colleges foster motivation by bolstering incentives and students' confidence that they can earn their degree.

3.  While community colleges assume that students have enough information to make choices on their own, occupational colleges devise extensive procedures to inform students, guide their choices, and prevent mistakes.

4.  While community colleges assume that students have professional social skills, occupational colleges teach these skills.

5.  While community colleges assume that graduates have job-search skills and can get jobs on their own, occupational colleges actively help graduates get jobs related to their studies.

We found many ways that traditional college procedures impede students' progress inadvertently, without imposing obvious barriers. They require students to have plans, motivation, information, soft skills, and job-search skills. Traditional middle-class students may have this skill set, but many nontraditional students do not. The resulting obstacles are the logical result of common assumptions about the necessity of traditional college procedures. The procedures are not inevitable. We find that the occupational colleges in our study use alternative procedures that reduce the need for these prerequisites, and students respond positively to them.

## ENHANCING STUDENT SUCCESS THROUGH INSTITUTIONAL PROCEDURES

Individual actions are sometimes the result of organizational context, as we repeatedly found. Student choices are not necessarily individuals' free and informed decisions; they are often constrained and informed by organizational procedures. Students' mistakes are not only caused by students; they are often structural, created by flaws in college procedures. Student job searches may not depend on student initiative; they can be guided along prescribed pathways defined by college-employer linkages. Student motivation may result from powerful trusted incentives as well as from student personality actions. A narrow focus on individuals misses the ways that institutions contribute to these student actions. Instead of assuming that individuals choose these actions, these occupational colleges use procedures that shift the burden from students to the institution in five distinctive ways.

### Information Overload Versus "Package Deal" Programs

Community colleges assume that students have clear plans and can assess which classes will lead to attaining those plans. They allow students to explore broadly, build a liberal arts background, and progress toward their goals at their own pace. When students have information problems, community colleges respond by piling on more information—more brochures, more catalog pages, and more meetings. Students unfamiliar with college and inexperienced at handling large amounts of information might end up with an information overload. Moreover, in providing many options, community colleges also create complex pathways, dead-ends, and few indications about which choices are efficient routes to concrete goals. They require students to learn to deal with an abundance of information, which may be a useful skill. However, this sink-or-swim method of information overload may not be the best way to teach it, especially at the beginning of college and for students who must contend with serious family, work, social, and financial problems. Community college procedures can be both overwhelming and confusing to students.

Community college procedures can also be confusing to counselors, who are responsible for helping students overcome their confusion. When students make bad decisions, counselors are often blamed (Grubb 2006). Yet students' problems may stem from organizational procedures rather than the messengers. Community colleges are like a complicated maze in which counselors must direct traffic using an incomplete map. Counselors must master and convey an unmanageable amount of ever-changing information. They must know about complex and changing course offerings and schedules for dozens of programs, and they must monitor the many possible mistakes of more than 800 students who don't have the time or awareness to ask for help. It is no surprise, then, that counselors sometimes provide bad advice, according to the reports of students and department chairs. Simply adding more and better counselors to direct traffic in such a maze may not solve the problems. As they try to advise students with such complex needs within such a complex structure, counselors' jobs are in many ways impossible.

In contrast, occupational colleges give students a package deal plan for attaining an explicit career goal in the time expected. Just as travelers choose a destination, and the travel agency provides a package deal plan with all arrangements (such as flights, hotel, and activities), students choose a goal, and occupational colleges offer a structured program that reduces the burden of collecting information and the risk of mistakes. Colleges select a few desirable occupations for which there is high labor-market demand, and for each, create one well-designed curriculum to prepare students in the shortest time and with the lowest risk of failure.

Of course, packaging limits students' choices. Americans place high value on offering many options (Powell, Farrar, and Cohen 1985), but options have costs (Schwartz 2004). Assessing options takes time, requires skills, and imposes great burdens on students. We found that many students either lack information, or don't know how to acquire it or use it effectively. Options also increase the risk of mistakes. We found that many community college students report taking the wrong classes that do not count for their degree. Moreover, options also make it more difficult for colleges to provide opportunities for steady progress. We found that community colleges had difficulty offering required courses during semesters and hours that were convenient (or even possible) for many students facing serious time constraints for completing their degrees.

On the other hand, because each occupational college program stipulates a specific set of courses in each program, even small colleges can offer the necessary courses every term in a predictable sequence, every student can make steady progress, and courses can be scheduled back-to-back so that less commuting and fewer schedule changes are required in a new term. A highly structured curriculum makes information manageable: it reduces information needs, simplifies logistics, and increases clarity and confidence. It creates clear information about students' past attainments, so advising becomes simple, and mistakes are avoided or easily discovered and corrected. If a third-term business student doesn't show up in a certain course on the first day, advisors contact the student immediately. Unlike community college students, occupational college students know exactly which courses they need, that these courses will be offered at the right time, and that they can make regular progress. Although some students may not need such structured programs, this option is valuable to those for whom certainty of timetable and completion are a high priority.

This is especially helpful to students who face multiple family and work demands. Students at occupational colleges can arrange work, child care, and family obligations around a predictable schedule rather than trying to fit ever-changing college course schedules into their already overburdened lives. Ironically, these structures can free students from the obstacles unintentionally created by flexible options, as explained in the next section.

In addition, these occupational colleges fix the counseling problem by simplifying procedures. Like students, counselors need to manage less information when fewer programs are offered and each is highly structured. At the same time, such structured programs and support systems reduce students' uncertainties and mistakes while supporting their progress, even if students enter college without much information. The occupational colleges use procedures that reassure students about these issues. Instead of trying to improve students' choices by piling on more information, the procedures reduce information demands and uncertainties about obtaining information, understanding costs and benefits, and trusting promised payoffs.

## Enhancing Motivation with Institutional Procedures

Motivation is not just an individual attribute. It also depends on context. Motivation requires that students have confidence that their efforts are worthwhile, that their short-term sacrifices will lead to long-term benefits. College entails many sacrifices: tuition, effort, time, and forgone earnings. If students are unsure that they can handle the costs or acquire the future benefits in a certain college context, their motivation may suffer. For many students, attending college may be seen as an experiment, a test of whether they can benefit from it (Manski 1989). However, given the wide variety of schools and programs within each college, students may feel uncertain about whether they are doing the right experiment (that is, one that will pay off)—an uncertainty suggested by the many students who transfer among two, three, or more colleges (Goldrick-Rab 2006).

Community colleges inadvertently make it hard for students to have confidence that they can anticipate and handle college demands. For instance, community colleges remove the barriers that arise from the standard Monday to Friday, nine to five course schedule by offering courses during early mornings, evenings, and weekends. Although removing these barriers accommodates work schedules, the resulting complex class schedules create other time problems. Students have difficulty attending classes at widely varying times of day and night, and have problems coordinating work and child care with these complex class schedules that change every semester. They cannot anticipate when courses will be offered in future semesters or whether they can be coordinated with other duties. Unsurprisingly, these complexities and conflicts make some community college students lose confidence about completing a degree on time.

Instead of assuming that students are sufficiently motivated, as community colleges do, occupational colleges devise procedures that increase students' confidence about course time schedule demands. These colleges simplify and compress course schedules into discrete time blocks, which are easily anticipated and coordinated with other demands. Students do not worry that progress toward their degree will be delayed by surprising time conflicts or unavailable courses.

Terms are also compressed, which reduces uncertainties. While community college students must anticipate possible competing obligations over a fourteen-week semester, occupational colleges operate on eight-week terms. While community colleges require students to anticipate competing demands over the next three to four years for an associate's degree (due to remedial courses and course scheduling difficulties), the same degree typically takes half as long (eighteen months) at some occupational colleges. Moreover, if a family crisis or other interruption forces a student to withdraw from a term—which is fairly common for nontraditional students—occupational college students in our sample lose just eight weeks, whereas community college students lose fourteen. Although short terms and short duration degrees intensify demands, with more class hours per week and fewer vacation weeks per year, demands are compressed into shorter time intervals. These occupational college students report increased confidence as they gain a sense of mastery by moving successfully from one term to the next.

At these occupational colleges, all students complete a sequence of compressed milestones. Even if they seek bachelor's degrees (which can be completed in as little as thirty-six months), they will first get a certificate (in as little as nine months) and associate's degree (in eighteen months). In contrast, community colleges often discourage interim credentials because some courses required for associate's degrees do not count for bachelor's degrees.

Frequent milestones have psychological and practical benefits. Psychologically, short-duration units make school seem less formidable, increasing the student's sense of mastery, which is also associated with increased motivation. Practically, they provide a quick sequence of payoffs, so students who do not reach their bachelor's degree goals are not left empty-handed. For instance, we interviewed an occupational college student aspiring to a bachelor's degree who became pregnant after twenty months of college. Pregnancy forced her to drop out without the bachelor's degree that she had planned, though she had earned an associate's degree in a career field by this time, which had improved her job and wages.

For many of these students, motivation is affected by context. When torn between the many competing demands for their time, effort, and money, students reported that complex and changing course schedules, long terms, and uncertain degree timetables reduce their confidence in college completion and their motivation. Procedures that help students see the light at the end of the tunnel and understand the intervening steps to the degree enhance motivation.

## Guiding Choices, Reducing Mistakes

Analysts often assume that students have suitable information about college requirements and can make good choices (Adelman 2003), but evidence to this effect is rarely collected. In one of the few related studies, interviews with forty-one students found that many students' decisions are poorly considered and based on little information (Grubb 1996, 67). Our interviews suggest the same conclusion.

We also examined the types of students who have information problems. Our surveys indicate that student information uncertainty is significantly higher for minorities and low-SES students than for whites and middle-class students. Similarly, community college students reported information uncertainties at rates much higher than their peers at occupational colleges. These differences in information uncertainty are not inevitable. Minority and low-SES students at our occupational colleges actually reported lower levels of uncertainty than whites and middle-class students at community colleges. Our analyses also found that information uncertainty differs by college major: it is significantly lower in health programs than in most other majors, and health majors at community colleges report no more information uncertainty than their counterparts in occupational colleges. Because information uncertainty strongly predicts students' perceived likelihood of achieving their degree goals, we examined how the procedures in the two types of colleges may affect information uncertainty.

Community colleges use traditional procedures that assume that students have information or know where to find it and know how to use it to make appropriate choices. Only a few counselors are provided at these schools, so only a few students can be served. Unfortunately, we found that many students reported difficulties in making choices, and that they reported making mistakes because of poor information, often not realizing their mistakes until it was too late. Many students have too little information about remedial courses, course requirements, realistic timetables, degree options, and job payoffs. Given strong pressures to complete degrees quickly, many students were disappointed to discover that they did not choose the right courses or an associate's degree that required fewer remedial courses.

In contrast, occupational colleges use several organizational procedures to inform all students, guide their choices, and prevent mistakes.

*Intake Procedures for Program Choice*    Admissions staff inform all students about the college's few programs, their requirements, and their placement rates, expected salary, and working conditions and expectations in relevant jobs, and they help students choose a program that fits their interests and achievement. Choice is reduced to a few options, each of which has high rates of degree completion and placement in high-demand, skill-relevant jobs.

*Frequent Mandatory Advising*    Occupational colleges offer systematic advising, which is mandatory for students and the primary duty of advisors. Information is presented in a timely manner, and mistakes are quickly detected. Advisors are required to initiate meetings with their students rather than placing the entire burden of responsibility on students, many of whom may not initially feel comfortable initiating such frequent contact or recognize the value of the meetings.

*Group Advising* Group advisory meetings give all students essential information. Peers share problems and solutions, and become role models for solving common problems and sources of positive peer pressures. Peers provide information and support, even when parents cannot.

*Student Information Systems* Systematic procedures keep track of student attendance and performance, so advisors can detect mistakes quickly, and contact students about incipient problems before they become serious.

*Standard Advice for Resolving Outside Conflicts* Standard advice is devised about how students can handle child care, and family and work conflicts, which is presented in mandatory advisory sessions. Sessions teach time-management skills so that students with multiple commitments can effectively plan time for classes and homework. They teach students to pick jobs that not only provide income, but also provide relevant training and career contacts.

While community colleges put the burden of acquiring information on students, these occupational colleges have analyzed their organizational information requirements and devised systematic procedures, employed staff, and arranged mandatory meetings to provide this information to all students. Not surprisingly, students are more confident that they understand college and program requirements.

## Beyond Academic Instruction: Teaching Soft Skills

Soft skills instruction is another difference between the two types of colleges. Although faculty report that many students lack professionally relevant workplace social skills at both public and private colleges, most community college faculty report that teaching these skills is not their job, and, if they try to enforce attendance or tardiness rules, they may not be supported by administrators. A few optional workshops provided information about self-presentation in job interviews. A few faculty members provided isolated advice about soft skills or work habits to their own students. But these reached few students, and such offerings were not considered an essential part of college.

In occupational colleges, on the other hand, mandatory advisory sessions and classes provide all students with individualized information about their dress, demeanor, vocabulary, and oral communication skills. These colleges also pose clear rules about attendance, punctuality, homework deadlines, and appropriate dress. When faculty impose their own rules based on occupational practices, the college supports them.

## Connecting Graduates to Appropriate Jobs

Schools are not usually considered active labor market participants. Labor markets typically involve only job seekers and employers. Our community colleges assume that they only have to give students human capital (that is, academic and job skills) and credentials (which are presumed to be recognized), and students will find jobs on their own. Colleges may offer a little assistance: sending out transcripts, posting job listings, and providing general career counseling and optional workshops for a few students. However, they focus on providing human capital.

In contrast, the occupational colleges in our study are active participants in the labor market. They invest in the "signaling process" (Spence 1974)—enhancing employers' understanding and trust of college information about students' qualifications and improving students' understanding of employers' demands.

Both economic and sociological theories say that schools convey credentials that improve employment outcomes. However, neither theory explains how schools make credentials understood, trusted, and valued by employers, especially for low-status students with low-status associate's degrees from unselective colleges. Why should employers value credentials from these colleges? This question is central to providing opportunities to disadvantaged students, and it is a serious problem that is largely ignored in sociology and economics. Occupational colleges have devised many ways to cope with that problem.

To improve employers' understanding, staff assist all students in preparing their résumés. They translate students' courses into skills employers recognize and value. This is another advantage of the standardized curriculum: it creates a skill set that every student in a given program has. Job placement staff know this skill set and how to signal it. Community colleges expect students to figure out on their own what skills they possess and how to present them to employers. Occupational colleges make sure that employers understand the information which their graduates present in transcripts, applications, résumés, and interviews.

To improve employers' trust, these occupational colleges provide employers with individualized information about graduates' qualifications. Information is made trustworthy through a process in which staff learn employers' needs and demonstrate to employers how the college's programs and graduates meet those needs. They also improve trust by providing this information in the context of trusted relationships with employers. Just as elite prep schools invest in staff who compile detailed student assessments and convey this information via trusted relationships (Persell and Cookson 1985), occupational colleges serve their student bodies, which includes many low-SES students. Placement staff cultivate employer relationships, which are similar to those of elite prep schools, and use them to benefit their students (compare Kariya and Rosenbaum 1995; Uzzi 1996). Employers can trust placement staff not to jeopardize their future relationship by misrepresenting a dubious student. In turn, staff at these colleges say they will continue sending graduates of dependable quality in the future only if an employer places their graduates in appropriate jobs.

As Grubb and Lazerson note, school-work "linkage mechanisms vary substantially, but all acknowledge (usually implicitly) that school-based occupational preparation needs to establish closer connections to employment if it is to work well" (2004, 186). They describe career-oriented guidance, credentials and licenses, and various forms of institutional connections (for example, school-employer partnerships, manpower forecasting, and co-ops). In particular, co-op programs develop trusted relationships with employers which serve the interests of both parties and permit communicating trusted information about graduates, particularly skills and attributes that employers need, but cannot easily assess in their hiring procedures. The occupational colleges we studied use many of these mechanisms. In particular, they create trusted relationships, which are used for hiring as well as for co-op experiences. Whereas community colleges focus only on providing human capital, occupational colleges also provide understandable and dependable signals about graduates. Obviously, employers need human capital, but they need trusted signals as well, and these occupational colleges provide both.

Although job placement seems to be a process of matching known attributes of students and jobs, contacts may do more than that. First, by learning the particular interests of each employer, placement staff can direct a marginal graduate to a recruiter who appreciates his distinctive hard-to-assess strengths, just as prep-school intermediaries and vocational-education teachers do (Persell and Cookson 1985; Rosenbaum 2001). Second, job duties are sometimes flexible, and placement staff report that employers sometimes upgrade jobs to get better graduates from their schools. Third, while employers may avoid applicants from disadvantaged backgrounds (due to employers' bias or applicants' poor interviewing skills), trusted evaluations may persuade employers to hire their graduates from disadvantaged backgrounds (Persell and Cookson 1985; Rosenbaum 2001).

Placement staff suggest that these processes occur, but we cannot test their contentions.

Besides improving the signaling process to employers, occupational colleges also improve the signaling process to students. By actively helping graduates get jobs, occupational colleges also help students perceive that their college achievements will be recognized in the labor market. Although we have no evidence about actual job outcomes, staffs' described activities seem likely to be helpful, especially for disadvantaged students who do not understand the labor market. In any case, students report that these activities are reassuring; these activities reduce their fears of being on their own in a labor market they do not understand.

Community colleges often assume that students exert effort because they perceive job payoffs, which in turn improves their chances to get a degree and a good job as in model 1:

$$\text{Effort} \rightarrow \text{Degree} \rightarrow \text{Job}$$

Yet many students we studied did not have confidence that they could complete degrees and get good jobs after college, which reduced their effort in their coursework (Rosenbaum 2003). Chapter 9 found that students' effort and degree confidence are increased if they perceive that school/teacher contacts can help them get good jobs. In turn, these perceptions are partly determined by college type, as portrayed by model 2:

$$\text{College type} \rightarrow \text{Perceive Contacts} \rightarrow \text{Effort \& Confidence} \rightarrow \text{Degree} \rightarrow \text{Job}$$

As chapter 8 showed, occupational colleges offer a more supportive environment for labor-market linkages; so it is not surprising that students at occupational colleges are more likely to believe that their school and teacher contacts could help them get a good job.

These findings imply that student effort and confidence should not be taken for granted; rather, colleges can take actions that improve them. Although these positive perceptions of contacts are less common in community colleges, they do exist there. When they do, they have the same positive impact on students' efforts and confidence.

Some community college faculty put much energy into building and maintaining trusted relationships with employers. Yet these activities come at the end of a long list of other duties that have higher priority. They are also totally discretionary, except in the health field, where they are supported by state licensing requirements. At some community colleges, rules require faculty and program chairs to have employer contacts, but no extra resources or time are provided for such activities. As a result, these busy faculty must decide whether to forge employer contacts, what form they will take, and how much time they will devote to those activities. Their employer contacts are unsystematic and highly variable across individuals and over time. Some reports indicated that relationships were stronger in the past or that they will be stronger in the future, but such changes do not inspire trust by employers or sacrifices by students. As we saw, some community college students doubted that their school and teachers could help them get jobs, and the doubts were related to students' decreased effort and confidence in completing their degrees.

## THE CHOICE PROCESS IN TWO ALTERNATIVE MODELS

These two types of colleges represent different models of the choice process. The models differ in how much colleges take responsibility for students' progress and structure choices for them so as to assure progress and limit mistakes. Although community colleges should be applauded for the opportunity they provide to millions of students, they can improve this success story by improving the models of human behavior that guide their institutional logic. The community college model puts the burden of decision making on individual students and requires students to make many appropriate choices. Unfortunately, as we have seen, students make many kinds of mistaken choices that hinder their progress. The occupational college model views choices as both an opportunity and a burden. It limits this burden and the risks of failure by reducing students' options to make mistakes and by monitoring and supporting their progress through college and into the labor market.

We found that community colleges' efforts to warm up plans and avoid stigma are not enough to improve graduation rates (chapters 3 and 4). In contrast, occupational colleges create a social context that controls students' choices and improves their outcomes. Community college students report serious information problems. Occupational colleges, on the other hand, create a social context that improves students' information and planning (chapter 5). While community colleges put the burden of navigating college requirements entirely on students, occupational colleges create a social context that reduces the risks of mistakes (chapter 6). While community colleges expect students to find jobs on their own, occupational colleges create a social context that supports the employment process (chapters 7 and 8). While community colleges put the burden on student motivation, occupational college procedures create a social context that improves effort and confidence (chapter 9). While community colleges assume that students can acquire social skills on their own, occupational colleges explicitly teach these skills (chapter 10). In each case, community colleges put the burden on students who often make poor choices, and occupational colleges provide a social context that structures, monitors, and implements choices.

Occupational colleges change the choice process. Rather than assuming that choice is an individual's burden, these colleges make it a joint process in which individuals and their institutions are both actors, and institutions take some responsibility for reducing mistakes and improving outcomes. Instead of making individuals obtain information, the occupational college model assumes that the institution is better able to ascertain which information is needed and which are the best choices required to get to desired outcomes most efficiently. Rather than consider each individual as having distinctive needs, occupational colleges consider groups of students with similar goals having common needs. Instead of viewing choice as a matter of individual preference, occupational colleges see a single choice that leads most efficiently to the desired outcomes. This approach limits choice but may better meet the needs of students for whom the risks of failure are the greatest concern.

## IMPLICATIONS FOR RESEARCH

Large-scale surveys risk asking the wrong questions or misunderstanding the answers. Before undertaking surveys, we must first understand our variables and how they operate. That is why we have done such detailed qualitative analyses of students, staff, and procedures within our sample of institutions. Such analyses permit us to discover processes that might not otherwise be seen. We identified organizational procedures that are often ignored by surveys, which may explain outcomes that are usually attributed to other causes. For instance, though students' college difficulties are often attributed to students' poor skills or colleges' poor instruction, our results suggest that organizational procedures may also be involved. What appears as low ability, low effort, or poor instruction might be due to confusing and inadequate organizational procedures.

Research is needed to examine these causal inferences. We have shown examples that suggest causation, and students report that they perceive causal relationships, but we have not proven causality or shown which combinations of procedures are necessary or adequate to increase rates of graduation. Nor do we know how some students manage to succeed in community colleges even without the procedures discussed here. Perhaps these students have something else going for them (sources of information, support, and incentives), or extraordinary support from individual faculty.

Research is needed to examine potentially new explanations for prior findings. Although analysts have noted that many community college students make slow progress because they take time out from their studies (Adelman 2003; Goldrick-Rab 2005), such analyses did not examine why students take time out. Our research suggests the possibility that time-outs could be caused by organizational failures—perhaps students do not understand job payoffs, or are disappointed at their slow progress (that is, discovering that their remedial courses did not count or that required courses were not offered when needed). Future research needs to consider which organizational procedures may affect these student problems, how they do so, as well as how many and which kinds of students are affected.

Research is also needed to examine professional social skills instruction. The incidence of required courses and advisory sessions at these occupational colleges is a matter of explicit policy and was easily verified. However, community college faculty's reports of teaching social skills on their own initiative arose in a small sample and have not been observed, and thus require further study. Moreover, further research is needed to examine the actual skills taught and how they are taught. Given that observers have criticized social skills as serving only employers' interests (Katz 1971), research needs to consider whether the social and communication skills taught in occupational colleges might be more generally useful in other contexts—in daily life as a citizen, a consumer, a parent, or a spouse. Furthermore, we need to consider whether these skills replace students' own ethnic distinctiveness or provide additional options to their cultural repertoire. Research needs to explore how these issues are handled by faculty and experienced by students.

Research should also examine whether the highly structured curriculum in occupational colleges deprives students of the opportunity to develop skills to make complex choices. We are skeptical about this concern. After all, many of these students have succeeded in making a remarkable decision to attend college, and have defied great odds in fitting college courses into already very complex lives. However, the issue deserves research attention. How do nontraditional college students develop decision-making skills for navigating complex bureaucracies, what techniques do they learn, and what is the failure rate for the various techniques? In contrast, to what extent are students in occupational colleges deprived of opportunities for acquiring these skills? Do some occupational colleges provide opportunities for training these skills, just as they train other social skills relevant to middle-class employment?

Other possible disadvantages of these procedures should also be studied. Occupational colleges' procedures may be more paternalistic than some students need. In our interviews with a small sample, only a few students expressed any negative feelings toward the occupational college procedures. More systematic research is needed on this question.

Given their apparent importance in our sample, more research should examine intake and advising procedures. At both colleges, intake procedures try to convince potential students to enroll, and the advising process tries to convince them to persist. Although procedures that encourage disadvantaged students to enter college might generally be seen as desirable, such processes inevitably risk overpromising rewards to students. One might worry about colleges doing so to boost enrollments, especially for-profit colleges. We did not observe these procedures firsthand, but we have begun such a study.

We have not examined graduates' jobs, and we have not compared the jobs that students get from comparable occupational programs in community colleges and occupational colleges. The programs seemed comparable, but community college graduates might get better jobs because stronger academic skills are taught, or occupational college graduates might get better jobs because of their employer contacts. We are now studying these questions.

Financial costs and benefits are another area of concern. We do not know about graduates' debts after graduation. Wilms' (1974) study found that some private schools were cost effective because students graduated sooner and secured higher earnings sooner. However, these are old results. New research is needed.

Contrary to conventional assumptions about students' ability to carry out their college plans, make informed choices, remain motivated, and develop social and job search skills, we have found that many students lack understanding in these areas. These phenomena vary by college type and by college procedures. Although we describe these problems and procedures in a few colleges, our study is better designed to pose new questions than to answer them. Research needs to examine students' problems with organizational procedures.

Unfortunately, most national surveys cannot address these questions because they have few indicators of the kinds of problems and procedures that we have identified. However, just as recent national educational surveys, such as HSB and NELS, have collected information on high school organizational features, future surveys can include questions on college organizational procedures, like those we have identified. Our research poses more questions than it answers, and points to promising new research questions on important issues.

## IMPLICATIONS FOR POLICY

These findings have implications for education policy: they suggest that organizational procedures can reduce student difficulties. Obviously, community colleges cannot precisely emulate occupational colleges. Community colleges serve many purposes and provide a wide diversity of offerings, including academic, transfer, and certificate programs; isolated academic and occupational courses, including contract programs; basic skills, GED, and ESL courses, and the like. Moreover, they face different challenges (Dougherty 1994; Grubb 1996) including severe budget constraints, which have gotten worse over time.

However, many people are rightly concerned about the poor degree completion rates in community colleges. Some observers have called for ending open admissions and remedial courses. These critics believe the problem is primarily academic, and that by restricting admissions only to students with strong academic skills, degree completion rates will improve. However, this proposal is not likely to get support or solve the problem. It will not get support because Americans strongly believe in preserving access to opportunity, for which college has become increasingly important. It will not solve the problem because it ignores an important obstacle to degree completion: the complex procedures that make college progress difficult for many students, including well-qualified students. These obstacles do not arise from open admissions, and though they impact low-achieving students, they affect others as well. They arise because of college traditions that are not aligned with today's students and their needs.

The present findings suggest several actions that might improve student outcomes. While community colleges cannot (and should not) implement these procedures college-wide, they could implement them in a limited number of programs. Limited forms of exploration could be offered, constrained so that every option ensures students dependable progress toward a degree. We briefly discuss the ways that each procedure, identified in our research at top occupational colleges, could be implemented in community colleges.

*1. Procedures to Provide a Structured Plan for Attaining an Explicit Career Goal*   Community colleges could give students a highly structured plan for attaining an explicit career goal within a distinct timeframe. Exploration is not always appropriate, especially if students need to make dependable progress in a timely manner without mistakes. Structured programs reduce information mistakes by counselors, faculty, and students. They also permit colleges to offer required courses each term so that students can make dependable progress. Although structures and timetables are especially helpful to disadvantaged students, even a Harvard graduate school dean (Dean Theda Skocpol) is currently urging all Ph.D. programs to stipulate clear timetables for students to attain milestones. Without such timetables, even very capable students tend to experience delays.

Although community colleges might continue to offer traditional programs to some students, a few programs with highly structured courses could promise students dependable progress with a known timetable. This would also allow community colleges to "fix the counseling problem," in which there are too few counselors and some counselors lack complete information on program requirements. Similarly, in large community college systems with several colleges in a relatively compact geographic area, specialization might be useful. Rather than each college offering structured programs in many areas, individual colleges could specialize in a few areas.

*2. Procedures to Bolster Incentives and Increase Students' Confidence in Handling Requirements*    Students need to be clear about the full costs and benefits of their program choices. This is especially difficult for students unfamiliar with college. Structured programs provide a first step toward such clarity. Community colleges could also clarify costs and benefits and boost incentives by compressing educational units into dependable time blocks, shorter terms, and a sequence of intervening short-term credentials, such as certificates and associate's degrees on the way to bachelor's degrees. Compressing the school day, the school week, the term, and vacations allows students to complete obligations more quickly and reduce the risks imposed by outside demands and crises. Moreover, dependable schedules and stability from term to term also reduce outside pressures.

Compressing school terms into shorter units may be difficult, especially for transfer credit. However, other kinds of compression may be feasible; for example, colleges could schedule the same number of instruction hours into fewer weeks.

*3. Systematic Procedures to Inform Students, Guide Choices, and Prevent Mistakes*    Community colleges could adapt many occupational college procedures: intake advising for program choice, frequent mandatory advising, group advising, peer cohorts, and student information systems. Although community colleges admit all students, they still assess students for assignment in remedial courses and selective programs. These assessments could have additional uses. As noted, community colleges offer numerous associate's degree programs of varying difficulty (AA, AS, AAS, AGS), and students who need several remedial courses for one type of associate's degree might need fewer for another. Many students (and perhaps even counselors!) do not know about these degree options, or the subtle differences between them. After assessment, students could benefit from knowing how much time they must spend in remedial classes for each degree, or what proportion of students with their level of preparation fail to complete each type of degree. Providing this information along with assessments could help students understand their expected timetables and make appropriate choices.

Like occupational colleges, community colleges could also shift the burden of information from students to advisors, who would take responsibility for assuring student progress as part of their job description. Some of the advising (for example, concerning courses, time management) does not need to be done one-on-one, and colleges could save money with some group advising, particularly if students are in similar programs or have similar goals. Mandatory frequent advising and student information systems (which closely monitor students' progress or difficulties) would be somewhat more expensive, but could have the valuable benefits of keeping students on the right track and catching their mistakes early. Peer cohorts could also serve some of these same purposes, though they may be difficult to implement for part-time students.

The best way to reduce remedial needs in college is to start in high school. Although student attributes certainly play a role in their remedial needs, students nonetheless need better information when they are still in high school. Because they are aware of open admissions policies, many high school students believe that high school effort is not important because they can get into college without working in high school (Rosenbaum 2001, chapter 3). If community colleges worked with high schools, they could warn students that attending college does not always mean taking college courses. If a version of the community college remedial placement tests were administered in high schools, students could assess their chances of taking actual college-credit courses. This might also lead them to increase their efforts in high school.

Some critics will object that these procedures are too expensive for community colleges. Many community colleges have faced repeated severe budget cuts, and, from our observations, policy makers often respond to budget cuts by striving to preserve course offerings while cutting everything else, including counseling. Funding agents should realize the harm that budget cuts impose. Moreover, community colleges should realize that counseling and other information sources may be necessary for improving degree completion rates, which may justify retaining counseling even if this requires cuts in course offerings. Unfortunately, funding formulas that pay community colleges for enrollment, but not for completion, create perverse incentives that do not encourage steps to improve graduation rates.

*4. Procedures to Teach Professionally Relevant Social Skills and Work Habits*    Besides providing academic and job skills, community colleges could also teach social skills and work habits. These skills are already systematically taught in health programs but are unsystematically taught in other community college programs by only a few faculty members. The primary obstacle to systematic implementation of such instruction is overcoming traditional conceptions of college, which do not recognize the need. However, having admitted new groups of students who have not been exposed to the norms and social skills of professional work places, community colleges must recognize the need to broaden their goals and their curriculum. Many occupational faculty already recognize the need, and we suspect that they would support such reforms.

*5. Employer Linkages and Job Placement Procedures*    To continue to make sacrifices for college, students need to trust that college has something to offer, especially for students who have always done poorly in school or who face conflicting outside pressures. Our community colleges already have some well-defined occupational programs, though their programs are rarely so clearly structured, their employer contacts are not systematic, and their faculty do not always have time for ancillary placement activities. Community colleges faithfully follow the four-year college model, but this model may not well serve their nontraditional students. Interestingly, the occupational college model comes closer to resembling the model of elite MBA programs, which tend to devote considerable resources to advising and job placement (compare Burke 1984; Grubb and Lazerson 2004).

Community college students tend to rely on family and friends for getting jobs. Some programs have tried to improve employment by helping low-income people think about how they could use their own contacts for getting jobs (Spaulding 2005). Unfortunately, most low-income people do not have many contacts to good jobs. The occupational colleges we studied not only improve students' skills, they also provide contacts to better jobs and help students get recognition for their value through trusted relationships.

Community colleges could provide information to employers through trusted avenues, either by providing time for occupational program chairs to work with employers, or by employing special job placement staff. As we have seen, community colleges already have many contacts with employers, which are unsystematic and are not used effectively. One approach would be to provide institutional rewards for faculty who develop these contacts; however, that approach may not reduce conflicting pressures on faculty or reduce the variability and uncertainty across different programs. Alternatively, community colleges could assign these tasks to job placement staff who create systematic dependable contacts for all students in all programs. Although high variability in contacts across programs and faculty may give rise to student doubts, institutional uniformity seems to inspire students' confidence that they can count on their efforts to be worthwhile.

Revolutionary changes have affected American society and community colleges. These colleges have begun an important revolution to improve opportunity, and this study has suggested ways to extend that unfinished revolution.

# NOTES

## CHAPTER 3

1. Dropout is defined as those students who had not attained a degree and were no longer enrolled toward a degree after five years.
2. Analyzing degree completion leads to the same conclusion. In terms of degree completion, cooling out improves degree completion for both groups, and warming up improves completion for those beginning with associate's degree plans but hurts degree completion of those beginning with certificate degree plans. Of course, degree completion in five years may not be enough time for those planning bachelor's degrees, however for those warming from certificate to associate, five years may be considered a suitable time frame.
3. This study does find that warming up was less prevalent at Southside than at the other two colleges. More of the students there decided to follow their original one- and two-year degree plans rather than opting to pursue transfer. We describe how, like faculty at Northwest and Central, faculty at Southside also resist cooling out in favor of warming up, despite institutional pressures favoring occupational programs.

## CHAPTER 4

1. The number of remedial course areas is based on students' reports of course titles that they had taken, which is probably a better indicator than their own count of number of remedial course areas, because students don't always realize that a course is remedial.

## CHAPTER 8

1. In semistructured interviews, all respondents were asked a core set of questions about their work and their interactions with representatives from their local labor markets. Faculty were asked about their actions, motivations, and the institutional and organizational practices that might enhance or inhibit

labor-market linking activity. Interviews were taped and transcribed. Analysis of transcripts began with deductive coding of responses to specific questions about labor-market linkage activities (including the instructors' own activities, institutional linking activities, and their perceptions of students' typical ways of finding jobs). Analysis also included open coding of broad employment-related themes, such as labor market influences on the curriculum, demand for employees in a given area, and so on. Later, the data was coded more specifically for those themes that had emerged as important across cases (for example, institutional mandates and individual's reasons for creating and maintaining employer links).

## CHAPTER 10

1. The author does not imply, judge, or consider the superiority or inferiority of differing cultural styles or preferences, or suggest that certain cultural behaviors should replace others.
2. Career services offices at the community colleges did not offer direct job placement services, but rather career exploration and the tools for students to do their own job searches. For a fuller description of these differences, see chapter 7.
3. Many of the examples presented come from interviews with program chairs. However, all these chairs are instructors who teach several classes every term. In some departments, they might teach as many as a third of the courses in a given program. They are, furthermore, highly visible and influential in that they play a central role in hiring decisions, evaluations of adjunct instructors, and the supervision and approval of the curriculum content.

# REFERENCES

Abbott, Andrew. 1988. *The System of Professions: An Essay on the Division of Expert Labor*. Chicago: University of Chicago Press.

Adelman, Clifford. 1996. "The Truth About Remedial Work: It's More Complex Than Windy Rhetoric and Simple Solutions Suggest." *The Chronicle of Higher Education* 43(4): 56.

———. 1999. *Answers in the Tool Box: Academic Intensity, Attendance Patterns, and Bachelor's Degree Attainment*. Washington: U.S. Department of Education.

———. 2003. *Principal Indicators of Student Academic histories in Post Secondary Education, 1970–2000*. Washington: U.S. Department of Education, Institute of Education Sciences.

Alba, Richard D., and David E. Lavin. 1981. "Community Colleges and Tracking in Higher Education." *Sociology of Education* 54(4): 223–47.

Anderson, Kristine L. 1981. "Post–High School Experiences and College Attrition." *Sociology of Education* 54(1): 1–15.

———. 1984. "Institutional Differences in College Effects." Unpublished paper. ERIC ED 256 204. Florida International University.

Apling, Richard N. 1993. "Proprietary Schools and Their Students." *Journal of Higher Education* 64(4): 379–416.

Arum, Richard, and Yossi Shavit. 1995. "Secondary Vocational Education and the Transition from School to Work." *Sociology of Education* 68(3): 187–204.

Astin, Alexander W. 1972. *College Dropouts: A National Study*. ACE Research Reports 7(1). Washington, D.C.: American Council on Education.

———. 1977. *Four Critical Years*. San Francisco: Jossey-Bass.

Bailey, Thomas R. 2002, April. *CCRC Currents*. New York: Community College Research Center, Teachers College, Columbia University.

Bailey, Thomas R., Norena Badway, and Patricia J. Gumport. 2002. *For-Profit Higher Education and Community Colleges*. Stanford, Calif.: National Center for Post-Secondary Improvement, Stanford University. http://www.stanford.edu/group/ncpi/documents/pdfs/forprofitandcc.pdf

Bailey, Thomas R., James Jacobs, Davis Jenkins, and Timothy Leinbach. 2003. *Community Colleges and the Equity Agenda: What the Record Shows*. Paper prepared for the American Association of Community Colleges National Conference, Dallas, Tex., April 6–8.

Barrick, Murray R., and Michael K. Mount. 1991. "The Big Five Personality Dimensions and Job Performance: A Meta-Analysis." *Personnel Psychology* 44(1): 1–26.

Barton, P. E. 2006. "High School Reform and Work: Facing Labor Market Realities." *Policy Information Report.* June. Princeton, N.J.: Educational Testing Service.

Baxter, Michael B., and John L. Young. 1982. "What Do Employers Expect from High School Graduates?" *NASSP Bulletin* 66(458): 93–98.

Becker, Gary S. 1975. *Human Capital.* Chicago: University of Chicago Press.

Berg, Ivar. 1971. *Education and Jobs: The Great Training Robbery.* Boston, Mass.: Beacon Press.

Bernstein, Basil B. 1990. "The Structuring of Pedagogic Discourse." In *Class, Codes and Control,* vol. 4. New York: Routledge.

Bettinger, Eric, and Bridget Terry Long. 2005. "Addressing the Needs of Under Prepared Students in Higher Education: Does College Remediation Work?" Working Paper 11325. Cambridge, Mass.: National Bureau of Economic Research. Available at: www.nber.org/papers/w11325.

Bills, David B. 1992. "The Mutability of Educational Credentials as Hiring Criteria: How Employers Evaluate Atypically High Credentialed Job Candidates." *Work and Occupations* 19(1): 79–95.

———. 2004. *The Sociology of Education and Work.* Oxford: Blackwell.

Bishop, John H. 1987. *Information Externalities and the Social Payoff to Academic Achievement.* Working Paper 8706. Ithaca, N.Y.: Center for Advanced Human Resource Studies, Cornell University.

———. 1988. "Vocational Education for At-Risk Youth: How Can It Be Made More Effective?" Working Paper 88-11. Ithaca, N.Y.: School of Industrial and Labor Relations, Cornell University.

———. 1989. "Why the Apathy in American High Schools?" *Educational Researcher* 18(1): 6–13.

———. 1992. "Workforce Preparedness." Working Paper 92-03. Ithaca, N.Y.: School of Industrial and Labor Relations, Cornell University.

Boesel, David, Lisa Hudson, Sharon Deich, and Charles Masten. 1994. *Participation in and Quality of Vocational Education.* National Assessment of Vocational Education, Vol. II. Washington: U.S. Department of Education.

Bourdieu, Pierre. 1984. *Distinction: A Social Critique of the Judgment of Taste.* Cambridge, Mass.: Harvard University Press.

———. 1992. "The Forms of Capital." In *The Sociology of Economic Life,* edited by Mark Granovetter and Richard Swedberg. Boulder, Colo.: Westview Press.

———. 2001. "The Forms of Capital." In *The Sociology of Economic Life,* edited by M. Granovetter and R. Swedberg. Colorado: Westview Press.

Bourdieu, Pierre, and Jean-Claude Passeron. 1977. *Reproduction: In Education, Society and Culture,* translated by R. Nice. Beverly Hills, Calif.: Sage Publications.

Bourdieu, Pierre, and Loic J. Wacquant. 1992. *An Invitation to Reflexive Sociology.* Cambridge: Polity Press.

Bowles, Samuel, and Herbert Gintis. 1976. *Schooling in Capitalist America: Educational Reform and the Contradictions of Economic Life.* New York: Basic Books.

———. 2002. "Schooling in Capitalist America Revisited." *Sociology of Education* 75(1): 1–18.

Boylan, H. R., and D. P. Saxon. 1999. "What Works in Remediation: Lessons from 30 Years of Research. Research Contracted by *The League for Innovation in the Community College.*" Available at: http://www.ncde.appstate.edu/reserve_reading/what_works.htm.

Brewer, Dominic J. 1999. *How Do Community College Faculty View Institutional Mission? An Analysis of National Survey Data.* New York: Alfred P. Sloan Foundation.

Brewer, Dominic J., and Maryann J. Gray. 1999. "Do Faculty Connect School to Work? Evidence from Community Colleges." *Educational Evaluation and Policy Analysis* 21(4): 405–16.

Brint, Steven. 2003. "Few Remaining Dreams: Community Colleges Since 1985." *Annals of the American Academy of Political and Social Sciences* 586(1): 16–37.

Brint, Steven, and Jerome Karabel. 1989. *The Diverted Dream: Community Colleges and the Promise of Educational Opportunity in America, 1900–1985.* New York: Oxford University Press.

———. 1991. "Institutional Origins and Transformations: The Case of American Community Colleges." In *The New Institutionalism in Organizational Analysis,* edited by W. W. Powell and P. J. DiMaggio. Chicago: University of Chicago Press.

Brinton, Mary C. 1993. *Women and the Economic Miracle.* Berkeley: University of California Press.

Brown, David K. 2001. "The Social Sources of Educational Credentialism: Status Cultures, Labor Markets, and Organizations." *Sociology of Education* Extra Issue(2001): 19–34.

Burke, Maryalice A. 1984. "Becoming a MBA." Unpublished Ph.D. dissertation. Northwestern University, Evanston, Ill.

Campbell, Paul. 1986. *Outcomes of Vocational Education for Women, Minorities, the Handicapped, and the Poor.* Columbus, Ohio: National Center for Research in Vocational Education, Ohio State University.

Cappelli, Peter. 1992. "Is the 'Skills Gap' Really About Attitudes?" National Center on the Educational Quality of the Workforce. Philadelphia: University of Pennsylvania.

———. 1995. "Employers Wary of School System." *New York Times.* February 20, p. 1.

Cappelli, Peter and Nikolai Rogovsky. 1993. "Skill Demands, Changing Work Organization, and Performance." National Center on the Educational Quality of the Workforce. Philadelphia: University of Pennsylvania.

Cappelli, Peter, Daniel Shapiro, and Nicole Shumanis. 1998. "Employer Participation in School to Work Programs." *Annals of the American Academy of Political
Science* 559(1): 109–24.

Carnevale, Anthony P. 2001. "Help Wanted . . . College Required." Presented at the
Business-Education Partnerships Conference. Chicago (January 8–9, 2001).

Cicourel, Aaron, and John I. Kitsuse. 1963. *The Educational Decision-Makers.*
Indianapolis: Bobbs-Merrill.

Clark, Burton R. 1960. *The Open Door College.* New York: McGraw-Hill.

———. 1973. "The Cooling Out Function in Higher Education." In *The Sociology
of Education,* edited by Robert R. Bell and Holger R. Stub. Homewood, Ill.:
Dorsey Press.

Coleman, James S. 1988. "Social Capital in the Creation of Human Capital."
*American Journal of Sociology* 94 Supplement: 95–120.

Collins, Randall. 1979. *The Credential Society.* New York: Academic Press.

Cox, R. D. 2004. "Navigating Community College Demands: Contradictory Goals,
Expectations, and Outcomes in Composition." Ph.D. diss., University of
California, Berkeley.

Crohn, Robert L. 1983. *Technological Literacy in the Workplace.* Portland, Ore.:
Northwest Regional Educational Laboratory.

Crook, J. and D. Lavin. 1989. "The Community College Effect Revisited." Paper
presented to annual meeting of the American Educational Research Association,
San Francisco.

Cross, K. Patricia, and Elizabeth F. Fideler. 1989. "Community College Missions:
Priorities in the Mid-1980s." *Journal of Higher Education* 60(2): 209–16.

Dale, Stacy B., and Alan B. Krueger. 1999. "Estimating the Payoff to Attending
a More Selective College: An Application of Selection on Observables and
Unobservables." Working paper 7322, Cambridge, Mass.: National Bureau of
Economic Research. Available at: www.nber.org/papers/w7322.

———. 2002. "Estimating the Payoff to Attending a More Selective College: An
Application of Selection on Observables and Unobservables." *The Quarterly
Journal of Economics, MIT Press* 117(4): 1491–527.

Deil-Amen, Regina. 2002. "From Dreams to Degrees: Social Processes of
Opportunity and Blocked Opportunity in Community Colleges." Ph.D. diss.
Northwestern University.

Deil-Amen, Regina, and James E. Rosenbaum, J. 2001. "How Can Low-Status
Colleges Help Young Adults Gain Access to Better Jobs? Practitioners'
Applications of Human Capital vs. Sociological Models." Presented to the
American Sociological Association. Los Angeles (August 12, 2001).

———. 2003. "The Social Prerequisites of Success: Can College Structure Reduce
the Need for Social Know-How?" *Annals of the American Academy of Political and
Social Science* March: 120–43.

———. 2004. "Charter Building at Low-Status Colleges." *Sociology of Education*
77: 245–65.

DiMaggio, Paul. 1982. "Cultural Capital and School Success: The Impact of Status-Culture Participation on the Grades of U.S. High-School Students." *American Sociological Review* 47(2): 189–201.

Dougherty, Kevin J. 1992. "Community Colleges and Baccalaureate Attainment." *Journal of Higher Education* 63(2): 190–214.

———. 1994. *The Contradictory College: The Conflicting Origins, Impacts, and the Futures of the Community College.* Albany: State University of New York Press.

Dougherty, Kevin J., and M. Bakia. 2000. "The New Economic Development Role of the Community College." CCRC Research Brief, No. 6. New York: Community College Research Center, Teachers College, Columbia University.

Dowd, Alicia. 2003. "From Access to Outcome Equity: Revitalizing the Democratic Mission of the Community College." Annals, V. 586(March): 92–119.

Duncan, Greg J., and Rachel Dunifon. 1997. "Soft Skills and Long-Run Labor Market Success." *Research in Labor Economics* 17(October): 1–42.

Eccles, J., and J. Appleton Gootman, eds. 2002. *Community Programs to Promote Youth Development.* Washington, D.C.: National Academies Press.

Eccles, J. S., C. Midgley, A. Wigfield, C. Miller Buchanan, D. Reuman, C. Flanagan, and D. MacIver. 1993. Development During Adolescence: The Impact of Stage-Environment Fit on Young Adolescents' Experiences in Schools and in Families. *American Psychologist* 48: 90–101.

England, Paula, and George Farkas. 1986. *Households, Employment, and Gender: A Social, Economic, and Demographic View.* New York: Aldine de Gruyter.

Erickson, F. 1973. "Gatekeeping the Melting Pot." *Harvard Education Review* 45(1): 44–70.

Farkas, George. 1996. *Human Capital or Cultural Capital? Ethnicity and Poverty Groups in an Urban School District.* New York: Aldine de Gruyter.

Farkas, George, Paula England, and Margaret Barton. 1988. "Structural Effects on Wages." In *Industries, Firms, and Jobs*, edited by George Farkas and Paula England. New York: Plenum.

Filer, Randall. 1981. "The Influence of Affective Human Capital on the Wage Equation." *Research in Labor Economics* 4(1981): 367–416.

Futures Project. 2000. *Policy for Higher Education in a Changing World: A Briefing on For-Profit Higher Education.* Providence, R.I.: Futures Project.

Garfinkel, Harold. 1967. *Studies in Ethnomethodology.* Englewood Cliffs, N.J.: Prentice-Hall.

Goffman, Erving. 1952. "Cooling the Mark Out: Some Aspects of Adaptation to Failure." *Psychiatry* 15(November): 451–63.

Goldrick-Rab, Sara. 2006. "Following Their Every Move: An Investigation of Social Class Differences in College Pathways." *Sociology of Education* 79(1): 61–79.

Granovetter, Mark. 1995. *Getting a Job: A Study of Contacts and Careers*, 2nd ed. Chicago: University of Chicago Press.

Grubb, W. Norton. 1991. "The Decline of Community College Transfer Rates: Evidence from National Longitudinal Surveys." *Journal of Higher Education* 62(2): 194–217.

———. 1995. *Education Through Occupations in American High Schools*, vol. I. New York: Teachers College Press.

———. 1996. *Working in the Middle: Strengthening Education and Training for the Mid-Skilled Labor Force*. San Francisco: Jossey-Bass.

———. 2006. " 'Like, What Do I Do Now?': The Dilemmas of Guidance and Counseling in Community Colleges." In *Missions Accomplished? Multiple Perspectives on Access and Equity in the Community College*, edited by Thomas Bailey and Vanessa Smith-Morest. Forthcoming, Baltimore: Johns Hopkins University Press.

Grubb, W. Norton, and Associates. 1999. *Honored but Invisible: An Inside Look at Teaching in Community Colleges*. New York: Routledge.

Grubb, W. Norton, and Marvin Lazerson. 2004. *The Education Gospel: The Economic Power of Schooling*. Cambridge, Mass.: Harvard University Press.

Grubb, W. Norton, and John Tuma. 1991. "Who Gets Student Aid? Variations in Access to Aid." *Review of Higher Education* 14(3): 359–82.

Hamilton, Stephen F. 1990. *Apprenticeship for Adulthood: Preparing Youth for the Future*. New York: Free Press.

Hamilton, Stephen F., and Klaus Hurrelman. 1994. "The School-to-Career Transition in Germany and the United States." *Teachers College Record* 96(2): 329–44.

Heckman, James J. 1999. "Doing It Right: Job Training and Education." *Public Interest* 135(Spring): 86–107.

Heckman, James J., Robert J. LaLonde, and Jeffrey A. Smith. 1999. "The Economics and Econometrics of Active Labor Market Programs." In *Handbook of Labor Economics*, vol. 3A., edited by Orley Ashenfelter and David Card. Amsterdam: North-Holland.

Heckman, James J., and Lance Lochner. 2000. "Rethinking Education and Training Policy: Understanding the Sources of Skill Formation in a Modern Economy." In *Securing the Future: Investing in Children from Birth to College*, edited by S. Danziger and J. Waldfogel. New York: Russell Sage Foundation.

Heckman, James J., and Yona Rubinstein. 2001. "The Importance of Noncognitive Skills: Lessons from the GED Testing Program." *American Economic Review* 91(2): 145–49.

Holzer, Harry J. 1996. *What Employers Want: Job Prospects for Less-Educated Workers*. New York: Russell Sage Foundation.

Hoxby, C. M., ed. 2004. *College Choices: The Economics of Where to Go, When to Go, and How to Pay for It, National Bureau of Economic Research Conference Report*. Chicago: University of Chicago Press.

Hughes, Katherine L. 1998. "Employer Recruitment Is Not the Problem." IEE Working Paper No. 5. New York: Teachers College, Columbia University.

Illinois Board of Higher Education (IBHE). 2002. *2001 Databook*. Springfield: Illinois State Department of Education.

Jacobs, Jerry A., and Sarah Winslow. 2003. "Welfare Reform and Enrollment in Postsecondary Education." *Annals of the American Academy of Political and Social Science* 596(March): 194–217.

Jencks, Christopher, Susan Bartlett, Mary Corcoran, James Gouse, David Eaglesfield, Gregory Jackson, Kent McClelland, Peter Meuser, Michael Olneck, Joseph Schwartz, Sherry Ward, and Jill Williams. 1979. *Who Gets Ahead? The Determinants of Economic Success in America?* New York: Basic Books.

Jenkins, Davis. 2002. "Participation of Women and Minorities in Information Technology Degree Programs in Illinois: How the Institutions Stack Up." Unpublished paper. Chicago: Great Cities Institute, University of Illinois at Chicago.

Karabel, Jerome. 1972. "Community Colleges and Social Stratification." *Harvard Educational Review* 42(4): 521–62.

———. 1977. "Community Colleges and Social Stratification: Submerged Class Conflict in American Higher Education." In *Power and Ideology in Education*, edited by Jerome Karabel and Albert H. Halsey. New York: Oxford University Press.

———. 2005. *The Chosen: The Hidden History of Admission and Exclusion at Harvard, Yale, and Princeton*. Boston, Mass.: Houghton-Mifflin.

Kariya, Takehiko, and James E. Rosenbaum. 1995. "Institutional Linkages Between Education and Work as Quasi-Internal Labor Markets." *Research in Social Stratification and Mobility* 14(1): 99–134.

Katz, Michael. 1971. *Class, Bureaucracy, and Schools*. New York: Praeger.

Kelly, Kathleen F. 2001. *Meeting Needs and Making Profits: The Rise of Nonprofit Degree Granting Institutions*. Denver, Colo.: Education Commission of the States.

Kempel, James, and Judith Scott-Clayton. 2004. "Career Academies: Impacts on Labor Market Outcomes and Educational Attainment." Presentation at a workshop on the school-to-work transition hosted by the Russell Sage Foundation, New York. May.

Kirschenman, Joleen, and Kathryn M. Neckerman. 1991. " 'We'd Love to Hire Them, But . . .': The Meaning of Race for Employers." In *The Urban Underclass*, edited by Christopher Jencks and Paul Peterson. Washington, D.C.: Brookings Institution Press.

Labaree, David F. 1990. "From Comprehensive High School to Community College." In *Research in the Sociology of Education and Socialization*, vol. 9, edited by Richard G. Corwin. Greenwich, Conn.: JAI Press.

LaLonde, Robert J. 1995. "The Promise of Public Sector-Sponsored Training Programs." *Journal of Economic Perspectives* 9(2): 149–68.

Lamont, Michelle, and Annette Lareau. 1988. "Cultural Capital: Allusions, Gaps and Glissandos in Recent Theoretical Developments." *Sociological Theory* 6(2): 153–68.

Lareau, Annette, and Erin M. Horvat. 1999. "Moments of Social Inclusion and Exclusion: Race, Class, and Cultural Capital in Family-School Relationships." *Sociology of Education* 72(1): 37–53.

Lin, Nan, Walter M. Ensel, and John C. Vaughn. 1981. "Social Resources and Strength of Ties." *American Sociological Review* 46(4): 393–405.

London, Howard B. 1978. *The Culture of a Community College.* New York: Praeger.

Lortie, Dan C. 1975. *Schoolteacher: A Sociological Study.* Chicago: University of Chicago Press.

Manski, Charles F. 1989. "Schooling as Experimentation." *Economics of Education Review* 8(4): 305–12.

Marcotte, David E., Thomas R. Bailey, Carey Borkoski, and Gregory S. Kienzl. 2005. "The Returns of a Community College Education: Evidence from the National Education Longitudinal Survey." *Educational Evaluation and Policy Analysis* 27: 157–75.

Martin, John P., and David Grubb. 2001. "What Works and for Whom: A Review of OECD Countries' Experiences with Active Labour Market Policies." Scandinavian Working Papers in Economics no. 2001:14. Uppsala, Sweden: Institute for Labor Market Policy Evaluation.

Maxwell, Nan. 2006. "Smoothing the Transition from School to Work: Job Skills." *The School-to-Work Transition*, edited by David Neumark. New York: Russell Sage Foundation.

Mazzeo, Christopher, Sara Rab, and Susan Eachus. 2003. "Work First or Work Only." *Annals of the American Academy of Political and Social Science* 586(1): 144–71.

McDonough, Patricia M. 1997. *Choosing Colleges: How Social Class and Schools Structure Opportunity.* Albany: State University of New York Press.

Meyer, John W. 1977. "The Effects of Education as an Institution." *American Journal of Sociology* 83(1): 55–77.

Meyer, John W., and Brian Rowan. 1991. "Institutionalized Organizations: Formal Structure as Myth and Ceremony." In *The New Institutionalism in Organizational Analysis*, edited by Walter W. Powell and Paul J. DiMaggio. Chicago: University of Chicago Press.

Mickelson, Roslyn A., and Matthew R. Walker. 1997. "Will Reforming School to Work Education Resolve Employer Dissatisfaction with Entry-Level Workers?" Paper presented at the annual meeting of the American Sociological Association, Toronto (August 12, 1997).

Miller, Shazia R., and James E. Rosenbaum. 1997. "Hiring in a Hobbesian World: Social Infrastructure and Employers' Use of Information." *Work and Occupations* 24(4): 498–523.

Monk-Turner, Elizabeth. 1983. "Sex, Educational Differentiation, and Occupational Status." *Sociological Quarterly* 24(3): 393–404.

Moss, Philip, and Christopher Tilly. 2001. *Stories Employers Tell: Race, Skill, and Hiring in America.* New York: Russell Sage Foundation.

Murnane, Richard J., and Frank Levy. 1996. *Teaching the New Basic Skills: Principles for Educating Children to Thrive in a Changing Economy.* New York: Free Press.

NCES (National Center for Education Statistics). 1996a. *Beginning Postsecondary Students Longitudinal Study.* Washington: U.S. Department of Education.

———. 1996b. *Integrated Postsecondary Data System* (IPEDS). Washington: U.S. Department of Education.

———. 1998. *The Condition of Education 1998.* Washington: U.S. Department of Education.

———. 2002. *Digest of Education Statistics 2001.* Washington: U.S. Department of Education.

National Center on Educational Quality in the Workforce (NCEQW). 1994. *The EQW National Employer Survey: First Findings.* Issue 10. Philadelphia: University of Pennsylvania.

Neckerman, Kathryn M., and Joleen Kirschenman. 1991. "Hiring Strategies, Racial Bias, and Inner-City Workers." *Social Problems* 38(4): 801–15.

Neumann, R. William, and David Riesman. 1980. "The Community College Elite." In *New Directions in Community Colleges: Questioning the Community College Role,* edited by George A. Vaughan. San Francisco: Jossey-Bass.

Nunley, Charlene R., and David W. Breneman. 1988. "Defining and Measuring Quality in Community College Education." In *Colleges of Choice: The Enabling Impact of the Community College,* edited by J. S. Eaton. New York: Macmillan.

Office of Planning and Research. 1997. *Fall 1996 Statistical Digest.* Chicago: Central Office, City Colleges of Chicago.

O'Hear, M., and R. MacDonald. 1995. "A Critical Review of Research in Developmental Education, Part I." *Journal of Developmental Education* 19(2): 2–6.

Orfield, Gary, and Faith G. Paul. 1994. "High Hopes, Long Odds: A Major Report on Hoosier Teens and the American Dream." Indianapolis: Indiana Youth Institute.

Osterman, Paul. 1988. *Employment Futures.* New York: Oxford University Press.

Palmer, James. 1990. *Accountability through Student Tracking: A Review of the Literature.* Washington, D.C.: American Association of Community and Junior Colleges.

Pascarella, Ernest T., Marcia Edison, Amaury Nora, Linda Serra Hagedorn, and Patrick T. Terenzini. 1998. "Does Community College versus Four-Year College Attendance Influence Students' Educational Plans?" *Journal of College Student Development* 39(2): 179–93.

Pascarella, Ernest T., Gregory C. Wolniak, and Christopher T. Pierson. 2003. "Influences on Community College Students' Educational Plans." *Research in Higher Education* 44(3): 301–14.

Perin, Dolores. 2001. "Academic-Occupational Integration as a Reform Strategy for the Community College: Classroom Perspectives." *Teachers College Record* 103(2): 303–35.

Perlstadt, Harry. 1998. "Accreditation of Sociology Programs: A Bridge to a Broader Audience." *Canadian Journal of Sociology* 23(1): 195–207.

Persell, Caroline H., and Peter W. Cookson, Jr. 1985. "Chartering and Bartering: Elite Education and Social Reproduction." *Social Problems* 33(2): 114–29.

Person, Ann E., James E. Rosenbaum, and Regina Deil-Amen. 2003. "The College Enrollment Revolution: Student Goals, Mistakes, and Plans in Differing Institutional Settings." Paper presented at the annual meeting of the American Sociological Association, Atlanta (August 2003).

Peterson, Trond, Ishak Spaorta, and Marc-David L. Seidel. 2000. "Offering A Job." *American Journal of Sociology* 106(4): 763–816.

Pincus, F. L. 1980. "The False Promises of Community Colleges: Class Conflict and Vocational Education." *Harvard Educational Review* 50(3): 332–56.

Powell, Arthur G., Eleanor Farrar, and David K. Cohen. 1985. *The Shopping Mall High School: Winners and Losers in the Educational Marketplace.* Boston, Mass.: Houghton Mifflin.

Richardson, Richard C., Elizabeth A. Fisk, and Morris A. Okum. 1983. *Literacy in the Open-Access College.* San Francisco: Jossey-Bass.

Roueche, John E., and George A. Baker III. 1987. *Access and Excellence: The Open-Door College.* Washington, D.C.: The Community College Press

Rosenbaum, James E. 1976. *Making Inequality: The Hidden Curriculum of High School Tracking.* New York: John Wiley & Sons.

———. 1984. *Career Mobility in a Corporate Hierarchy.* New York: Academic Press.

———. 1992. *Youth Apprenticeship in America.* New York: W. T. Grant Foundation.

———. 1998. "College-for-All: Do Students Understand What College Demands?" *Social Psychology of Education* 2(1): 55–80.

———. 2000. *Providing Career Options to the Forgotten Half.* Rose Monograph Series, American Sociological Association. New York: Russell Sage Foundation.

———. 2001. *Beyond College for All: Career Paths for the Forgotten Half.* New York: Russell Sage Foundation.

———. 2003. "Universal Higher Education: Challenges and Alternative Strategies for Serving the New College Student." Paper presented at the Educational Forum, Aspen Institute. Aspen, Colo. (September 22, 2003).

Rosenbaum, James E., and Takehiko Kariya. 1989. "From High School to Work: Market and Institutional Mechanisms in Japan." *American Journal of Sociology* 94(6): 1334–65.

Rosenbaum, James E., Takehiko Kariya, Rick Settersten, and Tony Maier. 1990. "Market and Network Theories of the Transition from High School to Work: Their Application to Industrialized Societies." *Annual Review of Sociology* 16(3): 263–99.

Rosenbaum, James E., Shazia R. Miller, and Melinda S. Krei. 1996. "Era of More Open Gates: High School Counselors' Views of their Influence on Students' College Plans." *American Journal of Education* 104(4): 257–79.

Rosenbaum, James E., and Jennifer L. Stephan. 2005. "College Degree Completion: Institutional Effects and Student Degree Likelihood." Paper presented to the Annual Meeting of the American Sociological Association, Philadelphia, Pa. August 12, 2005.

SCANS (Secretary's Commission on Achieving Necessary Skills). 1991. "What Work Requires of Schools: SCANS Report for America 2000." Washington: U.S. Department of Labor.

Schneider, Barbara, and David Stevenson. 1999. *The Ambitious Generation: America's Teenagers, Motivated but Directionless.* New Haven, Conn.: Yale University Press.

Schwartz, Barry. 2004. *The Paradox of Choice.* New York: HarperCollins.

Shaw, Kathleen M. 1997. "Remedial Education As Ideological Battleground: Emerging Remedial Education Policies in the Community College." *Education Evaluation and Analysis* 19(3): 284–96.

Shaw, Kathleen M., and Sara Rab. 2003. "Market Rhetoric versus Reality in Policy and Practice: The Workforce Investment Act and Access to Community College Education and Training." *Annals of the American Academy of Political and Social Science* 586(March): 172–93.

Spaulding, Shayne. 2005. "Getting Connected: Strategies for Expanding the Employment Networks of Low Income People." Field Report Series. Philadelphia: Public/Private Ventures.

Spence, A. Michael. 1974. *Market Signaling: Informational Transfer in Hiring and Related Screening Processes.* Cambridge, Mass.: Harvard University Press.

Stanton-Salazar, Ricardo, and S. Dornbusch, 1995. "Social Capital and the Reproduction of Inequality: Information Networks Among Mexican Origin High School Students." *Sociology of Education* 68(2): 116–35.

Steinberg, Laurence. 1996. *Beyond the Classroom.* New York: Simon & Schuster.

Stephan, Jennifer L., and James E. Rosenbaum. 2006. "Do Some Colleges Improve Students' Chances of Completing Degrees? How Propensity Score Methods Change the Question and Answer It." Paper presented to the Annual Meeting of the American Sociological Association, Montreal. August 12, 2006.

Stern, David, Neal Finkelstein, James R. Stone, John Latting, and Carolyn Dornsife. 1995. *School to Work: Research on Programs in the United States.* Washington, D.C.: Falmer Press.

Stern, David, Marilyn Raby, and Charles Dayton. 1992. *Career Academies: Partnerships for Reconstructing American High Schools.* San Francisco: Jossey-Bass.

Stigler, George J. 1961. "The Economics of Information." *Journal of Political Economy* 69(3): 213–25.

Stinchcombe, Arthur L. 1965. *Rebellion in a High School.* Chicago: Quadrangle.

Swidler, Ann. 1986. "Culture in Action: Symbols and Strategies." *American Sociological Review* 51(2): 273–86.

Tinto, Vincent. 1993. *Leaving College.* Chicago: University of Chicago Press.

Tuma, J. 1993. *Patterns of Enrollment in Postsecondary Vocational and Academic Education.* Prepared for the National Assessment of Vocational Education. Berkeley, Calif.: MPR Associates.

U.S. Bureau of the Census. 1994. "Educational Quality of the Workforce Issues Number 10." Washington: U.S. Bureau of the Census

U.S. Department of Education. 1998. *Digest of Education Statistics.* Washington: U.S. Government Printing Office.

Useem, Elizabeth L. 1986. *Low-Tech Education in a High-Tech World: Corporations and Classrooms in the New Information Society.* New York: Free Press.

Uzzi, Brian. 1996. "The Sources and Consequences of Embeddedness for the Economic Performance of Organizations." *American Sociological Review* 61: 674–98.

Velez, William. 1985. "Finishing College: The Effects of College Type." *Sociology of Education* 58(2): 191–200.

Wegener, Bernd. 1991. "Job Mobility and Social Ties." *American Sociological Review* 56(1): 60–71.

Weis, Lois. 1985. *Between Two Worlds: Black Students in an Urban Community College.* Boston: Routledge and Kegan Paul.

Wilms, Wellford W. 1974. *Public and Proprietary Vocational Training: A Study of Effectiveness.* Berkeley: Center for Research and Development in Higher Education, University of California.

Zwerling, L. Steven, and Howard B. London. 1992. *First-Generation Students: Confronting the Cultural Issues: New Directions in Community Colleges, 80.* San Francisco: Jossey-Bass.

# INDEX

Boldface numbers refer to figures and tables.